The Newcomer's Guide to North Carolina

Everything You Need to Know to Be a Tar Heel

Third Edition
Revised and Updated

Bill Lee

DOWN HOME Down Home Press, P.O. Box 4126, Asheboro, NC 27204

ISBN 1-878086-91-X

Library of Congress Control Number
2001 135667

Printed in the United States of America

Cover design by Tim Rickard
Book design by Elizabeth House

Down Home Press
P.O. Box 4126
Asheboro, N.C. 27204

Distributed by
John F. Blair, Publisher
1406 Plaza Drive
Winston-Salem, NC 27103

*To All North Carolinians
Past, Present and Future*

Preface

Since this book was first published in 1997, many things have changed. We have lost two of our prominent native sons, Charles Kuralt and former Governor Terry Sanford. Racing accidents claimed the lives of Adam Petty and Dale Earnhardt. Dean Smith retired. We have had three elections in which Democrats have regained the ground lost to Republicans in 1994. We gave our governor veto power. We named a woman from out of state as president of the university system. In 1999, this book was revised to update many of those changes. Now it must be done again. Just after that 2nd, Revised edition was published, Floyd, the most devastating hurricane in our history, flooded much of eastern North Carolina, destroying homes and lives. But it brought an unbelievable outpouring of financial help, relief donations and volunteer rebuilding in its wake. That is now part of our history, as is the 2000 census, which showed that we are becoming more urban. In 2001, a National Geographic writer came down to do a story on North Carolina–not as we are accustomed to, about the Appalachians or on the Outer Banks or our lighthouses, but on the town of Cary, which has grown from a one-stoplight town in 1960 to the seventh largest town in the state, due mainly to an influx of northerners who came there to work at local high-tech companies.

Changes. Changes. Nearly every chapter has required revision to keep pace with the changing times. Yet the core remains solid. This book covers the many unique things about North Carolina that distinguish us from others. Once read, visitors and new residents will understand us better and fit in more quickly.

As we go to press with this edition, more changes loom. The legislature must come up with a plan for Congressional Districts, as the state's population growth has given us a 12th congressman. Jesse Helms has announced his retirement, and what will change the political scene. Our state will inevitably change, sometimes too suddenly, it seems, more often gradually. The Newcomer's Guide to North Carolina is designed to give the reader a foundation to better understand these changes and how they affect us.

Contents

1

Who We Are

Welcome, welcome. It's nice to have you here in North Carolina.

We have a lot of ground to cover. We want you to know a little bit about our history and politics, our sports and tourist attractions, the foods we like and all.

And we want to help you get set up, know what your kid needs for school, where to go for your driver's license and what insurance you'll need and so on.

But to begin with, we need to introduce ourselves.

We ARE North Carolinians, otherwise known as Tar Heels. That name derives from the fact that we produced a lot of tar in the early days from our once-vast forests of long-leaf pine. And we like to say that generals said of North Carolina soldiers that they stuck in battle as if they had tar on their heels.

And we ARE from the Tar Heel State — or Old North State, which distinguishes us from our neighbors in South Carolina.

And speaking of our neighbors, we have been referred to as a "vale of humility between two mountains of conceit." The mountains, of course, are South Carolina and Virginia, where people consider themselves far more aristocratic than we who they think descend from all of the poorer cousins and ne'er-do-wells of their families who wandered away.

Our motto is *Esse Quam Videre* (and we know to pronounce the "v" as a "w"), which means "To be, rather than to seem." We are proud of that motto, because we think of ourselves as genuine people. We generally don't like to put on airs.

That's not to say that we won't dye our hair to hide the gray or sweep the dirt under the living room rug once in a while. But if caught, we're apt to grin sheepishly and own up to it.

We are an incredibly diverse lot. Historically, we are basically English, Scottish, Irish, German, African and Native American; mostly Baptist,

1

Presbyterian, Methodist, Episcopalian and Jew. But, as with most anyplace else in America, we are becoming even more diverse — a microcosm of the globe.

The 2000 census saw us gain 1.4 million people to put us just over 8 million. Hispanics showed the biggest percentage gain – from 1.2 percent up to 4.7 percent, placing them about equal to the percentage of Asians here. Nearly every town and hamlet, it seems, now has a real Mexican restaurant and grocery store.

Some of our families have been here for three hundred years. Some are newcomers, just like you.

Some family names have a special association for us. The Midgetts of the Outer Banks, for example, have been known for generations as the family devoted to saving shipwrecked sailors from "The Graveyard of the Atlantic." The Belks of Charlotte we know for the department stores that have carried their name in towns large and small across the state. The name Petty, as found in Level Cross, is synonymous with stock car racing. The Plotts are known to hunters as the mountain family who developed a special kind of hunting dog.

You probably already know a lot about us and don't realize it.

Surely you've seen at least one of the 249 episodes of the *Andy Griffith Show*, which never fell out of the Top Ten throughout its eight-year run and can still be seen in re-runs. It was pure show-biz. But it imitated life — our life. Mayberry was based on Mount Airy, Andy Griffith's home town. And much of the flavor of the show was drawn directly from his background, giving the settings, characters and stories believability.

Griffith, as Sheriff Andy Taylor, was a country boy at heart who took his jobs as sheriff and father seriously, was honest and had a homespun sense of humor and wisdom. If he ever acted in a non-genuine way, it was to pretend to be naive, the better to surprise those who might underestimate him.

A shortcoming of the show, however, was that it failed to include blacks. Ironically, the show ran during the height of the Civil Rights struggles in North Carolina and the South. Its first year, 1960, was also the year that students at A&T State University staged the sit-down protests at restaurants in Greensboro that resulted in desegregation of the lunch counters.

One of the student body presidents at A&T was Jesse Jackson, a South Carolina native who learned his *esse quam videre* lessons during those tumultuous days of the '60s. As with any politician of his stature, Jackson has a sizeable following. And, certainly, many others dislike him. But he is not wishy-washy. Friend and foe know where he stands on an issue and, as a result, where a sizeable number of blacks stand as well.

And speaking of up-front politicians, U.S. Sen. Jesse Helms stands head and shoulders above the crowd in that regard. Even though his name raised the blood pressure of many of us opposed to his views, the fact is we elected him to the Senate five times. In each of those races, it took a majority of us to do that.

And don't forget Elizabeth Hanford Dole of Salisbury, wife of Bob, but career woman in her own right. A former president of the American Red Cross, she flirted briefly with a bid for the Republican nomination for President in 2000, then became a contender for the U.S. Senate when Helms decided not to run again in 2002.

On the other side of the political fence, pay attention to our new U.S. Senator, John Edwards, who in 2001 was point man for the Democrats on the Patients' Bill of Rights and appears to be in the grooming stage for a presidential run. His political savvy, good looks and Southern charm were getting him more and more media attention.

Then there's Charlie Rose from Henderson. His across-the-table conversations with the hot newsmakers of the hour are late night fare on the Public Broadcasting System. He is known for his preparation, for incisive questioning and for his engaging — yet, no-nonsense — style.

And there are other media favorites who can give you a clue to the North Carolina character.

The late Charles Kuralt of Jacksonville and Charlotte was a familiar figure for decades, with his *On the Road* series for CBS and anchor spot on *Sunday Morning*. Always with a twinkle in his eye and a chuckling or sentimental tone in his voice, he would tell us stories of unsung folks across the country that exemplified the best of America.

David Brinkley of Wilmington teamed up with Chet Huntley for the NBC newscast in the early days of television. In later years, he led the younger newshounds quizzing the newsmakers on *Meet the Press*. He bowed out with an election-night shot at Clinton, calling him "a bore" who "has not a creative bone in his body." He later apologized, but did not recant.

We are several notches into the Bible Belt and have a considerable religious side. To represent us in that regard, we have the Rev. Billy Graham, born in Charlotte and now of Montreat, who has been our country's best-known preacher for decades. He has attracted crowds to the largest arenas and playing fields of the world in far greater numbers than athletic teams or rock stars. His broadcasts, newspaper columns and books have touched millions worldwide. Graham's only weakness seems to be a penchant for mixing with the powerful. If that is a fault, most of his followers don't mind, pointing out that he has counseled many presidents on spiritual matters and has served as the conscience of the nation.

Two of our basketball coaches, Dean Smith of UNC and Mike Krzyzewski of Duke, have reputations for honesty in a sport that has tempted many others to cheat. Smith, with two NCAA championships to his credit, retired in 1997 with 879 victories, the most ever for a college coach. Coach K won back-to-back NCAA championships in the early 90s and another in 2001. Both coaches are attached to their players, are concerned about their well-being beyond the college playing days and pushed them to graduate.

Richard Petty shows off a few of his racing trophies.

You may also have heard of Michael Jordan, of Wilmington. Jordan played basketball like no one else before. His approachability and smile have endeared himself to advertisers. After flirting with baseball, he returned to pro basketball and led the Chicago Bulls to three straight NBA championships. He retired in 1999, then announced a comeback in 2001.

Then there's Richard Petty, race car driver from Level Cross. That's in the heartland of the state, and Petty is a true representative of the North Carolina heart. He was competitive, with the most wins ever in stock car racing and was famous for it before TV began covering the races. He was a country boy who has been written about and photographed for New York magazines. Yet he remained humble and willing to talk to anyone who wanted to talk to him.

Now we watch his son Kyle, a new breed of Southerner who comes from the country culture and wins a few stock car races of his own, yet steeps himself in our literature, acknowledging the new voices trying to be heard.

You might also remember jowly old Sen. Sam Ervin, whom the liberals disliked for his stand on civil rights, but whom they loved for his handling of the Watergate investigation that brought down Richard Nixon. He is dead now, consigned to history.

You may have heard of a lot of other North Carolinians who have passed into history. Each can give you a clue to our character, and we are proud of them.

Dolley Madison, born near Greensboro while her mother was there on a visit, put Southern hospitality on the map as hostess for President Jefferson and First Lady for husband James.

Andrew Johnson, of Raleigh, stuck to Lincoln's generous plan of reconciliation for the union after the Civil War, but was outmaneuvered, then impeached by more vindictive forces who took over Congress.

Thomas Wolfe, of Asheville, a novelist obsessed with the passage of time, wrote in *Look Homeward Angel*, "You can't go home again."

William Sydney Porter, better known as O. Henry, moved from Greensboro to New York City and became famous for his short stories. Some were sentimental, such as *Gift of the Magi*, or humorous, such as *Ransom of Red Chief.*

Edward R. Murrow, born in Greensboro, was another of our TV personalities, one of the earliest, who gave us the news and experimented with interview programs and news specials. He foresaw the powerful potential of television and warned us of its dangers.

Many of the famous have lived out their last years in North Carolina. Maybe that says something about us.

Frances Bavier, better known as Aunt Bee, actually retired to Siler City, a town she had visited and had written into the scripts of the *Andy Griffith Show.*

Singer Kate "When the Moon Comes Over the Mountain" Smith died in Raleigh.

James K. Polk, left, Andrew Johnson, center and Andrew Jackson, on horseback, are the presidents that North Carolina gave the nation — although South
Carolina also claims the birth place of Jackson.

Betty Smith, who wrote *A Tree Grows in Brooklyn,* retired in Chapel Hill.

Carl Sandburg, poet and biographer of Abraham Lincoln, spent his last 26 years at Connemara, at Flat Rock, now a National Historic Site.

But many of our voices are alive and they're the ones that say more about us than any of the politicians or press agents. You should make a special effort to listen to these whose voices have risen in quality above many others.

— Doc Watson, an extraordinary guitar and banjo player and singer from Deep Gap near Boone, who has sung us the folk songs and hymns of the Appalachians.

— Maya Angelou, poet of Winston-Salem, who read her poem, "A Rock, A River, A Tree" at President Clinton's inauguration.

— Shirley Caesar, of Durham, one of the country's most adored gospel singers.

— James Taylor, raised near Chapel Hill and of the '60s generation, whose songs document a journey of inner turmoil to his finally coming to terms with life. If you stay, you'll come to find a special feeling in Taylor's song, *Carolina on My Mind.* You'll probably catch yourself humming *Carolina in the Morning* or *Carolina Moon.*

— Charles Frazier, Asheville native and resident of the Raleigh area, who wrote *Cold Mountain,* a best-seller and winner of the National Book Award for its authentic portrayal of Appalachian life in the Civil War era. Cold Mountain, a 6,000-foot peak west of Waynesville, looms large for his characters and setting.

You may also have learned a little something about us from the movies. True or half-true, there are clues in them to what makes us tick.

Thunder Road, for instance, starring Robert Mitchum as a mountain boy who ran moonshine — (that's home-made liquor, if you didn't know, also known as mountain dew, white lightning, bootleg whiskey or corn squeezin's) — in a hopped-up car that the police couldn't catch. He was going to give it up, but on his final run, he crashed and burned and died. Our fascination with moonshine is still alive. And you can get it today, but you should know your bootlegger. There's some awfully bad and poisonous stuff out there.

You may also remember *Norma Rae,* the movie about a union activist from Roanoke Rapids that won Sally Field an Oscar in 1979. In a state so dominated by textile mills, efforts by the Textile Workers Union of America to organize in our generally anti-union state led to sometimes-fatal clashes from the Depression era on. A particularly hard nut for the TWUA to crack was J.P. Stevens, which had plants throughout the state. The movie celebrated the courage of Crystal Lee Sutton, whose stick-to-it-iveness brought about a vote in favor of the union.

Then there are some things you may not know about us.

You'll find that we tend to get caught up in college basketball, especially during ACC tournament time. Newcomers are a little surprised how things can

Fishing methods of Outer Banks natives as depicted by John White during colonizing efforts of 1585-87.

come to a halt when Carolina plays Wake Forest or State plays Duke. We all have our favorites. There's even an ABC (Anybody But Carolina) faction out there for those jealous of UNC's success. We've also always liked minor league baseball and golf.

And we like our special foods. A trip to our southern coast is not complete without a stop at Calabash for a meal at one of the many seafood restaurants packed into that one tiny town. In Lexington, you must sample some of our best pit-smoked barbecue. And in the mountains, ramp suppers are popular during the spring. If you're brave, bite into a ramp — that wild, garlic-like fruit of the forest — just don't try to kiss your sweetheart for a couple of days.

Most of us are church-goers: primarily Baptists, Methodists, and Episcopalians, reflecting our British ancestry, Presbyterians our Scottish, and Lutheran and Moravian our German.

We descend from a variety of nationalities, and the character of our population has changed dramatically over the years.

The first of us, of course, were the natives. Most of the tribes were conquered by whites by the Revolutionary War. The Tuscaroras were the first to be eliminated, rising up against white settlement in the early 1700s. Most were killed. Those who survived moved north.

The Cherokees were also pushed back into the mountains, then removed to Oklahoma when gold was discovered on their land. But remnants of the tribe escaped removal and exist today as the Eastern Band of the Cherokees, living on a reservation next to the Great Smoky Mountains.

The Lumbee tribe of Robeson County is something of a mystery. Possibly descended from remnants of coastal tribes, the Lumbee have maintained a unique identity. They gained official recognition from the state in the 1950s. The Lumbee have a strong record in civil rights, having confronted and defeated efforts by the Ku Klux Klan to establish itself in Robeson County, and in education. Denied access to white schools, they raised money for their own. Their college is now known as the University of North Carolina Pembroke.

The earliest of the whites to come to Carolina were English. They drifted down from the Virginia settlements to claim free or inexpensive land along the rivers and sounds of the northeastern section of our state. French Huguenots also followed this track. The state's first town, Bath, was French. New Bern was established by early Swiss colonists.

The land that was to become North Carolina was part of a grant by King Charles to eight English lords who had helped him gain his throne. The people who settled the coastal plain were Europeans attracted by the rosy pictures painted by agents for the lords, who needed settlers to profit from their holdings, and by those who spilled over from the ever more crowded colonies in Virginia and South Carolina. They were mostly English, with smatterings of colonists from the continent.

The English, with a contribution from the Scotch-Irish, also first settled the

Cape Fear region. Once word of the successful settlement of the region drifted back, Scottish Highlanders poured into North Carolina through the Cape Fear. They had been on the losing side in a battle over who should be king of England, and many had come from clans whose chiefs had been killed and land confiscated by the British. The Scots established Campbellton, which eventually became Fayetteville, and joined the English in spreading out over the southern portion of the coastal plain.

Settlers of the interior of North Carolina came primarily from the northern colonies, many following the great wagon road down from Pennsylvania. Chief among these were the Scotch-Irish and Germans.

The Scotch-Irish were Presbyterian Scots who had been encouraged by the British to emigrate to Ireland in the 1600s to dilute the strength of the Irish Catholics. They became too powerful and came under British economic and political strictures. This encouraged them to emigrate again, this time to America. After landing in the Philadelphia area, they moved south, heavily settling the Piedmont counties of the state.

German protestants took essentially the same route. Theirs was a pilgrimage of religious freedom from the domination of a Catholic Germany. They too settled in the Piedmont. Emigrants from the German province of Moravia came first to Bethlehem, Pa., then established their own communities of Wachovia, Bethabara, Bethania and Salem near what is now Winston-Salem. The Quakers, an English religious sect, took the same route and established communities in the counties surrounding Guilford.

According to Cordelia Camp, writing in *The Settlement of North Carolina*, it was said of the early settlers that the English "have done most to make the government, the Scotch have done the most for education, and the Germans started most of the factories of those early days."

Blacks were among our earliest residents, brought into the Albemarle region by English settlers from Virginia. The earliest land grants gave an extra 50 acres per servant to settlers, so there was economic incentive to slavery. Because the colony lacked a good international port, most slaves were brought to North Carolina from South Carolina or Virginia. Our colonial government considered this a handicap to the region's economic development. Blacks were used mainly as farm labor, then in the naval stores industry. They worked the rice plantations and tobacco fields and resided mostly in the east. After the mid-18th century, blacks constituted about one-fourth of our population.

Historically, we are a state of small scale. Mostly, we started out as small farmers. Even our plantations down east were small compared to those of the Deep South. We also preferred small towns. To begin with, we have 100 county seats. Not all of them are like Mayberry, of course, but many are. Some of our towns, large and small, grew around crossroads and market centers, especially tobacco markets, or factories. The railroad age after the Civil War allowed each town to have its mill, providing a way to transport goods and to bring people to work from around the rural stations.

As our transportation systems improved, we changed too. While one son or daughter may have stayed to work the family farm, the rest moved into town or walked or caught a ride from the homeplace to work at the mill. This migration from the farm continued throughout the 20th century, as farms became more mechanized, were taken in by larger farms or were abandoned altogether. Many rural counties have steadily lost population, typically with the young people moving on to better opportunities and leaving the elderly behind.

But while farm life has been disappearing, most small towns have hung on. Even with many of the old textile mills closing, small towns still satisfy a need for central market places. Most of our county seats are relatively small. Many of our towns have found ways to lure tourists. Others have taken on new life as bedroom communities for the larger cities.

In 1990, the census labeled just about half our population as rural residents, living in towns of 2,500 or less or in unnamed communities – "out in the county," as we say. The new census found much of our growth took place in the cities, and our urban-rural ratio is sure to drop once that figure comes in.

Even in the cities, many North Carolinians of the Baby Boom era are only a generation or two removed from the farm. Many of us can remember childhood summers on the old family farm. We grew up knowing that a Mom-'n'-Pop country store was around the next bend, where we could get a Coke and a fried pie and a dollar's worth of gas. Many of us who moved to the big city grew up in small towns. We bought our jeans at a dimly lit dry goods store with dusty, hardwood floors. If we needed just one screw or a washer, we could get it from the hardware store where the owner would fetch it from one of a thousand little wooden drawers. And we'd eat lunch or get a milkshake at the local cafe where everybody knew each other.

A lot of us have retained elements of our rural or small town nature. It's ingrained, you might say. We still like country music, country cooking, church socials, working on cars and pitching horseshoes. But sometimes we look around and don't see a lot of the people we went to high school with and we learn that they've found opportunity out-of-state or in Charlotte, or somewhere. What we do see are more and more strangers, and sometimes we feel outnumbered. Instinctively, we know we're changing and the census figures bear this out.

In 1980, for instance, about 77 percent of us were North Carolina natives. In 1990, that figure had dropped to 71.7 percent. The new census is expected to lower that even further, as outsiders moved in to swell our population.

How we accept these changes varies from place to place and from person to person.

Those of us in the cities are used to change. Strangers moving in and out, old neighbors long gone, familiar buildings torn down and replaced with something else that may have been torn down and replaced.

Those of us in small towns and certainly in the rural areas are not as used to the uprooting that comes with change.

Southern hospitality still exists. Travelers have long written about the warm receptions received in the South, and if North Carolina was short on hospitality it wouldn't have fared as well with its tourist industry.

If you're coming here permanently, you'll still find us hospitable. But you'll have to take care to keep it that way. We'll usually think well of you until something happens to make us feel otherwise. If you find us standoffish, it could be an individual matter, or it could be that a stranger that preceded you has caused folks to withhold judgment for awhile.

Maybe a stranger came in and bought the local factory, then laid off some folks. Or maybe a retiree bought a farm, then started complaining about the odors from a pig lot that has always been next door. Or maybe a favorite hunting tract has now been posted.

What you need to remember is that North Carolinians aren't so averse to change itself as they are to being forced to change. We have always fought hard for our independence and we prize our individuality. If you come in with the notion that you're going to change things, you're likely to see the locals start building a lot of walls around them.

If we're standoffish, it might mean something else too. Because we are generally true to our characters, people we've lived with for awhile know us and accept us for what we are. They know where we're coming from, as the saying goes.

That's not so with you. We need to take your measure. Are you genuine? You may seem friendly enough. But are you genuinely that way? You may seem mean and nasty. Is that really you or are you just having a bad day? If you're truly an SOB, we can handle that. We just need to know.

It will help if you show a genuine interest in us and that's what this book is all about. Read it and you'll understand a great deal about us. Ask questions and show folks you've been studying up, and they'll appreciate it.

In any case, if you're a traveler or a new resident, welcome. And *Esse Quam Videre* to you.

Concealed handguns

There is one major exception to *Esse Quam Videre* that you need to be aware of.

That fellow who just broke in line ahead of you or who was driving the car that just crumpled your fender may be armed with a concealed handgun. So you might temper your response.

North Carolina is one of several states that allow citizens to carry concealed handguns provided they have a permit.

In general, a citizen needs to have stayed out of trouble, and completed a gun safety course in order to get the permit.

Concealed handguns cannot be carried into banks or government offices. But they can be carried most anywhere else unless the owner of a building posts a notice banning them.

One chain's efforts to ban guns from its premises resulted in boycott threats by the gun interests, and the signs came down.

Talking pointers

Some of us talk different than others, you may come to realize, and the new words and accents can be quite charming.

If you're a northerner, everything we say probably sounds funny to you. Of course we say "y'all." That's a perfectly good contraction used throughout the South. How else would you differentiate between "you" singular and "you" plural?

We tend to say "gonna" for going to. And we leave the "g" off of "ing" words (such as "goin' fishin' "). And when we say "My, my, I like fried pie" or "Why is the sky Carolina blue?" we soften our long "i" sounds. It's kind of hard to describe it in writing, but "my," for example, is somewhere between the "migh" of a straight accent and "ma." Sort of like "ma-a-a." Well, you'll just have to listen for it.

Then again, if you're from the Deep South, you may think we sound more like Yankees because our drawl may not be slow enough for your tastes.

But even we North Carolinians prick up our ears at the talk of some of our own.

Native residents of the Outer Banks, for instance, have an Elizabethan brogue — or so it's been called. They sound English. They say "Hoy toid" for high tide and "Moi, moi, Oy loik froid poy."

In the upper tier of counties, next to the Virginia line, there's another different accent. It doesn't pervade all speech, as does the Outer Banks brogue, but is evident mainly with the "ou" sound. They pronounce it "oa," so that "out and about" becomes "oat and aboat." This is referred to as a "tidewater" accent and has been transplanted from the Virginia coastal areas through migration.

The Appalachians also have a special culture, including a way of saying things.

When one fellow retired recently from a western North Carolina company, he got this note:

I understand that a give-out has been made of your impending retirement. Well, I guess you're on the down-go that we're all going to retch sometime. We sure air gonna miss ya! I'm sure that atter awhile you'll miss us too. You can be as ornery as all get-out, but also pretty nice at times. I know I shouldn't benasty ya, but you deserve a little "biddy-pecking." Here's a list of retirement do's and don'ts.

Do:
Be careful not to get bodaciously ruint out cootering around during all your free time.
Take that every-day gal of yours, pack a go-poke and go somewhere to enjoy your-selves.
Drink some water and suck your thumb too or you'll fleshen up real quick. Then you'll have to hoof a whoop and a holler to lose the extra pounds.
Eat garden sass in large quantities in order to avoid this hazard."

Don't:
Wait a coon's age to come visit either.
Sit around digging up old dead cats. Life is too short.
Write me a return letter full of butter-mouth bull.

Luckily for us and for the man who got this letter, the writer — a mountain woman — included a translation list for the Appalachian vernacular she used. Here it is:

A give-out = an announcement.
On the down-go = declining in age or health or economic status.
Retch = reach.
Air = are.
Atter = after.
As all get-out = very much so.
Benasty = degrade.
Biddy-pecking = to nag mildly.
Bodaciously ruint = seriously injured.
Cootering around = walking aimlessly or idly.
Everyday gal = steady sweetheart.
Go-poke = traveling bag.
Drink some water and suck your thumb = eat a small meal.
Fleshen up = put on weight.
Hoof = walk.
A whoop and a holler = a considerable distance.
Garden sass = vegetables.
Coons age = a long time.
Digging up old dead cats = recalling disagreeable subjects.
Butter-mouthed = flattering.

Some say that our mobile society, the influence of television, the fact that we are talking less to each other face-to-face all threaten to diminish our special regional characteristics, particularly our speech.

In fact, one recent study showed that young folks on Ocracoke Island were losing their brogue. Because tourism has increased so over the past 30 years, Ocracoke has lost the isolation that allowed the islanders to pass down the brogue through the generations. Now the young folks are picking up regular talk from TV and their contact with outsiders.

So to help us preserve some of our uniqueness and to keep us from all becoming alike, you newcomers might throw out a "ya'll" now and then or "haven't seen you in a coons age" or something along those lines. After awhile you'll get used to it. And we won't even know that you're from somewhere else.

Books

Beck, Ken and Clark, Jim. *The Andy Griffith Show Book.* St. Martins's Press, 1985.

Camp, Cordelia and Wilson, Eddie W. *The Settlement of North Carolina.* Durham, 1942.

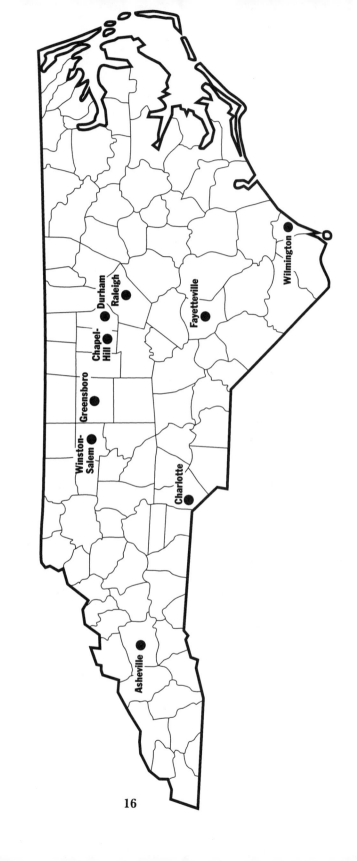

Durham
Raleigh

Chapel-
Hill

Greensboro

Winston-
Salem

Fayetteville

Wilmington

Charlotte

Asheville

16

2

Our Land

North Carolina is divided into four parts — the tidewater, the coastal plain, the Piedmont and the mountains. Each has its special characteristics that separate it from the others. Each has beauties and secrets that the natives knew and exploring whites uncovered. They were impressive, and the discoverers wrote back to tell others.

Ralph Lane, governor of an unsuccessful attempt to colonize Roanoke Island in 1585, called our land "the goodliest soil under the cope of heaven, so abounding in sweete trees, that bring sundry rich and most pleasant gummes, grapes of such greatnes, yet wild. . .so many sorts of Apothecarie drugs, such several kinds of flaxe, & one kinde like silke...and sundry other rich commodities, that no parts of the world, be they West or East Indies, have, here we finde great abundance of."

We have liked Lane's description so much that the state's office of tourism has used "the goodliest land" to describe North Carolina in its advertisements.

Lane, of course, was a partner in a business enterprise that stood to profit by luring more people to the new land. So this and other, similar, luscious descriptions of what was to become North Carolina have to be read in that context.

There is no question, however, that the land delivered on its promises. Even when it was bypassed — largely because of its geography — as an initial focus of settlement, its reputation for rich soil and hospitable climate drew the adventurous from more populated areas to stake a claim.

Another phrase the state has used to entice tourists is "Variety Vacationland," which emphasizes the contrast between mountains and shore. At sea level, you can watch the sun rise big and orange over ocean waves. At the other end of the state, from a peak more than 6,000 feet high, you can watch the sun set, soft and subdued over waves of blue mountain ranges. Climates can range from Canadian in the Balsam range on the Blue Ridge Parkway to subtropical around Wilmington. The land is simple and flat in the coastal plain, complex and folded in the mountains. So big, varied and complicated is the land that it can take even a born-and-bred North Carolinian a lifetime to learn it.

A description

A line of narrow barrier islands, known as the Outer Banks, forms the state's eastern profile, extending for about 300 miles from Virginia to South Carolina. The islands are sandy, with dunes rising to their highest at Kill Devil Hills. Three major turns in directions of the banks are marked by Cape Hatteras, Cape Lookout and Cape Fear. Midway between Lookout and Hatteras and north to Virginia, the banks are separated from the mainland by large, shallow sounds, mainly Currituck, Albemarle and Pamlico. Three inlets — Oregon, Hatteras and Ocracoke — allow entry to the sounds. South of Ocracoke, the banks are smaller and the sounds narrow. Inlets too are smaller and more numerous. Along the entire coast, only the Cape Fear River flows directly into the Atlantic, and its mouth is marked by the treacherous Frying Pan Shoals.

Across the sounds to the west begins the tidewater region, extending from 30 to 80 miles inland and characterized by marshes, swamps — including the Great Dismal — and natural lakes. This region gives rise to the coastal plain, the relatively flat stretch of land which continues another hundred miles or so inland.

At about 400 feet above sea level, the Piedmont begins. The terrain is more rolling and hilly, with several small mountain ranges — the Uwharries near Asheboro, the Brushy range that rises to Pilot Mountain (2,700 feet) in Surry County, the South Mountains below Morganton and the Sauratown Ridge in Stokes.

These hills and small chains are a prelude to the Appalachians that rise abruptly from the Piedmont. The chain runs southwest to northeast, from Alabama to Maine. It is in North Carolina that the peaks are highest — 49 above 6,000 feet, 174 above 5,000 feet. Mt. Mitchell, at 6,684 feet is the highest point east of the Mississippi River. In North Carolina, the range is made up of two chains — the Blue Ridge, to the east, paralleling the Unakas, or Smoky Mountains, to the west. Joining the chains are cross-ridges, such as the Cowees, the Balsams and the Blacks. This rugged landscape of alternating peaks and valleys covers about 6,000 square miles.

Climate

North Carolina is a Sun Belt state, a catch-all term for the states of the South and Southwest that distinguishes us from the states to the north with cooler environments. But actually, we need to distinguish ourselves from the Sun Belt too. We're not nearly as hot as most of the other states in the southern tier.

We do have our heat waves. Temperatures can climb over 100 for days at a time. And we have our cold snaps as well. The thermometer has been known to dip below zero even east of Raleigh. But these are unusual circumstances, and represent weather extremes.

As you might expect, average temperatures drop as you leave the coast and travel to the mountains. Wilmington's highs range from about 56 degrees in January to about 89 degrees in July. Raleigh-Durham's highs for the same months range from 50 to 88 degrees. Asheville's range is 47 to 84 degrees. Some areas south of Wilmington, warmed by the Gulf Stream, have a subtropical climate, comparable to northern Florida. On some of the highest peaks of the Appalachians, the climate is comparable to areas of southern Canada.

Rainfall varies widely as well. Wilmington's annual rainfall is about 53 inches, Raleigh-Durham's about 43 and Asheville's about 38. Asheville is the central weather station for the mountains, but its rainfall amounts are deceiving. Actually it sits in a dry pocket of our mountains, most of which receives between 50 and 60 inches of rain annually. The rainiest areas of the state — of the entire eastern United States, in fact — is between Rosman and Cashiers, which records about 80 inches a year.

Geology

The theory of plate tectonics — that the earth's surface rides on a number of subsurface plates that migrate and rub and bump against each other — now shapes our thinking about how our state was built.

The geology of the mountains is difficult to interpret. The Appalachians sit on billion-year-old rock, ancient sea bottom hardened by heat and pressure. Overlying this are compacted layers of sediment, pebbles and mud. But violent land movements have disrupted the geologic record. Layers have been thrust over layers, rocks broken and stood on end or scattered among strangers so that the whole doesn't always make sense. Thus, geologists differ about how the mountains were formed.

One theory holds that the Appalachians are the product of at least four different mountain-building periods. The last occurred about 270 million years ago when the African continent collided with the North American continent, creating along the seam a great welt that is today the southern Appalachians.

1969 photograph from Apollo 9 of the North Carolina coastline from near the Virginia line to a point just west of Cape Lookout.

What is missing for this theory is evidence of a suture from the collision and traces of material from the African plate.

So a second version holds that "suspect terrains," or pieces broken from plates, were swept before the migrating continent and plastered onto North America. The compression of these smaller plates between the larger created a buckling of land that became the Appalachians.

Compression also could have built the smaller mountain chains of the Piedmont or they could have been features of the smaller plates. In any case, they too sit on a hard rock base. The soil of the Piedmont is claylike, combining rock crushed to varying consistency with mud and pebbles.

North Carolina began forming its ocean shoreline about 200 million years ago, when the African plate reversed course and began moving away, tearing the giant continent of Pangea apart. Water poured into the seam and lapped against the hard rock base of the Piedmont.

Over time, eroded sediment and the bones of sea animals built up beyond this ancient coast and, as the sea receded, became exposed as the porous, sandy soil of the coastal plain.

Actually, the sea has risen and fallen many times during that 200 million years. And the giant sand banks that protect our coast have marched back and forth with the shoreline. It doesn't take much change in sea level to alter our coastal profile. The terrain is so flat that a small rise in the water level can cover land far inland or a small reduction can expose the shallow sands of the sounds.

Water

The Blue Ridge chain has been called "The Mother of Rivers." It's a natural place for rivers to begin. A great deal of rain falls on the southern Appalachians. Groundwater is consistently recharged, and all over the mountains, springs trickle to the surface and begin their trips downhill. These creeks join, and the many folds of the mountains create vast and complicated watersheds that collect the rain itself and direct it into the creeks. Even the fog and mists that envelope the mountains can develop measurable amounts of water that drips from leaves where it collects. So, as fishermen know, these creeks can become large enough to support nice-size trout at surprisingly high places. And they quickly become the beautiful, boulder strewn rivers of the mountains that can flow gently in the flats, turn to whitewater on downhill courses, then tumble madly over ledges as waterfalls.

The water can be treacherous as well. Because of the size of the watersheds, because of the steep and rapid descent of the water and because the waterways can be quite narrow with steep banks, a heavy rain can bring flash flooding in the mountains, while the rise in flood waters is more gradual and predictable in flatter terrain.

Actually, water — with a little help from climate — took over the work of sculpting our mountains after geological forces had quieted.

Our mountains are old, rounded and mature with good soil and abundant plant growth. Contrast them with the naked and jagged peaks that character-ize the much younger Rockies or Sierras. The flow of water has created the many hollows and valleys of the Appalachians. And, although no glaciers reached as far south as North Carolina, ice age temperatures froze water trapped in fissures, prying rock apart, then loosening it as temperatures warmed. Today, winter-spring climate changes continue this ice-sculpting activ-ity on a smaller scale, and mountain-wise drivers are conscious of the rock falls that thaws can bring.

As a rule, the peaks of the Unaka chain are higher than those of the Blue Ridge. But the Eastern Continental Divide rides the ridge of the lesser chain. This means that water rising as creeks or falling as rain on the east slope of the Blue Ridge eventually ends up in the Atlantic. Water originating on the west slope finds its way around those high Unaka peaks to the Mississippi River, then to the Gulf of Mexico. All of the major rivers born on the western slope — the French Broad, Pigeon, Tuckaseegee, Nantahala and the Little Tennessee — flow into the Tennessee, except for the New, which flows north from Ashe and Alleghany counties, and enters the Ohio by way of the Kanawha.

Rivers rising on the eastern slope of the Blue Ridge — the Yadkin, Catawba, Green and Broad — sooner or later flow into South Carolina, as does the Lumber farther east. Several eastern rivers, among them the Roanoke and the Chowan, originate in Virginia.

Still others we can claim from beginning to end. The Deep and the Haw rise in the Piedmont and join to form the Cape Fear. Near Durham, the Eno and Flat merge to form the Neuse. And near Roxboro, the Tar begins, becom-ing the Pamlico before it flows into Pamlico Sound.

The Piedmont's coarse soil and hard rock base have given in to the river waters over time, but not to as great a degree as in the mountains, where rapid falls produce more force, or in the coastal plain which has more yielding soil. So at the fall line, the ancient shore where the Piedmont meets the coastal plain, rivers generally change character from quicker, narrower courses to a deeper, wider and more gentle flow.

Lastly, there are a number of rivers that begin in the tidewater region, ris-ing from the swamps for short but life-abundant runs to the sounds. Among them are the Pasquotank, Perquimmans, Alligator, Pungo, Little, and another New River at Jacksonville.

Nothing has changed our landscape more this century than the construc-tion of dams which have backed up water all across the state, from Lakes Fontana (1945), Hiwassee (1940) and Nantahala (1942) in the west to Lake Gaston (1963), Jordan (1974) and Falls (1981) in the eastern Piedmont.

Some, such as the mountain Lakes Lure (1928) and Toxaway (1903, rebuilt 1961) have been constructed by private resorts. Man-made reservoirs for growing towns have been built all across the state. The Tennessee Valley Authority and other private manufacturing and power companies built the larger lakes in the mountains for water power to turn turbines for the manufacture of electricity. The lakes also provided for flood control.

Duke Power made the Catawba River its domain with power-producing dams at Lakes James (1923), Rhodhiss (1925), Hickory (1928), Lookout Shoals (1915), Norman (1963), Mountain Island (1924) and Wylie (1926).

On the Yadkin, Lakes High Rock (1927) and Badin (1917) were built by aluminum companies to manufacture power. Lake Tillery (1928) on the Pee Dee was built by Carolina Power & Light Co.

The construction of these dams often led to massive relocations of people, homes and communities. But the memories of those inconveniences have dimmed because of the recreational values of the lakes, which have made fishing and boating available within a reasonable drive of just about any location in the state.

East of the fall line, a number of natural lakes occur. Some of them — such as Lake Phelps — are thought to have been dug out by a meteor's impact. The largest natural lake is Mattamuskeet, in Hyde County, which is actually three feet below sea level and which a company tried to drain at one point in order to farm the rich bottom.

Flora

The first British explorers who arrived off our coast in July, 1584, not only saw a paradise from off-shore, but smelled it as well — "so sweet and so strong a smel, as if we had bene in the midst of some delicate garden abounding with all kind of oderiferous flowers."

More than 400 years of clearing land for homesteads, farms, cities, subdivisions, highways and other sprawling aspects of civilization has altered our landscape drastically from the time when the first whites sniffed paradise. As settlement progressed, our natural gardens were celebrated only until they occupied a particular spot of land that was needed for something else. The vast forests of pines in the coastal plain and hardwoods to the west not only got in the way of progress but provided important natural resources to the settler as well. Almost every nook and cranny of the state has been logged. Only a few small patches of virgin forest remain in the remotest sections of the mountains. And along the Black River, a stand of 1,400 year-old cypresses — the oldest trees east of the Rockies — has survived progress.

Still, the extent of our woodlands is impressive, as is the diversity of the plant kingdom within our borders. North Carolina can claim the extremes of a Canadian-style landscape in its balsam fir forests and, on the other hand, the lowland swamps and savannahs suitable to a Florida environment. And there is much in between.

B.W. Wells, in his book *The Natural Gardens of North Carolina*, said that whoever laid out the state's boundaries "succeeded so well botanically that one might think of them as possessed with less political sense than vegetational acumen." Wells divided the state's plant kingdom into eleven communities, and it is convenient to summarize his groupings to acquaint newcomers with our plant life and with some of the unique landscapes where they thrive. They are:

1) The dunes. Moved about by wind and tides, the sand is a difficult environment for plants. Sea oats are the most common plant and, because they help provide dune stability, are protected by state law. Also found are low shrubs, such as sea elder and sea kale, and on the sound sides, scattered patches of salt grass. The predominant trees are live oak and yaupon, which often must bend drastically with the wind to survive. Here and there, where landside flats are large enough, stands of trees become established. But the blowing sand and migration of the banks reclaim many of them over time.

2) The salt marshes. Beautiful in their green expanse, extensive areas of salt grasses, rushes and low shrubs mark the transition of the shallow sounds to dry land. Because they must exist in salt water, the grasses are related to the drought-resistant strains of drier climates.

3) Fresh-water marshes. Where you see cattails, you see the fresh-water marsh habitat. Many other plants are featured in the marsh, adapting part of themselves to air, part to water and part to water-soaked soil. Differences in vegetation in both the fresh- and salt-water marshes usually signal a change in water depth. Noteworthy are the marshes of the fresh-water Currituck Sound.

4) Swamp forests. A uniquely southern environment that features stands of gums and cypress thriving in swamps where water stands up to two feet deep. The gums have wide bases and spreading root systems for stability in the muck. Cypress also have "knees," above-water protuberances that breathe for the submerged roots. Shallow waters of the swamps have seen great stands of white cedar, which have been heavily logged. Rattan and cross-vine climb high into the trees along the swamp edges.

5) Aquatic vegetation. Fresh-water plants are adapted land forms, which have learned to live entirely in or below the water. Outside of the water, they would be too thin and weak to stand, but depend on their buoyancy for support. Because of the vastness of the eastern waters, aquatic vegetation is most common. Duck food plants, the pondweeds, create a duck hunter's paradise down east.

6) Shrub bogs, or pocosins. The pocosins are generally wetlands, or at least boggy, but can be dry during spells of drought. They are transition areas between wetlands and dry ground that cover large areas of the eastern counties and the higher, but still poorly drained areas of the Great Dismal Swamp.

The bogs are characterized by expanses of evergreen shrub, such as gall berry, loblolly bay, titi and wax myrtle, punctuated by small pines and stands of cane or reed. The soil can be peatty, deep in undecayed organic matter.

7) **Grass sedge bogs, or savannahs.** Where fire visits frequently, the pocosins become savannahs. Grasses and low, flowering plants thrive because they hide their most vital parts — the roots — underground out of fire's reach. Wildflowers exist to one degree or another in all of our habitats, but they thrive almost year-round in wet soils of the coastal plains and excel where the debris from a previous year's growth is burned away. In the savannahs are found the unusual trumpet plants which capture, drown and digest small insects. And around Wilmington is the habitat of the Venus fly-trap. Darwin called it "the most wonderful plant in the world." A wayward insect triggers the clamping of its jaws like a steel trap and is dissolved by juices excreted by the plant.

8) **Sandhills.** The driest and most sterile of our habitats, the sandhills exist along the coast and in the southern coastal plain around the golf resort of Pinehurst. The long leaf pine and the turkey oak are the only trees that can survive in the sandhills. Once there were vast forests of the pines, but logging, the turpentine industry and fires have reduced their numbers. Where stands of the pines have been replanted, the needle carpet gives a glimpse of what once lay underfoot throughout this region. Wire grass, a few shrubs and a number of hardy, flowering plants exist in the sandhills as well as less desirable weeds such as the sand-bur.

9) **Old field communities.** Where you see abandoned land that has not yet returned to forest, you see the transitional old field communities. If left undisturbed, the field will return to what it was before. First the ground cover, such as crabgrass, takes over, followed by weeds. In about the third year, broom sedges move in and over a period of years consolidate their hold on the field. Finally, small pines rise above the sedge and develop into pine forests. And if a hardwood forest once existed on the site, that will replace the pines. The vacant lots of failed subdivisions, abandoned family farms, logging sites — wherever man has cleared land and left it — there you find the old field communities.

10) **Great forests.** Our most diverse plant communities, the great forests also cover the most territory. They are found in all areas of the state, where rainfall and drainage are good, and soils retain water. But they are predominant in the Piedmont and mountains below 5,000 feet. Oak and hickory are the mainstays. Where moisture is better, we have beech, maple and sweet gums and, where drier, loblolly pines. But in most areas of the Piedmont and mountains, pines are indicative of clearing and, if left alone, a transition back to hardwoods. Under the deciduous canopy are smaller trees such as the dogwood, and shrubs: among them azaleas, hydrangea and redbud and, in the mountains, laurel and rhododendron. All provide spectacular colors during flowering.

11) Boreal, or high mountain forests. Above 5,000 feet, the balsam and spruce thrive in a Canadian-like climate. On some peaks where high winds retard tree development, the rhododendron can reign. Other treeless peaks, known as balds, are botanical puzzles. Are these grass or heath-covered areas natural or manmade? Both sides are argued — and the answer may be some of each. But many balds that are no longer grazed must be maintained by man, usually with controlled burns, or plant succession begins. For others, particularly the heath balds, fire naturally comes often enough.

Color is used by our plant communities to advertise themselves. Azaleas have a wide range of color; the white of dogwoods and mountain laurel, yellows of hydrangea, and pinks of the rhododendron, fruit trees and redbuds are mid-level visual delights of spring and summer. Down low are the wildflowers that bloom in all of our plant communities, but are most spectacular in the great forests, the sandhills, the savannahs and marshes. Wildflower hikes are a popular pastime in North Carolina. Take along a good identification guide, hike in different areas and in different seasons and because our plant habitat range is so great, you can find most of the flowers in the guide within our borders.

And certainly, there are edible plants out there. Every kid knows the blackberry bush. But be careful with the mushrooms. Some are deadly poisonous. There are guides to the edible kind but most of us steer clear and get our mushrooms at the grocers. The natives and early settlers also used plants as medicines, creating teas, poultices and baths from herbs and plants, wild and domestic, to cure everything from sore eyes, toothache and itch to fever, cancer and consumption. Even today, healing herbs such as ginseng are sought in the backwoods and can be sold for high prices.

Fauna

The diversity of plant environments within our borders provides for a tremendous range of wildlife habitats.

Even though our land has been intensively logged and developed over the years and the impact of human endeavor is constantly diminishing wildlife habitat, some 850 species of vertebrates can be found in the state. Most are permanent residents. But many are birds who winter here or who stop to rest on flights between their summer and winter quarters.

Most animal life exists around us unseen. Alligators bask in the eastern swamps. Loggerhead turtles crawl onto the beaches late at night to lay their eggs. Privacy-loving black bears roam the Great Smokies, seldom seen except for those who have become spoiled with tourist handouts. Salamanders abound in the Smokies' moist places.

Most of us, rushing to and from our jobs and other appointments, see little of our state's wildlife other than the common birds and squirrels of our urban yards and parks. We know they're out there, these wild animals. We see them mostly as road kill — the possums, skunks and occasionally deer — that meet their deaths by automobile. Driving along, we occasionally spot a hawk atop a telephone pole or fence post. Even in the city, we can hear the woodpeckers and sometimes owls and, in summer, the nighttime symphony of bullfrogs, treefrogs, crickets and cicadas.

But most wild birds and animals avoid the cities and highways. To really see them, you need to get out of town. Pack a lunch and something to drink, take along binoculars and your camera, and go . . . where? A paperback called *North Carolina Wildlife Viewing Guide* by Charles Roe, identifies 90 sites across the state where humans can observe wildlife in natural habitats. Each site discusses the birds and animals that can be seen and tells you how to get there. No matter where you live in the state, you don't have to go far to enter the world of the wild.

The coastal islands, from Bald Head to Currituck, are a paradise for bird watchers. Spring and fall migrations provide the best opportunities for filling out the birdwatcher's list. The maritime forests attract landbirds, and there is plenty of room for waterfowl and shorebirds. Terns, gulls and the brown pelican can be seen year-round up and down the coast. The southern islands, warmed by the Gulf Stream, provide habitat for bird species more typically found farther south or in the sub-tropics. Farther north, in the Cape Hatteras National Seashore, the salt-water lakes and marshes of Pea and Bodie islands provide habitat for large flocks of wintering ducks, geese and tundra swans. Summer residents of the coast include herons and egrets. And among those who stop over in their migrations are hawks and owls and, occasionally, peregrine falcons and bald eagles.

Overshadowed, perhaps are the land animals of the islands — frogs and turtles, otters, minks and muskrats, snakes, salamanders and lizards, rabbits, foxes and deer, and others. The observant beach-goer can also sometimes see dolphins and porpoises offshore. Much of the coastal islands' area is protected as state and national parks or wildlife refuges.

In the coastal plain, sound marshes, such as at Swan Quarter, and natural lakes, such as Phelps and Mattamuskeet, also provide wintering quarters and stopover points for migratory waterfowl. Mattamuskeet, a National Wildlife Refuge, has an especially large population of Tundra swans in winter, and hosts snow geese, Canadian geese and migratory shorebirds in huge numbers.

Wildlife refuges also exist along the Alligator River and at Dismal Swamp. At Alligator River, red wolves have been reintroduced after nearly dying out in the '80s. It also is home to the endangered red-cockaded woodpecker, bald eagles and, of course, the alligator. The Great Dismal Swamp has a diversity of birds, especially woodlands species, as well as reptiles and amphibians.

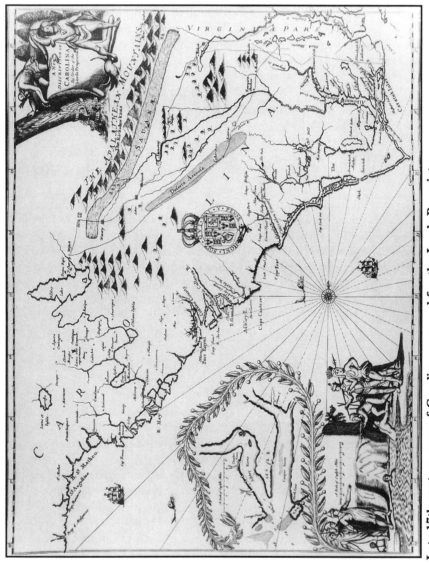

Late 17th century map of Carolina prepared for the Lords Proprietors.

Mammals include the black bear and bobcat.

Lake Waccamaw is known for its aquatic life, with many fish species and mollusks living there that are unique to the world. In the Sandhills, the rare Bachman's sparrow nests, and the state's most unusual butterflies can be found.

Mammals that inhabit areas of the coastal plain include river otters, minks, muskrats, deer, foxes, bats, squirrels, rabbits, beaver and so on. Reptiles abound, including many varieties of frogs, turtles and snakes. All four of North Carolina's poisonous snakes — coral, cottonmouth water moccasin, rattlesnake and copperhead — can be found in the coastal plain.

We think of the Piedmont as mostly urban, but the cities are surrounded by woods and fields that are abundant with wildlife. The habitats are not quite as diverse as those of the barrier islands and coastal plains. Most support wide varieties of woodland birds, including turkeys, quail, vultures and ravens, as well as many types of reptiles and amphibians. Beavers, river otters, flying squirrels and other common small animals thrive as do white-tail deer.

Where water is impounded, many of the same native and migratory species of birds can be seen as at the coast. Jordan Lake may be the best place in the state to catch site of bald eagles which nest in the upper lake regions, often in large numbers.

The state parks and wildlife viewing areas of the Piedmont are abundant and usually more accessible to on-road vehicles than those down east, which are often sandy or swampy. It's also easier to get out and hike, find a quiet spot and wait for animals to appear. Another, still quieter way to enter wildlife habitats is by canoe into the backwaters of the larger lakes or along the tamer rivers such as the Eno.

Just as the warm habitats of the southeast permit subtropical species to live within our borders, the higher mountains of western North Carolina mark the southern limits of some birds and animals that are more commonly found in colder climates. Among these are the saw-whet owl, black-capped chickadee and other birds, as well as the northern flying squirrel and New England cottontail. Good places to try for sightings are Grandfather and Roan mountains, Mt. Mitchell and the higher elevations of the Blue Ridge Parkway.

In addition to the seldom-seen black bears and bobcats, the Appalachians are home to many more easily seen animals, such as chipmunks, groundhogs and deer. The common raven flies over many of the wooded areas of the western half of the state. A hike along a mountain trail can turn up ruffed grouse, wild turkeys, owls and red-headed woodpeckers. Red wolves have been reintroduced in the Great Smoky Mountains National Park. The park is also home to more species of salamanders than can be found in any one area outside of the tropics.

A particularly troublesome animal in the park is the European wild boar. A number of these animals were brought to a private game preserve near

Murphy and escaped into the wild in 1920. They reproduced and spread, finding the wilds of the park a perfect environment. They have voracious appetites for small plants and animals and root intensively for their food. Since the '50s, they have been the biggest biological problem for the park, and hunting rights have brought on political problems. A trapping/relocation program seems in recent years to have reduced their numbers.

Settlement

Geography had much to do with the kind of people that we became. The Outer Banks were difficult to navigate. Treacherous shoals and shifting inlets buried many a ship in "The Graveyard of the Atlantic." After early failures inside the banks at Roanoke Island, English efforts to gain a foothold in the New World moved north and south. So the colonies of Jamestown and Charleston became centers of commerce and government, attracting merchants, shippers, bureaucrats, artisans, tradesmen, laborers, schemers, etc. Those who came to North Carolina wanted to escape the "city" for more elbow room and freedom. And, as will be discussed in the chapter on history, difficulties of governing this remote region of Carolina made our forebears even more independent.

Geography influenced us in many other ways. Many of our towns and cities began as settlements along sounds, rivers and trading routes. Because forests, swamps and rivers made overland travel extremely difficult, the earliest settlers claimed land along the shores of the sounds and the large rivers feeding them. Water provided the transportation routes. And while there were no deep water ports enabling trade directly with Europe, shallow-draft boats engaged in commerce across the sounds and in and out of the inlets with other colonies. Our earliest towns — Bath, New Bern and Edenton — were situated on these water routes. Settlement extended up the rivers, then up the creeks. As long as they could float a boat, the colonists had access to the world. Once land along the milder waters of the sounds had been claimed, settlers — particularly the Highland Scots — tackled the Cape Fear, creating the towns of Brunswick and Wilmington on the coast, then Fayetteville inland. Geography was not kind to Brunswick. Although it played a prominent role in the Revolutionary War, Brunswick became a ghost town as Wilmington,which was better protected against storms, pirates and gunboats, prospered.

Long before whites came, the natives had followed the lay of the land in establishing paths for trading and war parties. These paths criss-crossed the state and where possible, the settlers widened them for their own use. The earliest routes, connecting a landlocked farmer with a watercourse, or one coastal settlement with another, or with the Virginia ports, often were blazed through swamps under very difficult circumstances. One early strategy was the "corduroy" road, brought from Europe, in which trees were laid lengthwise along the route with smaller cuttings crosswise and often surfaced with sand.

Where rivers could not be forded, ferries — unreliable as they were — were put into operation. And by 1728, when the line between North Carolina and Virginia was established, surveyors reported crossing seven north-south roads along their 240-mile-route due west from the coast.

The Great Wagon Road from Pennsylvania became one of the most important overland routes in the development of North Carolina. Down this road came the colonists who populated the backcountry from the 1740s into the 1760s, fanning out from the Winston-Salem area west to the Blue Ridge, east until they met the settlers pushing inland from the coast, and south to Salisbury and Charlotte and beyond the state's borders into South Carolina and Georgia. Outposts sprang up where the new wilderness roads carried settlers, adventurers and their supporting commercial ventures. Where roads crossed navigable rivers or other roads or where there was a good mill site, settlements such as Charlotte and Salisbury took root and grew.

But the roads were bad, muddy when rainy and often impassable. Ferries were unreliable and bridges went unrepaired. Travel diaries throughout the 18th century were critical of North Carolina's roads. So the colonists still preferred to be near watercourses. Those along the Yadkin and Catawba and their tributaries became more closely tied to South Carolina because that's where the water took them. During the colonial period, this led to friction between the backcountry colonists and the ruling/taxing entity of North Carolina.

The sectionalism that retarded progress in the state until shortly before the Civil War was caused mostly by geography. Power resided in the east, which had been settled earlier, mostly by the British. Because of its location, this area retained the seat of colonial rule, which had the better trade outlets over water, enabling farms to be larger and requiring more slaves. Although they didn't approach the level of the Deep South plantations, the aristocratic easterners differed greatly from the Germans, Welsh and Scotch-Irish of the west, who had come down the inland routes from the north, had less access to markets and thus farmed on a much smaller scale.

But of course the west was bigger, and eventually population growth helped shift power from the east. In the decade before the Civil War, a plank road was built from the towns of Winston and Salem to Fayetteville, at the head of the Cape Fear's navigable waters. But more importantly, railroads were built — among them a north-south line connecting Wilmington and Weldon, and a main line running west from Goldsboro to Morganton. The railroads connected towns which had shown promising growth and helped them consolidate that growth. They also attracted settlements. And new towns, such as Rocky Mount, Durham and Burlington were born. High Point exists only because the railroad crossed the plank road there.

Other overland routes — primarily the old post road system that relied on able-bodied residents to keep open the mail links between settlements — remained primitive at best. Private companies pushed roads through the mountains prior to the Civil War, but all work on new roads and railroads stopped with the war. With the exception of Mecklenburg, which enacted a county tax to build roads of macadam — stone and gravel on a well-drained soil base — good roads were built only when the automobile phased out horse-drawn conveyances. The state built a primary road system in the '20s by selling bonds and paying them off with a gasoline tax and license fees. It took over maintenance of the secondary roads in the '30s. In the '40s, another large bond issue financed "farm-to-market" roads. In the '50s and '60s, limited-access interstate highways were built. In the '70s, four-lane highways were pushed into the mountainous backcountry. In the '80s and '90s, the last of the interstate links were completed and old sections widened and improved. Today, drivers can cross the state north-to-south on Interstates 95, 85, 77 and 26 and east-to-west on I-40. New interstates are on the drawing boards, and circumferential routes around some of our cities, such as Charlotte, are in various stages of construction. A trip from Wilmington to Murphy, which once required weeks, now can be done in eight hours or so.

Transportation improvements continue to affect our geography. Little burgs of 20 years ago around our larger cities became "bedroom communities" for workers who wanted to escape urban problems. Now they have growth problems of their own as more people and businesses have followed them out of town.

Small towns of the mountains and the coast have also been affected. The four-lane highways have drastically cut the time it takes to drive from the Piedmont into the mountains. You used to count on being stuck on a winding, two-lane highway behind a logging truck or camper; now you just zip right around these slow-pokes. A trip to many parts of the coast used to involve ferries as well as the two-lane roads. Now modern bridges span the sounds and many of the inlets. Towns such as Boone and Manteo have welcomed the business, but struggled to cope with the environmental problems that have resulted.

Environmental issues

Because of its abundance of resources and the demands people have placed on them, a number of environmental battles have been waged in North Carolina. Some have resulted in large tracts of land set aside for the public, others in regulations: watershed protection, land use planning, coastal development restrictions and endangered species protection.

Logging, drainage for agriculture and land development have changed drastically the landscape of the early settlers.

As more people drifted in, more trees were cut for clearing and for homes. But individual cutting tended to be selective, with only the biggest trees chosen for use. As commercial uses of the forests increased, logging became more indiscriminate.

In the eastern part of the state, cypresses were cut for all-purpose lumber and white cedar for boat-building and shingles. Most significant, however, was the logging of the forest of long-leaf pine, which once covered the eastern third of the state. Early on, the tree became a source for the "naval stores" industry. Its long trunks were used for masts and spars. Its resin was drained for pitch, tar and turpentine.

Only a few virgin long-leaf pines remain, protected now in Weymouth Woods Preserve near Pinehurst, but a few scattered second-growth forests can be found in protected areas of the coastal plain. These require careful management.

In the west, hardwoods were logged heavily beginning late in the 19th century. Logging companies owned much of the Appalachians and built railroads and primitive roads deep into the hills to bring out the harvested trees. Where hills were too steep for vehicles, logs were skidded down large wooden troughs.

Beyond the depletion of trees as a resource, heavy logging created erosion and water runoff problems, as well as loss of habitat for animals and plants. Indiscriminate logging was the catalyst for efforts to protect forests. The Weeks Law allowed forest lands to be purchased by the U.S. government. The Pisgah National Forest was created in 1916, mostly out of the Vanderbilt Estate forests which were the first in America to be scientifically managed. The Nantahala Forest was created in the southern section of the state's mountains in 1920. The Croatan Forest was established in the coastal plain in 1933, and the Uwharrie National Forest in 1961 in the central part of the state. Some land within the national forests is state-owned, and some privately owned. But the logging that takes place within the forest is managed by the U.S. Forest Service.

Debates continue over logging practices on public lands — whether to clear-cut or to cut selectively in any given area, for example, or whether to harvest downed or diseased wood — but the debates and their resolutions take place within the framework set up by the national forest system. Currently, the debate is over salvage timber cutting legislation passed in 1995 on behalf of foresters. Environmentalists say the law allows timber other than that classed as "salvage" to be cut. The cutting that has taken place so far has created more of a furor in the northwest, but the debate rages here as well.

The national forests have served a number of other purposes — recreation, education, game management, sites for fish hatcheries.

Concerns over logging also led to the creation of the Great Smoky Mountains National Park. It took more than 50 years from the earliest efforts by proponents until Franklin D. Roosevelt finally dedicated the park in 1940. Land for the park — nearly 160,000 acres — was bought with private funds and money raised by bond issues in North Carolina and Tennessee and deeded to the federal government.

Much of the timber in the park area was logged, but virgin forest remains in the park's most inaccessible places. Remnants of virgin forests also can be found in the Linville Gorge and Joyce Kilmer-Slickrock Wilderness areas of the mountains. But even where heavy logging took place, such as in the Great Smokies Park or at Mount Mitchell State Park, impressive second-growth forests have been established.

But there are new environmental threats to the mountains — acid rain and automobile exhaust pollutants that affect plants, soil and animals; and the balsam woolly adelgid, an insect that is killing the fraser firs. An insect blight killed off the chestnut trees in the 1930s. Another that kills hemlocks threatens to enter from the north. Flowering dogwoods in the deepest parts of the forests are being destroyed by a fungus.

Drainage of wetlands for agriculture and timber has been and remains a source of environmental concern — primarily for the coastal plain, but also to some degree in hardwood bottomlands and even in mountain bogs.

Historically, swamps, bogs, even some lakes were looked on for their drainage potential. Swamps were viewed as disease-carrying blighted areas better off ditched and drained. Boggy soils, when accessible, provided rich nutrients for crops. Lake Mattamuskeet was the scene of a giant drainage project in the teens and '20s that eventually failed.

Drainage projects have been actively promoted by the state and federal governments since the 1820s. At first, canals were dug by hand, later with steam-powered dredges. The extension of railroads into the back areas encouraged further drainage for crops and timber products. In recent decades, paper companies have drained wetlands to plant pine trees, and corporations have established farming on a massive scale in several coastal counties.

Kevin Moorehead, writing in *N.C. Wildlife* magazine in 1995, estimated that half of North Carolina's wetlands have disappeared through drainage projects, not only for timber and agriculture but also for mining, grazing, diking, filling for roads, stream channelization, mosquito control and urban sprawl.

In recent years, wetlands have become increasingly valued for their environmental benefits. Through their soils and the vegetation they support, wetlands can retain water from heavy rainfalls and allow for a more controlled period of absorption into the earth and streams. They can filter out harmful sediments and pollutants. Wetlands also nourish a wide variety of plant and animal life. They provide habitat for wildfowl and many land animals and for important elements of the food chain for fish and game. An estimated 70 percent of the plant and animal species on the state's rare and endangered lists depend on wetlands habitats.

A section of the federal Clean Water Act requires landowners to get a permit for any activity that would alter a wetland. But it doesn't prohibit wetlands development. It merely weighs the economic benefits of the project against the potential environmental effects, and most of the permits are approved. Through the Coastal Area Management Act, the state can protect salt-water marshes, but its authority does not extend to inland fresh-water wetlands.

Prior to World War II, few people visited the Outer Banks. Travel was limited by the lack of bridges, good roads and accommodations. Outside of a few settlements, not much was happening on the dunes, and they were left mainly to the lighthouse keepers, sea rescuers and fishing and hunting guides. The war opened up the banks, however. German submarines harassed shipping off the coast and, in turn, were sunk. A buildup took place on the banks to protect the coast from attack. The bridges and paved roads that resulted brought tourists after the war, and the necessary motels and cottages and support services followed. Later came the condos, subdivisions for second homes and golf courses.

But natural forces reign on the Outer Banks. Man has been unable to tame the maritime forces that play freely along the banks and ensure for himself a permanent, safe habitat.

During some storms, depending on the direction of wind and ocean current and on the situation of the beach, sand can build up along the shore. Other storms wash away sand. Some storms open new inlets; during others, old inlets are closed. Geologists say that the banks are moving toward the mainland, that what is now on the land side of an island eventually will be on its shoreside, and with more time washed away.

Developers, fishermen and businessmen say they need protection from these natural forces so they can operate in a stable environment.

The developer points out that as a landowner, he should be able to build seawalls and jetties to protect his property from washing away. The geologist replies that seawalls can actually speed up the beach erosion process by disrupting the natural wash-over activity of waves and deepening their cut. Jetties, he says, may keep your sand from washing down-current. But it robs the neighboring landowner of the sand he needs for renourishing his beach.

Fishermen also want jetties to protect the channels through inlets in the banks that allow them to get to sea. Again, the reply is that jetties rob sand from elsewhere and that a single storm can close the inlet or fill it back up and all of this expense would be for nothing.

The Cape Hatteras Lighthouse is a case in point. It was built in 1870 some 1,600 feet from shore. By 1987, the ocean was lapping but 120 feet away. Over the years, the lighthouse grounds had been sandbagged and protected with walls and jetties. But it became clear that in order to save it, the lighthouse had to be moved. A complicated project, that later was designated the nation's Outstanding Civil Engineering Achievement of 1999, was developed to move the lighthouse to 1,600 feet inland on rails and with hydraulic jacks at a cost of about $10 million.

Scientists and geologists from all over the country were in Duck in 1994 to

Sea oats help anchor dunes at Hammocks Beach State Park near Swansboro.

study beach erosion problems. The advanced instruments used in their experiments and computer models based on the data should provide us soon with our best information on how our shoreline is shaped. What is clear is that nature has so far won this battle and may continue to do so. What is left for us to decide is whether this effort to harness nature on the Outer Banks can ever be practical and who is to pay for it.

A number of battles between environmentalists and developers have taken place on the islands, with each side scoring victories. As with the mountain forests and the state's wetlands, environmentalists view the banks as having special, important ecological systems. Developers say that the land is their's to do with as they please, that they have learned to build responsibly, that their projects provide jobs and an expanded tax base. Environmentalists reply that any development risks injuring this fragile ecology, that any tax base gain is offset by the need for more government services, that construction jobs are only temporary and that jobs catering to tourists are seasonal and don't pay well.

And the arguments go on.

Plenty of development has taken place. Nags Head, the Bogue Banks, Topsail Island, Carolina Beach all boast the traffic jams, neon strips, tourist attractions, condos and housing developments typical of heavy coastal development anywhere.

The developers of Bald Head Island won a major battle of the '70s when several environmental groups sued to prevent construction of a marina, the only access to the island unless you land your own boat on the beach. Bald Head is the only semi-tropical island in the state. It was once on the list to become a state park, but funds didn't come through. Now a resort community of condos and homes has been built around a golf course. But much of the island remains wild.

Plenty of the Outer Banks has been preserved from development, particularly north of Bogue Banks. Buxton Woods, with 3,000 acres the largest maritime forest in the state, and Jockey's Ridge, the 140-foot-high dune near Nags Head, were saved from development by citizen action and are now protected. Nags Head Woods, which traps rain to recharge the only source of underground fresh water for the town, was bought by the Nature Conservancy. The state has parks along the coast at various points of interest, including the entire island at Hammocks Beach.

The largest protection is provided by the National Park Service, however, with the Cape Hatteras and Cape Lookout National Seashores. Cape Hatteras Park was established in 1953, and is accessible by automobile through Manteo. It stretches 70 miles from Bodie Island south to Ocracoke and is broken by the Pea Island National Wildlife Refuge and several Hatteras Island towns. Cape Lookout Seashore consists of three islands — Portsmouth (or North Core), South Core and Shackleford — and stretches for 56 miles. It is accessible only by ferry or private boat, and is undeveloped except for a few primitive camping and fishing areas.

The rivers have also been the scene of a number of the state's environmental battles.

Efforts by a power company to dam the New River in Ashe County were defeated by environmental groups who succeeded in winning Wild and Scenic River status for the north-flowing stream.

The Champion Paper Co. in Canton has been sued by Tennessee landowners downstream on the Pigeon River who said their land had been devalued as a result of toxic waste pollution. One federal case resulted in a hung jury and a $6.5 settlement. A state court suit is unresolved. In 1998, Tennessee and North Carolina regulators and the EPA cut a deal to give Champion a wastewater permit which would require the company to cut its tea-colored discharges by half by 2001.

The Neuse has been the focal point of a controversy that came to a head in 1995 when heavy rains caused hog waste lagoons to overflow into the river. As far back as 1988, the state has tried to protect the Neuse from too many nutrients that cause excessive algae growth and rob the waters of oxygen. Meanwhile, the state's hog industry has boomed with subsequent problems of waste storage and spillage. In 1998, the state established a two-year moratorium on hog farm expansion, and extended the ban in 2001.

A few state statistics

Total area: 52,669 square miles
Rank: 28
Land area: 48,843 square miles
Forested land: 20,043,300 acres
Bounded by: Virginia, South Carolina, Georgia, Tennessee

County seats

North Carolinians who pride themselves on their knowledge of geography have had to overcome some quirks in the names of our towns and cities. Some counties and towns have names that would seem to link them together, although they may be many miles apart.

Greenville, for instance, is not in Greene County but in Pitt. That's where you'd think Pittsboro would be, but no. It's in Chatham County. And Greensboro is in Guilford County. Jackson County, to avoid confusion, should be home to Jackson or Jacksonville. But they're in Northampton and Onslow counties respectively. Jackson County does have Cherokee, however. It's certainly not in Cherokee County.

It just doesn't seem to make sense does it?

The list goes on:

Franklin is in Macon County, not Franklin.

And Franklinville is in Randolph.

Graham is in Alamance, not Graham.

Waynesville is in Haywood, not Wayne.

Yanceyville is in Caswell, not Yancey.

Mooresville is in Iredell, not Moore.

Columbus is in Polk, not Columbus.

Rockingham is in Richmond, not Rockingham.

Asheville is in Buncombe, not Ashe. And Asheboro is in Randolph.

This is by no means an exhaustive listing, but you get the point — which is that you can't assume a town-county pairing by the names.

That said, let us point out those combinations that do make sense.

Camden, the town, can be found in Camden, the county. Durham is in Durham, Gastonia in Gaston and Gatesville in Gates. Halifax is in Halifax. Hendersonville is in Henderson (although Henderson, the town, is in Vance). Lincolnton is in Lincoln and Nashville is in Nash. Rutherfordton is in Rutherford, Warrenton in Warren, Wilkesboro in Wilkes, Wilson in Wilson and Yadkinville in Yadkin.

Origins of cities

Here is a list of the state's cities and towns that had at least 23,500 people in the 2000 census.

Charlotte: Settled around 1750 by Scotch-Irish, mostly from Pennsylvania, who migrated down two colonial trading routes, the Occoneechee Trail to Concord and its extension, the Catawba Trading Path, that ran about where Tryon Street is today. Named in 1762 for Charlotte of Mecklenberg, German queen of England's George III.

Raleigh: Established in 1792 as the state's capital by vote of a legislative commission. Named for Sir Walter Raleigh, who financed the failed British attempts to settle Roanoke Island.

Greensboro: Established in 1808 as a county seat in the geographical center of Guilford County. Named after Gen. Nathaniel Greene, patriot hero of the Battle of Guilford Courthouse nearby.

Winston-Salem: Salem, begun in 1766, was the principal town of the Moravian settlement of Wachovia. Winston was founded in 1849 as the seat of the newly created Forsyth County. Named for Joseph Winston, a Revolutionary war hero and politician; Salem means "peace."

Durham: Established in 1854 as a North Carolina Railroad station. Named for Dr. Bartlett Durham, who owned the land on which the station was built.

Fayetteville: Created in 1778 by combining Scottish communities of Campbelltown and Cross Creek on the Cape Fear River. Named for Gen.

LaFayette, French hero of the American Revolution.

High Point: Established as a commercial center shortly after 1854, when the North Carolina Railroad was built across the route of the plank road between Salem and Fayetteville. Named so because it was the highest point of the railroad between Charlotte and Goldsboro.

Asheville: Laid out in 1794 as a county seat where the Swannanoa River joins the French Broad. First named Morristown, it was renamed in 1797 after Gov. Samuel Ashe.

Wilmington: Incorporated in 1739 from two communities — New Liverpool and New Town — near the junction of the Northeast and Cape Fear rivers. Named for Spencer Compton, earl of Wilmington.

Gastonia: Incorporated in 1877 at the crossing of two railroad lines. Replaced Dallas as the county seat in 1911. Named for William Gaston, 19th century congressman and state Supreme Court judge.

Rocky Mount: Established in 1816 as a mill site on the Tar River; moved two miles in 1845 to the Atlantic Coast Line tracks. Named for rocky mounds and ledges along the river.

Greenville: Centrally located in Pitt County and with good access to the navigable Tar River, it was established as the county seat in 1786. Named for General Green, Revolutionary War hero.

Cary: Begun in 1852 when A. Frank Page established a sawmill. Named Page's Turnout at first; renamed in 1871 for U.S. Sen. Samuel F. Carey of Ohio, a temperance lecturer who passed through North Carolina. "E" was lost through a clerk's error.

Goldsboro: Begun in 1845 where the Wilmington-Weldon Railroad passed near old Wayne county seat of Waynesboro, two miles away. Incorporated in 1847 and became the county seat in 1850. Named for Matthew Goldsborough, a railroad official.

Burlington: First known as Company Shops, when it was built around the shops of the North Carolina Railroad in 1856. The name was changed to Burlington in 1887. It was said to have been chosen by Katherine Scales, daughter of the governor, from a list of suggested names posted on a store front.

Chapel Hill: Chosen by a legislative committee in 1793 as the site for the newly authorized university. Named after a Church of England chapel on the site.

Wilson: The town was a merger of an early 19th century church and trading post settlement named Hickory Grove and a Wilmington-Weldon Railroad depot named Toisnot. Incorporated and renamed in 1849, it became the seat of a new county. Both town and county were named for Louis D. Wilson, a state politician who was killed in the war with Mexico.

Jacksonville: Established as a county seat at a ferry landing on the New River. Known as Onslow Court House until 1849, when it was renamed in honor of President Andrew Jackson.

Kannapolis: Established in 1905 along the Southern Railway as a location for James William Cannon's textile mill. The name is a combination of the family name plus *polis,* the Greek word for city.

Hickory: Site of a stage coach stop and log tavern built in the 1750s and licensed as Hickory Tavern in 1786. Became the nucleus of a settlement with the arrival of the railroad shortly before the Civil War.

Concord: Incorporated in 1798 after a dispute over where it should be situated. Things were settled peacefully, and that's how it got its name. It is the county seat of Cabarrus.

Kinston: Early known as Atkins Bank, a landing on the Neuse River. Later occupied by a chapel, then in 1857 a tobacco warehouse. Incorporated in 1762 as Kingston after George III, the "g" was dropped after the Revolution.

Salisbury: Established in 1755 on an old Indian trading path as a "jumping-off" point into the wilderness. Named after a town in England, or perhaps after its namesake in Maryland where some of its early settlers were from.

Rivers and lakes

From the tiny trout streams and rapids-filled rivers of the mountains to the gently flowing rivers and lakes of the Piedmont to the wide, navigable waterways and swamps of the coastal plain to the sounds and Atlantic Ocean of the coast, North Carolina has an abundance of water resources.

Here is a listing of them, working generally west to east.

Rivers	Beginning	Course	Mouth
New	Formed Alleghany-Ashe line from north, south forks	NW through Virginia, joins Kanawha at Charleston, W.Va.	Gulf
French Broad	Formed Rosman in Transylvania from north, south forks	NW through Asheville, joins Holston near Knoxville to form Tennessee River	Gulf
Pigeon	Formed SE Haywood from east, west forks	NW through Canton, joins French Broad in Tennessee	Gulf
Tuckaseegee	Formed SE Jackson from Panthertown, Greenland creeks	NW into Swain, joins Little Tennessee at Lake Fontana	Gulf

Nantahala	Rises SW Macon, joins Little Tennessee	NW into Graham, Fontana Lake	Gulf
Little Tennessee	Formed Rabun County, Georgia, from two creeks	N into Macon Co., NW to Fontana, joins Tennessee in Tennessee	Gulf
Hiwassee	Rises in Towns County, Georgia	NW through Chatuge, Hiwassee lakes; joins Tennessee in Tennessee	Gulf
Yadkin	Rises in south Watauga near Blowing Rock	NE into Wilkes, then SE to High Rock, Badin, Tillery lakes, joins Uwharrie to form Pee Dee	Atlantic
Deep	Formed Guilford at High Point Lake from E&W forks	SE through Randolph, joins Haw in Chatham to form Cape Fear	Atlantic near Southport
Haw	Rises in Forsyth	E to Alamance; SE through Jordan Lake; joins Deep to form Cape Fear	Atlantic near Southport
Catawba	Rises in SW McDowell	E, SE; dams at lakes James, Norman; into S.C. near Charlotte	Atlantic
Lumber	Formed on Moore, Richmond line from two creeks	Flows SE, crosses Robeson, in S.C. joins Pee Dee	Atlantic
Roanoke Albemarle	Formed Montgomery County, Va., from N&S forks	Enters Warren as Lake Gaston, flows SE, E	Sound
Chowan Albemarle	Formed at Gates-	Flows SE	

			Sound
	Hertford-Va. line from Nottaway, Blackwater rivers		
Tar (becomes Pamlico in Beaufort Co.)	Rises in Person east of Roxboro	SE, E by Rocky Mount, Greenville, Washington	Pamlico Sound
Neuse	Formed in Durham County from Eno, Flat rivers	SE through Falls of Neuse lake, by Kinston, New Bern	Pamlico Sound
New	Rises in Onslow near Jones line	SE across Onslow	Atlantic at Onslow Bay
Cape Fear	Formed by Deep, Haw in Chatham	SE and S by Fayetteville, Wilmington	Atlantic near Southport

Lakes	County Located	How formed	Date
Hiwassee	Cherokee	Dam, Hiwassee	1940
Purpose: TVA flood control, power generation, recreation			
Santeetlah	Graham	Dam, Cheoah	1928
Purpose: Power generation for aluminum plant, recreation			
Nantahala	Macon	Dam, Nantahala	1942
Purpose: Power generation for Nantahala Power & Light			
Fontana	Swain-Graham	Dam, Little Tenn.	1945
Purpose: TVA flood control, power generation, recreation			
Lake Lure	Rutherford	Dam, Broad	1928
Purpose: Resort development, recreation			
James	McDowell-Burke	Dam, Catawba	1923
Purpose: Power generation for Duke Power, recreation			
Norman	Iredell-Catawba-Lincoln-Mecklenberg	Dam, Catawba	1963
Purpose: Power generation for Duke Power, recreation			

High Rock	Rowan-Davidson	Dam, Yadkin	1927

Purpose: Power generation for aluminum company

Belews Creek	Stokes-Rockingham	Dam, Belews Creek	1971

Purpose: Power generation, recreation

Badin	Stanly-Montgomery	Dam, Yadkin	1917

Purpose: Power generation for aluminum company

Tillery	Stanly-Montgomery	Dam, Pee Dee	1928

Purpose: Power generation for Carolina Power & Light

Jordan	Chatham	Dam, Haw	1974

Purpose: Flood control, reservoir, recreation

Hyco	Caswell-Person	Dam, Hyco	1964

Purpose: Power generation for Carolina Power & Light

Falls	Durham-Wake-Granville	Dam, Neuse	1981

Purpose: Flood control, reservoir, recreation

Kerr	Vance	Dam, Roanoke (Va.)	1952

Purpose: Power generation, reservoir, flood control, recreation

Gaston	Warren-Northampton	Dam, Roanoke	1963

Purpose: Power generation, recreation

Phelps	Washington	Natural
Mattamuskeet	Hyde	Natural
Waccamaw	Columbus	Natural

Books

Houk, Rose. *Great Smoky Mountains National Park. A Natural History Guide.* Boston, 1993, Houghton Mifflin.

Kaufman, Wallace and Pilkey, Orrin H. Jr. *The Beaches Are Moving. The Drowning of America's Shoreline.* Durham, N.C., 1983, Duke University Press.

North Carolina Atlas & Gazeteer. Freeport, Me., 1993, 2nd ed., DeLorme Mapping.

Powell, William S. *The North Carolina Gazetteer. A Dictionary of Tar Heel Places.* Chapel Hill, 1968, The University of North Carolina Press.

Roe, Charles E. *North Carolina Wildlife Viewing Guide.* Helena, Montana, 1992, Falcon Press.

Taylor, Walter K. *Wild Shores: Exploring the Wilderness Areas of Eastern North Carolina.* Asheboro, 1993, Down Home Press.

Waynick, Capus. *North Carolina Roads and Their Builders.* Raleigh, 1952, Superior Stone Co. 2 vols.

B.W. Wells. *The Natural Gardens of North Carolina.* Chapel Hill, 1967, the University of North Carolina Press.

3
History

We have introduced you to the people of North Carolina, then told you a bit about the geography and how it has shaped us.

Add to those elements the ebb and flow of human affairs and the happenstance of natural phenomena. Study the records of all of these elements, try to understand them and how they relate to each other and you create history.

North Carolina has a tremendously rich history, stretching back more than 400 years.

As one of the 13 original colonies, it shared the nation's history of early settlement, struggles with the natives and the changing relationship with England that led to the Revolutionary War.

With the Southern region, it shares the history of the Civil War, Reconstruction and the era of Civil Rights reform.

But its special blend of geography, population and circumstance have created a history unique within our borders that can be absorbed only through time. Here we'll give you a base on which to build a more thorough knowledge of the state's history.

We cannot cover in depth the history of the area you are visiting or in which you've settled. This local history — involving the old families, city development and growth, special institutions, building projects, tragedies and disasters — are what give your area its special character.

Histories have been written for nearly all of the state's 100 counties and many of its towns and cities. And many local citizens have recorded their memories in books and pamphlets. Your library will have most of these.

This chapter necessarily makes short order of our long, 400-year story. A bibliography at the end of the chapter will guide you to other books on a variety of subjects in North Carolina history and you can read them for greater detail.

The first here

The land that became known as North Carolina was settled more than 10,000 years ago in the latter stages of the great migration from Asia, when humans crossed the Bering Strait and, over time, fanned out across the continent.

These first claimants to the land shared it with large animals, such as mammoths, camels, horses and bison, and plenty of small game that they hunted and wild plants that they gathered. These people, called Paleo-Indians by archaeologists, chipped stones to make spear points and other tools. They tended to follow the animal herds and not to settle into permanent homes and villages.

About 8000 b.c., a warming climate began to change the landscape and caused many larger animals to become extinct. An increased population put further pressure on the meat supply. Game, especially larger game, became more scarce, and hunting more difficult.

During this period, known as the Archaic, humans confined themselves to a smaller area. To cope with the challenging survival conditions, they became intimate with their environment and learned the habits of plant, animal and sea life. They carved bowls, cooked in skin-lined pits in water brought to a boil with heated stones, and developed spear throwers to hurl their weapons with more force. Still, they tended to wander.

But between about 1000 and 500 B.C., the natives settled down and became farmers. They cleared fields — primarily along waterways where the soil was rich — and planted squash, corn and other vegetables. They supplemented their planting with hunting and fishing. They built homes, some with frameworks of woven saplings covered with bark and skins. They also began to make pottery, with clay rolled into long ropes and coiled into bowls. Spears were abandoned in favor of the bow and arrow.

They honored their dead, and some built ceremonial burial mounds. These were known as the Woodland people.

Another cultural tradition, the Mississippian, existed here as well. The Mississippians were also agrarian, but had more complex political systems that could unite several villages under one kingdom. They also built large pyramid-shaped mounds for religious rituals. Town Creek Indian Mound, operated as a tourist site in Montgomery County, was built by natives of the Mississippian tradition who displaced Woodland people for awhile.

The Cherokees were Woodland people who adopted some of the traditions of the Mississippians. You can still see today some of the Cherokees' ceremonial mounds along the rivers of western North Carolina.

Elements of both the Woodlands and Mississippian traditions were alive when the Europeans arrived.

What we know of the history of native Americans prior to the coming of the whites has been told to us by archaeologists who sift through the debris of civilizations and make educated guesses about what they find.

What we know of native history after the contact is told to us by European historians in the context of their own experience. They write of a heathen, uneducated people who were often child-like, often barbarous and in need of schooling and religion.

But most of all, the Europeans felt that the natives needed to be moved out of the way so that the colonists could establish themselves on a piece of land, fortify and develop it, then expand onto neighboring ground. When the natives fought to retain their land, they were killed. Those who acquiesced soon lost their prime hunting and planting grounds and died of hunger. Many others were killed by the new diseases brought by the Europeans. In the North Carolina region, it took the Europeans about 250 years to move the natives out of the way.

The Lost Colony

In 1587, fewer than a hundred years after Columbus had stumbled upon the New World, England attempted to gain its first foothold in America.

With Sir Walter Raleigh as sponsor, 113 people packed into three small ships and after 76 days at sea landed on Roanoke Island and began to set up a colony in the name of England. We know a great deal about this enterprise — how it was financed, the difficulties of the voyage, how things went during the first month of the colony's life.

What we don't know is what happened to it. The colonists disappeared with little trace. They are known to us as The Lost Colony. And theirs is our favorite story.

The Europeans' knowledge of our region had developed slowly. The Italian Verrazano, sailing for France, first saw it in 1524. But the sand banks prevented him from finding a protected anchorage, and boat parties did not spend much time exploring.

Hernando de Soto, a Spaniard, passed through the mountains in 1540. He was looking for gold but didn't find any. So the early explorers ignored Carolina for more fruitful territory.

Interest grew in Europe over the mystery and promise of America. The English, although latecomers to exploration, decided to get in on the action. Raleigh was Queen Elizabeth's choice to explore the possibilities for a colony, and he outfitted an expedition that arrived off Cape Hatteras in the summer of 1584.

From a base on Roanoke Island, the party explored the inner coast for about six weeks, compiled reports and made drawings of the new land and its inhabitants and brought two natives, Manteo and Wanchese, back to England.

The expedition stirred up immense excitement, and Raleigh was showered with money, praise and a knighthood. The new land was named Virginia for Queen Elizabeth (the Virgin Queen), and plans were made for a return.

The next summer, 108 colonists — most of them British and most soldiers — arrived at Roanoke Island aboard six ships financed largely by Raleigh and commanded by Sir Richard Grenville. A fort and a few houses were built, and the governor, Ralph Lane, sent explorers as far north as the Chesapeake Bay and well inland in all directions.

In August, Grenville went to England for supplies, but was delayed in returning. It was the next summer before he could get back to America. Just days before he arrived, the colonists left with Sir Francis Drake, whose fleet had called at Roanoke Island. Although their crops were doing well, the colonists were running short of supplies, and the natives were increasingly hostile over their presence. Also while Drake was there, a severe storm hit and apparently hastened Lane's decision to go back to England.

Grenville looked high and low for the colonists, then gave up and sailed back to England, leaving a dozen or so soldiers behind.

Raleigh, his resources now dwindling, quickly joined with a number of British merchants in a new attempt at colonization. This colony, which included women and children, would emphasize settlement instead of exploration.

Raleigh's orders were that the new colony be established in the Chesapeake region. But the commander of the fleet arrived off the coast in July, 1587, much later than anticipated, and he refused to take the colonists beyond Roanoke Island.

So the colonists, under Governor John White, began repairing the old buildings of the previous Roanoke colony and prepared to set up their own community. Early events were ominous. They had arrived too late to plant crops. The only trace of the military contingent left behind was a skeleton. And one of the settlers was killed by Indians after he'd strayed too far while crabbing.

But a few things happened that cheered the colonists. Manteo, to whom the colonists turned for advice on survival, was christened in the first Protestant baptismal service in America. And Eleanor Dare, wife of Ananias Dare and daughter of Governor White, gave birth to a daughter. She was named Virginia and was the first child of English parents born in America.

It quickly became obvious that someone would have to return home for supplies. Those brought over would not last until harvest time the next year, and the Indians could spare no food. So White went back to England on one of the ships, intending to return quickly.

But it was nearly three years before he did so. War with Spain, difficulties in raising new funds for supplies and the organizing of the fleet delayed him. Finally, on August 15, 1590, White's ship came in sight of Roanoke Island. He could see smoke from the location of the fort, and he was encouraged. But the landing was costly. Stormy waters created difficulties and eleven men drowned in the high surf.

Once ashore, the English found only felled trees and grass on fire, probably started by lightning. They found no sign of the colonists, except for the letters "CRO" carved into one tree and "CROATOAN" carved into another.

That indicated to White that the colonists had moved to Croatoan, Manteo's tribal village at Hatteras, and because there was no cross carved to indicate danger, that they had gone willingly. But there was no way to check on them. The storm nearly prevented the landing party from returning to the ship. And the weather prevented them from sailing south. The relief ships were forced to return to England, and the mystery of the colonists' fate was left behind.

The first successful English colony was established 17 years later at Jamestown, in the Chesapeake Bay region where the original colonists were supposed to go. Rumors that some of the Roanoke Island colonists had survived reached Jamestown now and then, but efforts to track them proved fruitless.

Thus, the enterprise became known as the "Lost Colony." Its fate has been debated by generations of historians. Some think the colonists were all killed. Others believe a fleet may have offered them passage back to England and that they perished at sea.

Some think they intermarried with the Indians. John Lawson, an early surveyor of the colony, wrote in the early 1700s that Hatteras tribesmen told him that several of their ancestors were white and that they could read from books. But the truth can never be known.

Except for the war years of the early '40s, the story has been retold each summer night since 1937 in a symphonic drama, *The Lost Colony*, written by the late North Carolina playwright Paul Green. The pageant takes place in an outdoor amphitheater in Manteo and is an excellent way to soak up some North Carolina history on the very sands where the events took place.

Colonial times

The difficulties of navigating through the shifting inlets of the Outer Banks, the shallow sounds and lack of a port protected from the weather discouraged further efforts to settle North Carolina directly from overseas. Successful settlements were begun in Jamestown, then in Charleston.

As a result, North Carolina was first settled by those who found themselves a bit constrained in the established colonies. Word circulated that the soil was good for agriculture and that the natural resources were desirable and plentiful. It took the more adventurous to leave civilization — that as it was — to settle in North Carolina. But beginning in the 1650s and throughout the colonial

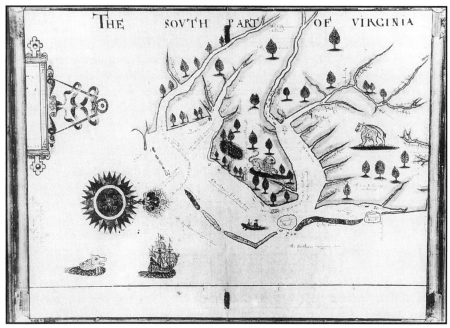

A version of the map drawn in 1657 by cartographer Nicholas Comberford.

period, the overland migrations from the south and the north populated North Carolina from the coast to the base of the Appalachians. And the political experience of this very independent group of people was typical of the evolution of thought and action that led the colonies to revolt.

In 1663, after a civil war restored the monarchy to England, Charles II granted a charter to eight Lords Proprietors — powerful men to whom he owed political debts — that granted them all lands south of what is now Virginia into Florida. The territory stretched west all the way to the Pacific and was named the Province of Carolina, in honor of the king.

The charter established a royal government, but it also set up an assembly elected by the people that was to advise in the enactment of laws. The charter gave the colonists all the rights of English citizens and provided for religious freedom. The Lords Proprietors were given the power to set up a government, to collect taxes and establish an army to defend the colonists from the Indians and the Spanish.

Albemarle, to the north, and Clarendon, along the Cape Fear, were North Carolina's first counties and a third, Craven, encompassed most of what is now South Carolina. Bath, in 1706, became the first town to be formally laid out and incorporated.

Early on, difficulties arose over the instructions to the colonial governors from England. Many proved unworkable in the real world of the frontier. Good governors to this backwoods area were hard for the Lords Proprietors to find. And they seemed indecisive about how to govern, at times allowing the colonists great freedom, at other times trying to reassert their authority. Colonial leaders felt that they better understood how to make the colony run smoothly, and the simmering resentment over British authority often boiled over into conflict. The degree of that conflict between the colonial assembly and the governor and his council was usually related to how committed the latter were to carrying out the Lords Proprietors' dictates.

In 1677, one of the first popular uprisings against the royal government in America occurred when acting Gov. Thomas Miller, himself a Carolina colonist, arrested a sea captain and George Durant, a rival colonist, for violating trade laws. But Durant's supporters, chief among them one John Culpeper, rose up and jailed Gov. Miller, seized tobacco he had collected for taxes, then tried and sentenced him, and ruled the colony themselves for a year. Miller eventually escaped and made his way to England to tell what had happened. Culpeper then was sent by the colonists to England to give their side of the story. Culpeper was arrested and convicted on several counts, including embezzlement of tax revenues, but was then released and pardoned, thus ending the episode known as "Culpeper's Rebellion."

Division of the Province of Carolina began in the 1690s when the Lords Proprietors decided to install the main governor at Charles Town, with a deputy governor over the northern territory. The deputies were mostly from among the settlers and the land "North and East of Cape Feare called North Carolina" assumed its own identity. In 1712, the Proprietors sought to regain administrative control, naming a governor of North Carolina who would be independent of Charleston.

The steady growth of the colony was interrupted about this time by the Tuscarora Indian wars. The Tuscaroras inhabited the lands that were being steadily encroached upon by settlers. In some cases, Indians were paid for their land. But typically, they were tricked out of it and taken advantage of by traders. Many were kidnapped and taken north into slavery. A struggle for the governor's office had divided and weakened the colony, and a large, well-armed faction of the Tuscarora tribe attacked outlying settlements. Hundreds of settlers were killed, and survivors had to flee to the communities along the rivers.

The war lasted for about a year, and the Tuscaroras were quelled only with the help of settlers and friendly Indians from South Carolina. It took some time for the colony to recover, but gradually economic activity and immigration picked up. New counties were established and new towns incorporated. Edenton, begun in 1722, became the colony's first capital. Brunswick was established on the Cape Fear River in 1725. Merchant ships from the north

Chowan County Courthouse at Edenton, built about 1767.

came calling more often for tobacco and pine products, chiefly tar. Pirates skulked along the Outer Banks and had to be put down.

In 1729, King George II bought most of the colony from the seven of eight Lords Proprietors willing to sell. The boundary with Virginia was surveyed, and North Carolina became a royal colony, subject to the control of the governors appointed directly by the king. Their instructions were to make the colony a productive part of the empire and to enforce the king's dictates.

As might be expected, these plans did not sit well with most colonists who had been cushioned from direct contact with the Lords Proprietors and had become accustomed to a large measure of self-rule. The independence won during the early colonial period provided the backdrop for their struggle against a succession of five royal governors who held office during the nearly 50 years leading up to the Revolution.

Matters large and small boiled down to one basic question. Would the assembly, elected by the people, act independently and represent their will? Or would it blindly rubber-stamp the king's dictates as expressed through the governor?

The first governor, a man named Burrington, ran into trouble immediately in his efforts to collect property taxes. His high-handed manner and inability to compromise soon caused him to be replaced by Gabriel Johnston, a Scotsman. Johnston alarmed the colonists with quick decisive actions to collect property taxes soon after his arrival in 1734, threatening to seize the property of those who would not pay. But he was willing to compromise on other matters and proved himself an able administrator over time. Until his death in 1752, the colony grew and prospered.

Quarrels erupted with the third royal governor, Arthur Dobbs, over the assembly's powers and the judicial system. At times, the assembly would use its power to allocate public funds as leverage to attain its goals. Once, when asked by the governor to act on legislation deemed intolerable, the assembly refused to meet, claiming that a majority of members could not be rounded up. This enraged Dobbs to the point that he called them "as obstinate as mules."

Wars with the French and the Indians, the Cherokees in particular, came during Dobbs' administration. The war with the French took place up and down the American frontier and was significant both for the British, who consolidated their hold on the colonies, and for the colonists, who saw what they could accomplish when they worked together.

The Cherokees were among the tribes stirred into action against the colonists by the French. Attacks on outlying settlements led to the establishment of Ft. Dobbs near Statesville. When that was attacked, in 1760, an army was sent into Cherokee country but defeated. The next year, under Col. James Grant, an army of colonists and Scottish Highlanders met and defeated the Cherokees, pushing them far into the mountains and breaking forever their power to halt the westward movement of the whites.

The pace of events leading to revolution picked up during the five-year term of Gov. William Tryon, who was the best known of the royal governors. We have today the restored Tryon Palace, which was built for him in the late 1760s in New Bern, the new capital of the colony. Built of brick and trimmed in marble, Tryon Palace was said to be the finest government building in all of the colonies. But even though the popularly elected assembly allocated the money for it, the palace was hard for many North Carolinians to swallow, especially those who lived far from New Bern and never expected to see it. They complained bitterly over the taxes that had to be collected for its construction.

Complaints over excessive taxes and fees and the high-handed manner in which they were collected by the royal appointees brought on a series of protests, arrests and counter-protests that escalated into the Regulator movement. This rebellion of frontiersmen centered on Hillsborough, but involved settlers throughout the inland areas of the colony. It reflected sectional differences with the eastern colonists, who were in control of the assembly and who were seen as British collaborators by the westerners. The movement gathered momentum over a three-year period and ended in armed conflict when Gov. Tryon sent in a force of about 1,500 troops to protect judges assigned to a special term of Superior Court.

The Battle of Alamance took place a few miles southwest of what is now Burlington in May, 1771. In two hours it was over, a clear victory for the governor's militia. Twenty or so Regulators were killed on the battlefield, another half-dozen hanged for treason. The movement was broken, largely with the help of eastern colonists who opposed the Regulators' cause. Later, the regions would side together against the king over some of the same issues — unfair taxation and oppressive government — that the Regulator movement had raised.

Actually, some who supported Tryon against the Regulators had acted earlier against the crown over the Stamp Act. An effort by England to raise funds in the colonies, the act required many documents, including newspapers, legal papers, surveys and shipping documents to be published on stamped paper that had to be bought from the government. In 1765, when a ship carrying stamped paper arrived at Brunswick on the Cape Fear, a group calling itself Sons of Liberty blocked the unloading. When two ships were seized for not carrying stamped papers, a group of North Carolinians marched on Brunswick and convinced British agents to free the vessels.

Resistance throughout the colonies caused the British to back down, but they followed with a series of measures, including one that established import duties on a variety of products. Virginia called on other colonies to join a "Non-Importation Association." As the North Carolina Assembly began to discuss the matter, Tryon abruptly ended the session. But assembly delegates reconvened on their own and approved the association. Again, England backed down in the face of the colonies' actions and removed the duties on all products except for tea. Following the more famous tea dumping in Boston Harbor, a group of ladies staged the Edenton Tea Party in October, 1774, stating their intention to support the American cause by drinking no more tea.

As with the other colonies, North Carolina heeded the call to send delegates to a Continental Congress. Three men, William Hooper, Joseph Hewes and Richard Caswell, were elected in a statewide convention to which all of the counties sent representatives. The state and county groups continued to meet, quickening popular sentiment for self-rule. The Mecklenberg Committee, for example, declared the laws of the king to no longer be in force. May 20, 1775, the date of this so-called "Mecklenburg Declaration of Independence," is on the North Carolina state seal and flag. That same month, the last royal governor, Josiah Martin, fled the colony aboard a British warship.

In the vacuum created by his absence, North Carolina formed a provincial government and raised a militia, which helped fight against loyalists in Virginia and South Carolina. Meanwhile, the ousted Martin concocted a plan wherein Scots still loyal to the king would join British troops under Sir Henry Clinton and Lord Cornwallis at Wilmington, then march inland to split the colonies and fan north and south to regain control. But colonists got wind of the plan and 1,100 militiamen met the 1,600 Scots attacking at Moore's Creek Bridge north of Wilmington and stopped the advance.

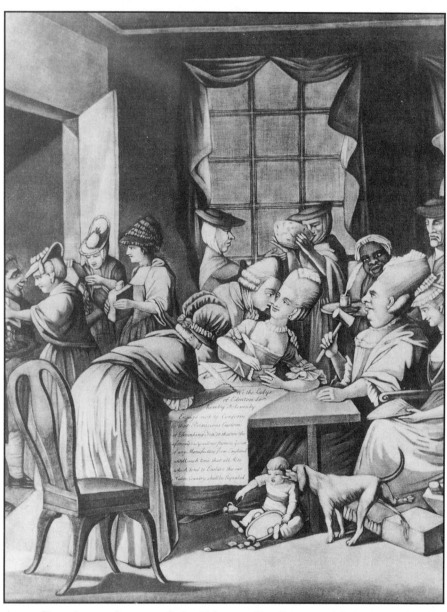

An unflattering caricature of the Edenton Tea Party, published in a British magazine.

Diorama scene
depicting
the battle of
Moore's
Creek Bridge
in 1776.

Statue of
Gen. Nathanael
Greene at
Guilford
Battleground
Park.

Many in North Carolina of British extraction were generations removed from the home country. Many more were of non-British ancestry, and the kinship with England was felt less and less through the decades of the colony's growth. Still, many were saddened by the split with England. But when King George declared the colonies in rebellion and began military actions against them, most colonists became convinced that independence was their only course. In the Halifax Resolves of April 12, 1776 (the other date on the state flag and seal), North Carolina's provincial congress expressed the same sentiments for independence that were later embodied in the more famous national Declaration of Independence of July, 1776. The signing of that national document led to great celebration in the province. The provincial congress adopted a state constitution in December, and in January, 1777, the first slate of state officers was sworn in, with Richard Caswell as delegate-appointed governor.

The Revolutionary War

After the battle of Moore's Creek Bridge, North Carolina was relatively free of fighting for four years. Its troops took part in battles up north, then in the south after the fall of Savannah in 1778. Josiah Martin, the former royal governor of North Carolina, tirelessly argued that Loyalist strength in the state would help the British reclaim the territory. So when Charleston fell to Cornwallis in May, 1780, the British were confident that North Carolina would prove fairly easy pickings and give them another stepping-stone northward in their war with the colonies. Because British troops did not fare well in the heat and humidity of summer, Cornwallis decided to wait until autumn to advance. The delay gave the state militias time to reorganize, and troops were sent from the north to help. Meanwhile, the Loyalists were organizing too. One of their gatherings — at Ramsour's Mill near Lincolnton — resulted in a battle with state militiamen. Their defeat sapped the Tories' strength and made them useless to Cornwallis.

The Americans, attacking the British in August at Camden, S.C., were decisively beaten, but still Cornwallis delayed his advance. The Americans reorganized again, and the British threat mobilized a force of frontiersmen who had settled beyond the Appalachians in what is now northeastern Tennessee. Cornwallis finally moved toward Charlotte in mid-September. His troops were harassed the entire way by partisan guerrillas. When he finally made Charlotte, he found himself surrounded not by the Loyalists he had expected, but in a "hornet's nest" of rebellion.

As the Overmountain Men neared Charlotte, they were met on Oct. 7 by British Col. Patrick Ferguson, who placed his men on Kings Mountain just inside South Carolina. It was a position he thought impregnable. But the mountain men, who were crack shots and at home on the terrain, killed

Ferguson and routed his troops. The battle, which lasted only about an hour, forced Cornwallis back into South Carolina.

Now George Washington named Gen. Nathanael Greene of Rhode Island to lead the southern forces. During the winter of 1780-81, Greene lured Cornwallis into pursuing his army. Things started badly for the British, when a large force of Redcoats were beaten at Cowpens, S.C., by a segment of Greene's army led by Gen. Daniel Morgan. Cornwallis, still convinced that Loyalist sympathy remained strong in North Carolina, tried but failed to reinforce his army as he chased Greene through the icy winter. In February, Greene crossed into Virginia, where he rested his troops. His army gained strength as eager colonists, sensing victory, joined Greene's forces. Finally, when he returned to the state in March and faced Cornwallis at Guilford Courthouse, outside of Greensboro, Greene outnumbered the British by about 2 to 1. The British forces, however, were better trained, and after a hard day of fighting, were left in control of the battlefield. But Greene's was a tactical victory of the lose-the-battle, win-the-war variety. Cornwallis' losses were so severe that he retreated to Wilmington, which had been taken by the British a few weeks earlier. There he decided to move on Virginia and, after taking that state, return to North Carolina to mop up. He marched north out of Wilmington and into Virginia, maneuvering in frustration until at last, in October, he was boxed in at Yorktown and surrendered.

Shaping the state

At the close of the war, North Carolina territory stretched to the Mississippi River. And the land over the mountains quickly began to attract settlers. New counties were established and, in 1794, Nashville was chartered as the county seat of Davidson. Like those who had left established colonies to settle in North Carolina earlier, the pioneers who went west were an independent bunch, and they soon began to set up their own state of Franklin. Elections were held. John Sevier became the first governor, and elected sheriffs began collecting taxes. Representatives petitioned Congress to recognize the new state, but this was not granted. With economic incentives and threats, North Carolina wooed the westerners back into its fold. But the territory was finally ceded to the new United States, and the state of Tennessee admitted to the union in 1796.

North Carolina's own entry to the union was rocky. Soon after the Constitution was drawn up by the Philadelphia convention of 1887, forces in the state divided over how much power the federal government should have. In its first vote on the Constitution, in August 1788, the state convention turned it down, objecting mainly to powers of federal taxation and court jurisdiction in the state and over the lack of a bill of rights. A second convention was called for November, 1789. Federalists, who favored the constitution, waged an educational campaign around the state, and popular opinion began turning the tide. Also, the Bill of Rights had been introduced. The Constitution was ratified by this assembly, with the Bill of Rights winning approval the following month. North Carolina was the 12th state to ratify the constitution. Of the 13 original colonies only Rhode Island acted later. The delay kept North Carolina out of the first U.S. Congress, and the state had no say in the election of George Washington as first president.

As settlement in the new state expanded westward, New Bern was considered to be too far east to continue as the capital. The question was referred to the same 1788 convention in Hillsborough that voted against the Constitution. Delegates dictated that the new capital be located within ten miles of Isaac Hunter's Tavern in Wake County. In 1792, the land for the city of Raleigh was bought, and construction began on a capitol building.

The state's constitution of 1776 provided for one or more universities, and a bill sponsored by William R. Davie and passed by the legislature in 1789 established the first state-supported university in the nation. It was built at a crossroads near the center of the state on land donated by local farmers. The place was called Chapel Hill after an old Anglican chapel on the site, and the university opened its doors in 1795. Early on, it gained a reputation in the state for liberal thinking. This "hotbed of federalism," as it was called then, angered legislators who tried to cut off some state funding. But a state court restored that funding, ruling the university had a basis in the constitution and thus was protected from the whims of the legislature.

Cherokee removal

Six hundred miles to the west of Roanoke Island's *Lost Colony* amphitheater is another built into a Great Smokies mountainside, where on each summer night a drama about the Cherokee Removal, *Unto These Hills,* is performed. Of all of the American tribes, the Cherokees tried the hardest to learn the white man's ways and become "civilized," according to his standards. But in the end, the Cherokees met the same fate as other tribes and were removed to a reservation far from home. Only a few remained in the North Carolina mountains and their ancestors live there today.

The Cherokees' ancestral homeland spread across part of four of today's states: North Carolina, Georgia, Tennessee and Alabama. Twice, the Cherokees fought for the losing side — against the British during the French and Indian wars and with the British during the Revolution. The wars had a devastating effect on the tribe, with the crowning blow in 1776, when a fierce campaign by colonial forces under Gen. Griffith Rutherford wiped out many Cherokees and their villages.

So when George Washington's administration developed a program to teach natives the ways of the whites, many Cherokees saw it as the only way to preserve their nation. They learned modern agricultural practices and transformed their hunting and trading economy. A few put together large plantations and owned slaves. Privileged Cherokee children learned English and elements of white culture at schools set up by religious groups. Literacy was promoted throughout the Cherokee nation, even among those who did not learn English. Sequoyah developed a Cherokee syllabary of 85 symbols in the 1820s, and a newspaper was established for the tribe.

Western migration of whites continued to create a demand for land, and the discovery of gold in Cherokee territory in northeast Georgia in 1828 increased pressures on the federal government to obtain Cherokee lands for white settlement. U.S. policy then was to obtain native lands only through treaty, and the Cherokees refused to sign. But in 1835, an unauthorized group of Cherokees did sign a treaty and, despite a tribal petition disclaiming the deed, it was ratified by the Senate. In the winter of 1838, the removal to the west began, with U.S. Army soldiers rounding up 16,000 Cherokees to begin the long walk to their new reservation in Oklahoma. About 4,000 of them died along the way, and the survivors called it the "Trail of Tears."

Years earlier, a group of Cherokees known as the Oconoluftee had opposed the tribe's cultural transformation and seceded from their nation. Individuals were granted titles to tracts of land which were not affected by the 1835 treaty. So, ironically, the natives who had spurned "civilization" were able to remain on their lands, while those who had tried so hard to become good citizens were the losers.

Another thousand or so Cherokees escaped removal by hiding. Among these rebels was Tsali and his sons who were hunted intensively after they killed two soldiers. The Army offered to allow the rebels to remain in the mountains if Tsali would give himself up. He did so and was executed.

The scattered remnants of the tribe joined the Oconoluftee to form the Eastern Band of the Cherokee Nation. Their lands were consolidated within the Qualla Boundary and are held in trust by the federal government. The town of Cherokee exists today at the eastern entrance to the Great Smoky Mountains National Park. Tourism and gambling are its economic mainstays.

The Rip Van Winkle State

Between the turn of the century and 1835, North Carolina took a long snooze. Somewhere along the way, it was dubbed the "Rip Van Winkle State" after the Washington Irving character who fell asleep and was oblivious to events around him.

The period was characterized by lack — lack of industry, lack of education, lack of transportation and markets, lack of money and, most of all, lack of political will to do anything about the state's problems. The philosophy that "the government that governs least is best" was practiced in the extreme.

Agriculture prevailed, with only a few weak stabs at establishing any kind of industry. Most of the farming was at the subsistence level — families scratching out a living on small plots. Where larger plots could be combined, cotton and tobacco were the mainstays. Both crops wore out the soil. Conservation measures, such as crop rotation, were not practiced and there was an incessant need for new fields. Both crops also required a great deal of manpower, hence a greater need for slaves to plant and pick and to clear forested land. Actually, slavery had dwindled in North Carolina late in the 18th century, but the invention of the cotton gin sped up processing, created a huge demand for cotton and helped bring about the expansion of slavery.

Political power rested in the east and was dominated by the wealthy and privileged. In general, they liked things the way they were. They did not feel compelled to educate the masses. Internal transportation improvements would not benefit them greatly, as they already had access to the rivers and sounds and could export their products by water.

So discouraging were the times that many North Carolinians moved away to other states where there were better opportunities. Among these were families whose children — such as Andrew Jackson, James K. Polk and Andrew Johnson — went on to do great things for their new states and for America.

Of course, not all of the state's best and brightest emigrated. There were a few progressive thinkers who stayed behind and dreamed of better things for their slumbering home state. Chief among these was Archibald Murphey of Caswell County, who was a circuit court judge and, in his travel in the western and central part of the state, saw first-hand the deprived conditions of North Carolinians. He wrote about what he saw and appealed to the General Assembly to adopt his programs for improvements in education, agriculture, public works and the constitution.

Ante-bellum years

Fortunately for the world of metaphor, Rip Van Winkle did wake up. And so did North Carolina. The 25 years before the Civil War were marked by a tremendous spurt of progress. Much of it was patterned after Murphey's vision, although he did not live to see it. Murphey had lacked the political ability to overcome the power of the eastern establishment. Not so David Swain, an able and respected lawyer from Asheville, who engineered a constitutional convention in 1835. Amendments to the Constitution lessened the requirements of wealth for representation in the General Assembly and effectively gave control of the House to the common man, predominant in the west.

Before the decade was out, the legislature established a public school system, and during the '50s state superintendent of schools Calvin Wiley molded it into one of the best in the nation. Schools were also set up for the deaf and

The State Capitol in Raleigh, built in 1840.

for the blind. Based on a study by Dorothea Dix of Massachusetts, a hospital for the mentally ill was built.

The legislature worked in partnership with private financing sources to back construction of railroads within the state. The first to be built was a line between Wilmington and Weldon, which was of strategic importance during the Civil War. Another line was built from Goldsboro through Raleigh and the Piedmont, along a curve that ended in Charlotte. Towns along this route began to grow rapidly and today make up the urban areas of the Piedmont Crescent. Another line extended the railroad to Morganton.

Turnpikes and plank roads improved transportation throughout the state, making markets more accessible to farmers and nurturing industrial activity. Literacy rates improved, and newspapers thrived. A better educated citizenry traveled more and exchanged ideas with progressive forces in other states. North Carolina was drawing notice nationally and internationally over its new-found era of progress.

But a cloud hung over it all and it grew darker and darker. Disputes between the North and South over the extension of slavery and the question of states rights within the union brought war that ended this period of progress.

The Civil War

When Abraham Lincoln won the presidency and secession fever spread through the South, many North Carolinians didn't want to leave the union. Even after the Confederate States of America was formed in February, 1861, North Carolinians voted against a convention to consider joining.

But after the action at Fort Sumter in April, when Lincoln ordered states to provide troops for the quelling of the insurrection and ordered a blockade of Southern ports, popular opinion quickly shifted and North Carolina joined the Confederacy.

"First at Bethel; farthest at Gettysburg; last at Appomattox." This is a catch-phrase that schoolchildren have learned over the years about North Carolina troops during the Civil War.

Big Bethel, near Yorktown, was the scene of the first skirmish of the war. Raw recruits of D.H. Hill's 1st North Carolina Regiment made up the bulk of the small Confederate force that routed a much larger Union force under Gen. Benjamin Butler. The first Confederate casualty of the war was from North Carolina — one Henry Lawson Wyatt of Edgecomb County.

Gettysburg, of course, was the three-day battle in the small Pennsylvania town that marked the turning of the tide for the South and Gen. Robert E. Lee, who had fought so well against great odds. Two North Carolina regiments led the futile attack up Cemetery Hill, known as Pickett's Charge. More than 4,000 troops from the state were killed at Gettysburg, about a fourth of the Southern total.

At Appomattox, Lee finally surrendered to Union Gen. Ulysses S. Grant. North Carolinians made up a fifth of his Army of Virginia at that time, and members of Gen. William R. Cox's brigade are said to have fired the last shots there.

More than 40,000 North Carolinians died in the Civil War, the most of any other Confederate state. Besides Gettysburg, the state suffered most heavily during the Seven Days battle near Richmond in 1862, at Chancellorsville and at Fredericksburg.

Even so, relations between the state and the Confederate government were never very good, a fact attributed to Jefferson Davis' irritation that it took the state so long to secede. Wartime Gov. Zebulon Vance also was protective of the state when he deemed Confederate actions excessive.

No battles on the scale of Gettysburg, Antietam or Shiloh were fought in North Carolina. There were no sieges here to compare with those at Atlanta, Vicksburg or Petersburg. But several major areas of engagement took place in the state.

A main concern for the Union was the southern coastline. Because many nations remained neutral in the conflict, the South would be able to trade for war goods, so the North put quick pressure on the ports — including

Wilmington — with blockades. The North also wanted access to eastern North Carolina because it could surround Virginia and cut off the Wilmington-to-Weldon railroad which supplied Richmond from the South. The best way to accomplish this was over the sounds and up the rivers, so the forts guarding the Outer Banks inlets were early targets.

A naval force under Butler took two forts guarding the Hatteras Inlet in August, 1861, setting the stage for an expedition early the following year by troops under Gen. Ambrose Burnside. On February 7, the small Confederate force at Roanoke Island surrendered after Yankees had landed more than 7,500 men.

Several days later, Elizabeth City fell. In March, New Bern and Little Washington were occupied. In April, Ft. Macon, which guarded Morehead Inlet, fell, and in December the town of Plymouth was taken.

(*In any first reference to Washington, N.C. in conversation, one should always say "Little Washington" to avoid confusion with the nation's capital. If, during the conversation, there is any danger of confusion continue to use "Little."*)

Ft. Fisher, which guarded the entrance to the Cape Fear River, held for most of the war and, because it was so difficult to blockade, Wilmington remained open as a Southern port. The Wilmington and Weldon Railroad, which carried supplies imported from friendly countries and agricultural products from our fertile coastal plain north to Richmond, became known as "The Lifeline of the Confederacy."

As attention turned to fighting Lee in Virginia, the North was never able to spare the troops to take full advantage of *their* position in North Carolina's east. Yankee raids carried out on towns farther inland met with only limited success. An attempt to capture Goldsboro and sever the railroad line in December, 1863, was driven back. It took a great deal of the state's already strained resources to quell these raids. And they became such a bone of contention with the Confederacy that Davis and Lee finally ordered Gen. Robert F. Hoke to clear out the Yankee troops.

In April 1864, Hoke recaptured Plymouth with the help of the Albemarle, a 150-foot ironclad ram that had been built by North Carolinians to sink blockading ships. But Hoke too was soon called back to Virginia. Union troops reoccupied Plymouth and soon controlled eastern North Carolina again. And they sank the Albemarle in the process.

Ft. Fisher, dubbed "The Gibraltar of America," had withstood two major attacks during the war. But late in 1864, the North determined to capture it to clear the way to Wilmington, the last Confederate port to remain open. A landing on Christmas eve by 3,000 troops resulted only in a few skirmishes. But it enabled them to see the fort up close. And perhaps that helped when on January 13, a huge fleet of ships opened a heavy three-day barrage on the fort. At 3 p.m., every ship sounded a whistle and forces that had landed above the fort began an attack. While the fort's defender's were occupied with the main

Scene at Bennett Place near Durham as Confederate Gen. Johnston surrendered to Gen. Sherman.

attack, a second force gained a foothold on a weakly defended side. As federal troops poured in, fierce hand-to-hand fighting took place, and by 9 p.m., the fort had fallen. It took Union forces a little more than a month to fight their way up the Cape Fear to capture Wilmington.

In the far western counties, where slavery was not as pervasive as in the east, there was considerable sentiment against secession even after the mood had changed in the rest of the state. To escape being drafted by Southern recruiters and, in many cases because they considered it their duty, many mountain men left home to fight for the Union. The families left behind suffered at the hands of Confederate sympathizers. Violent incidents on both sides brought retaliation. "Bushwhacking," or killing rivals from ambush, was commonplace, and children quickly learned who their families' enemies were. These divisions were often the basis of family and political feuds that have lasted into our time.

The worst incident took place late in January, 1863, at Laurel Creek in Madison County where a band of Yankee sympathizers had a hideout from which they conducted raids on nearby towns. After a Southern force looking for the hideout was ambushed, a fight took place in which the commander reported killing 13 men and taking 20 prisoners. But Vance, from Asheville, reacting to rumors of a massacre, opened an investigation that revealed a number of the prisoners, including old men and boys, had been shot. The commander, Col. James A. Keith, was forced to resign in disgrace.

The bloodiest battle of the war — and in all of North Carolina history — came as Gen. William T. Sherman was marching on Goldsboro and was met about 25 miles west of there, at Bentonville, by a force under Confederate Gen. Joseph E. Johnston. Some 2,600 southerners and 1,600 northerners fell in this battle, which took place on March 19-21,1865, three weeks before Robert E. Lee's surrender at Appamattox.

Retreating ever westward before Sherman's forces, Johnston finally surrendered on April 18, three days after Lincoln's assassination, and the formal agreement was signed at Bennett Place just west of Durham. Johnston's was the last major Southern force to surrender, although skirmishes continued sporadically here and there across the South.

In fact, a number of these were related to a Federal foray from Tennessee by troops under Gen. George Stoneman, who occupied Boone in March and burned a number of buildings. His troops swept through Lenoir, Wilkesboro and Mt. Airy, then moved into Virginia. They returned to North Carolina through Danbury and Mocksville to Salisbury, where they destroyed military and railroad supplies and other public and private buildings. Stoneman returned to Tennessee through Statesville and Taylorsville, but some of his men rampaged through Charlotte, Morganton, Marion and Asheville. It was to elements of these troops that Gen. James G. Martin surrendered the last force in western North Carolina at Waynesville on May 6, 1865.

Sherman, realizing that the war was about to end and remembering the reluctance with which the state had seceded, had tried to rein in his men who had blazed their way through Georgia and South Carolina. But any goodwill that he may have established was negated by the destruction of property suffered during "Stoneman's Raid." It was the last straw in a war that had totally wasted North Carolina and the South, exhausting resources and leaving hardly a family untouched by property loss and death.

Reconstruction

If you're from the North, you'll probably be called a Yankee, maybe even a damned Yankee at some point, and you'll probably understand that since before the Civil War that has been a Southern term for Northerner. You may also be called a carpetbagger, a term that came out of the Reconstruction period.

Reconstruction, which lasted until 1876, was to Southern states the equivalent of a military occupation. Northern troops were stationed here. Yankees arrived in droves, many of them with all of their belongings stuffed into luggage of bright-colored cloth that looked like swatches of carpet. Some of these carpetbaggers were idealistic and wanted to build a new South. Others came merely to exploit.

Whites who had held office before or during the war were removed and newcomers installed. Most white Southerners had supported the Confederacy and were not allowed to vote. Thus they had no voice in electing their new leaders, had no influence over new laws that were enacted nor over the new Constitution that had to be written for the state to re-enter the Union.

A hatred of these Northerners developed that was deeper than that Southerners felt during the war. An active resistance evolved that was largely underground, and the white Conservatives — heirs to the North Carolina spirit of independence — who joined it were viewed as heroes for generations to come. But the resistance had its dark side. Secret societies, most notably the Ku Klux Klan, brought violence down on the former slaves who not only now could vote but controlled the government with the despised Northerners. Anyone else who helped further the freedmen's cause were also targets.

Lincoln and President Andrew Johnson, a native of North Carolina, had favored a lenient course for a Southern state to rejoin the union. Generally, 10 percent of its men could swear allegiance to the U.S. Constitution and abolish slavery, then form a new state government and petition for re-entry. North Carolina took the prescribed actions at a convention in 1865 called by William W. Holden, an interim governor appointed by Johnson. It also set up elections for that November, and Holden was defeated by Jonathan Worth. New representatives to Congress also were elected.

But radical, more vindictive forces in Congress opposed the lenient terms for re-entry and refused to seat the Southern senators and representatives. A joint committee was set up to design stricter requirements for readmission, and in 1867 Congress passed its own Reconstruction Act, which included dividing the conquered South into military districts. Meanwhile, Southern states had signaled their intentions toward blacks by various acts, including the "Black Codes" adopted by the North Carolina legislature that failed to grant blacks equality or the right to vote. As a result, the congressional plan for readmission required Southern states to ratify the 14th Amendment, which defined citizenship to include blacks, protected the civil rights of all citizens and allowed the federal government to step in when those rights were threatened or abridged.

Equality of blacks and the threat to "state's rights" were abhorrent to the South, but the 14th Amendment was ratified by the required majority of states and became part of the Constitution. The amendment also took the vote away from leaders of the rebellion, so that when a new state constitutional convention was called in 1868, many of the leading citizens could not take part in it. Delegates to the convention were of both races and of all shades of opinion, but most were North Carolina natives. Most also were pro-union and Republican, a new party in the state composed of outsiders, the freedmen, and native whites who were tired of the old rule of the planting aristocracy or who had sympathized with the Union during the war or who were just tired of fighting and wanted to rejoin the United States.

The new constitution was more democratic and most of its provisions have survived despite the attack on it by conservative forces who gained control after Reconstruction. The court system was modernized, with judges to be popularly elected instead of being appointed by the legislature. Property qualifications for voting and holding office were eliminated, and suffrage was granted to all males. The governor's term was established at four years and his powers expanded. But he was denied the veto — a throwback to hostile relations with governors during colonial days.

With the ability of conservative whites to vote still limited, the new constitution was approved and the radical Holden was elected governor. The Republican-dominated legislature ratified the 14th Amendment, and North Carolina was readmitted to the Union on July 20, 1868.

Conservatives now laid the groundwork for a return to power. Those who had been disenfranchised because of their activities during the war could now vote under the new constitution. But outside the political realm, whites organized local dens of the Ku Klux Klan to terrorize blacks and those whites — many of them Northerners — who through the Union League or the Freedmen's Bureau worked to advance their cause. Typically, the Klansman wore a flowing white robe with a hood that concealed his face. The Klan rode after dark, and their vigilantism ranged from threats and whippings to property damage and murder. Klan activity peaked in Caswell and Alamance counties after the 1868 elections. After the murder of a Holden confidante in Yanceyville, Holden asked for a federal force to help fight the Klan.

Troops from Tennessee under Col. George W. Kirk spent the last half of 1870 arresting men named in a list provided by Holden, who took the position that only military justice, not the state courts, could deal impartially with the Klan. Not one on Holden's list was convicted, as lawyers petitioned federal judges to release their white clients on the grounds that they had been denied due process of law — a provision of the 14th Amendment meant ironically to protect blacks.

The momentum had been building for a conservative return to power in the 1870 elections, and corruption in the Holden administration helped doom the Republicans. The new legislature impeached and convicted Holden on eight charges. It then put the two-year-old Constitution to another popular vote, expecting it to be rejected. But it passed, and the legislature had to turn to amendments to get its way. At a convention in 1875, nearly 30 amendments were approved, including one that established separate but equal education for blacks, another that outlawed mixed-race marriages and another that outlawed secret societies.

Federal troops were withdrawn from North Carolina in 1870 and from the rest of the South by 1876. Reconstruction ended with the union restored and the slaves freed, but with conservative whites embittered by the experience and determined to chip away at blacks' gains in any way possible. The experience of the Civil War and Reconstruction flavored North Carolina's history and politics for a century and more to come.

Postwar development

Human and capital resources were exhausted by the Civil War, but the spirit of progress shown in the state prior to the war began stirring anew. It took time to build momentum again, but by the end of the century North Carolina had a strong industrial base in tobacco products, textiles and furniture that complemented the state's three agricultural mainstays — tobacco, cotton and wood.

James B. Duke began peddling tobacco off his family farm near Durham and built the American Tobacco Co. into a giant monopoly that at one point controlled 75 percent of the nation's tobacco industry. R.J. Reynolds in Winston and Julian S. Carr in Durham also made their names in the tobacco industry.

Families, such as the Battles in Rocky Mount and the Holts in Alamance County, which had established textile mills earlier in the century now expanded their capacity and began new mills in other towns. Communities across the state raised money for their own mills, most of which operated well into the 20th century and helped spread out the state's population.

In High Point, business leaders banded together to start furniture factories. Hardwood was plentiful, as was labor, and rail transportation was accessible. Households that had been through war and ensuing hard times were in need of furniture. By the turn of the century, High Point's preeminence as a furniture city had been established. Its move into national markets encouraged nearby towns to start their own plants, and by 1921, when the Southern Furniture Exposition Company opened, High Point was a national force in the furniture world.

The state's industrial rebirth was a marriage of North-South resources. Much of the brain, most of the brawn and some of the money came from within the state, while some of the brain and much of the money was imported or invested from outside.

While businessmen in the city prospered, things were different for the farmers. The ante-bellum plantations of the east were broken up into smaller farms, and the number of farms more than doubled between 1860 and 1880. Many former slaves and poor whites, unable to buy land, became tenant farmers or sharecroppers, who rented farmland and shared the crops with the landowner.

The Executive Mansion, home for the North Carolina governor since the 1890s.

Cotton and tobacco were the principal crops. But typically, throughout the post-war years of the 19th century, surpluses caused prices to drop while production costs and taxes rose. And typically, the farmer became dependent on a system of borrowing at high interest rates for immediate farm and family needs with proceeds of the next harvest as collateral. When a harvest was poor or when market prices were below expectations, the financial crisis that ensued often resulted in the loss of the farm.

Leonidas L. Polk, a farmer-politician, emerged as a leader of the farm movement. He worked to establish a state Department of Agriculture and in 1877 became its first commissioner. In 1886, he began publishing the *Progressive Farmer*, a newspaper for farmers. He became president of the National Farmers' Alliance and was poised to lead a populist third party, the Peoples' Party, in the 1892 presidential election when he died one month before the nominating convention.

Farmers blamed the state's ruling Democrats for many of their problems, complaining that their policies favored industry. So in 1894, after a financial panic that only made things worse for agriculture, the farmer-led populists joined with Republicans to capture both houses of the legislature and, in 1896, the governorship. Blacks still embraced the Republican party of Lincoln, and

The Wright Brothers Memorial on July 20, 1969, when man first stepped on the moon.

those elected in these years were the last to serve in the legislature until the 1970s.

Under the Republicans, the state's election laws were liberalized, resulting in increased black voter registration and, particularly in the eastern counties, a number of black office holders.

By raising the race issue at every opportunity, Democrats played on the fears of whites that blacks were gaining control of government. By 1898, a "White Supremacy" campaign returned control of the legislature to the Democrats. And in 1900, Democrat Charles B. Aycock was elected governor.

Also in 1900, North Carolina voters passed a constitutional amendment that made it difficult for blacks to vote. It denied illiterates the right to register, but contained a "grandfather clause" that said no one who had registered to vote prior to January 1, 1867, or his lineal descendant, would be denied voting rights. Most whites therefore could skirt the illiteracy issue but, as that date preceded the Reconstruction Act, blacks had no recourse.

The Wright brothers

It's hard to imagine the Outer Banks of Dare County without the condominiums, motels, tourist shops and restaurants that line the island's roads today. But it was a wilderness of blowing dunes and sandflats in 1900 when Orville and Wilbur Wright, two bicycle-makers from Dayton, Ohio, chose the Kitty Hawk area to fly their experimental aircraft.

The coastal winds would give them lift. The high dunes would be their launching places. The sand provided a soft place to land. And the isolation would allow them to conduct their flights and study the results of their tests without distraction.

There was no bridge to the island then, and the Wrights had to ferry all their supplies and equipment across Albemarle Sound. The first year, they erected a tent, and in succeeding years they built primitive wooden structures in which to live, work and protect their increasingly sophisticated craft from the elements.

Their flying took place during late summers and autumns, the off-season for bicycle makers. The first year, the Wrights studied the actions of a small glider by flying it like a kite. Later, one or the other would lie in the glider and the other would get it airborne for their first manned flights. The second year, they experimented with a larger glider; the third, with one still larger.

Their trips to Kitty Hawk were preceded by months of brainstorming, experimentation, wind-tunnel tests and the actual manufacture of their aircraft. Over the years, they tackled and solved problems of control and balance, wing size and design, materials and so on. Finally, they had to build their own gasoline engine because none at the time could meet their specifications.

They kept meticulous records of all their tests, both in the lab and on the dunes. At times they became discouraged. But because of their scientific approach and because of their early success — at Kitty Hawk, they were breaking all gliding records — the leading proponents of flight began to see the Wrights as their best hope and urged them on.

In September 1903, the Wrights ferried across to Kitty Hawk the parts to the machine that they hoped would power them into the air. But of course, they had to undergo trial after trial before success. Storms broke over the Outer Banks and confined the brothers to their crude structure. Aircraft parts wouldn't fit properly, or broke altogether, requiring lengthy delays for repairs. Finally, in late November the machine took shape.

It had two parallel wings — about 40 feet in length — fastened together by struts and wires. A smaller set of wings was built onto the front of the craft, with a pair of rudders fastened to the rear. Two propellers turning in opposite directions were mounted on the rear to push the craft along. Their shafts were fitted with bicycle sprockets and chains, linking the propellers to the engine. The engine was placed off-center to counter the weight of the pilot who would lie on his stomach, face forward, to work the craft's controls. The landing gear was a pair of runners, like a sled's. Wheels would have just stuck in the sand. For takeoff, the Wrights designed a track made of two-by-fours and a truck with modified bicycle hubs for wheels that ran along it and on which their aircraft was placed. It gave them about 60 feet to work up the speed for take-off.

On December 14, with the help of a crew from a sea rescue station, the Wrights moved the plane into position to attempt the first powered flight. Wilbur took the controls after winning a coin toss. He cranked the engine, let go of a restraining wire, moved down the track and took off. But Wilbur nosed up too fast and stalled.

Three days later, Orville, because he had lost the toss, was the pilot of the first successful flight, over a distance of 120 feet in 12 seconds. Two more flights increased the time and distance, and the fourth of the day, flown by Wilbur went for more than 852 feet in 59 seconds. A sudden gust of wind later in the day uprighted the craft, damaging it so that it was never flown again.

The news was reported by the Norfolk Virginian-Pilot, based on information from a telegraph operator who handled the Wrights' telegram home to Dayton. Most of the information was wrong, except for the fact that they flew. Although the news was mostly forgotten for awhile, the Wrights' continued success with newer and better craft gradually gained more and more attention until they were famous worldwide. Most of their later work was done in Ohio, although they did return to Kitty Hawk for more flying in 1908.

The U.S. government built the Wright Memorial on the site in 1932 and today operates a visitor center where you can study the story of the Wrights and see where they first flew. Their flying machine is on display at the Smithsonian Air and Space Museum in Washington, D.C.

New age of progress

Charles B. Aycock, elected along with other Democrat reformers in 1900, is known as the governor who launched a new era in education. He and other state leaders campaigned across the state for communities to organize school districts and build schools. During Aycock's term, more than 1,200 new schools were built, with the state increasing the amount of funds for education to supplement local taxes. Compulsory attendance for children soon followed, high schools were built and terms lengthened. When Aycock assumed office, the state ranked last among the states in education. By the depression it had improved, but still ranked in the bottom ten. The construction programs of the '20s and the '40s carried the school systems into the baby boom period of the mid-'50s and on.

A Highway Act was passed in 1921 under Gov. Cameron Morrison, who became known as the "good roads" governor. During the '20s, the state spent a hundred million dollars to push roads of concrete, asphalt, sand, clay or gravel into all sections of the state. During the Depression, all construction and maintenance of roads became the responsibility of the state. Advancements were made in rail service, also improving the state's transportation picture. A new port at Morehead City and port improvements at Wilmington, construction of the Intercoastal Waterway and work to deepen the Cape Fear to Fayetteville were aimed at increasing sea-going trade.

During the first third of the century, electrification spread rapidly through the state. Duke Power, developed by tobacco tycoon James B. Duke, built ten dams along the Catawba River to serve the Piedmont. In the east were Carolina Power and Light, Tidewater and Virginia Electric and Power. By 1935, North Carolina ranked tenth in power production and was one of the top three states in capacity.

As transportation and power sources developed, so did industry. At the beginning of the century the value of manufactured goods was only slightly greater than agricultural products. By 1930, it was triple. During the three decades, the value of textile products grew from $30 million to $450 million, tobacco products from $16 million to more than $400 million and furniture from $1 million to $54 million.

The state contributed more than 86,000 men to the Armed forces during World War I, more than 2,300 of whom lost their lives. Many of them served in the 30th — the Old Hickory Division, which played a major role in breaching the German defenses. Ft. Bragg was among the military camps established during the war, and it has become the largest military facility of its kind in the country.

Soldiers returned home to find that the Woman Suffrage Amendment was being passed in most states, although North Carolina's legislature rejected it until after it had been ratified. The rest of the country was also voting "dry," although it mattered little in our state, which had enacted its own prohibition against liquor in 1909.

Along with the rest of the country, North Carolina was swept up in a tide of patriotism in the extreme, in which domestic reforms, international politics and unconventional ideas were attacked. Lobbying by university presidents, including William Louis Poteat of Wake Forest College, helped stave off anti-evolution legislation in 1927.

North Carolina suffered along with the rest of the nation as the economy collapsed in 1929. As buying power was lost, prices for goods were cut along with wages. The downward spiral forced mill closings. Farm prices dropped. Banks failed. People and businesses went bankrupt; farms and homes were lost.

The state benefited along with others from national recovery efforts. But it took a few of its own steps as well. Loss of income during the early stages of the Depression had reduced tax collections by state and local governments. The state could not balance its budget; local governments defaulted on bonds. Under Gov. O. Max Gardner and J.C.B. Ehringhaus, the state was reorganized. A number of departments were consolidated, including the universities, and programs and state salaries were cut. Business and corporate taxes were raised, and a three percent sales tax was enacted. The state took over the public roads and public schools, removing those expenses from local governments, who then were able to meet their bond obligations and reduce property taxes to boot. By 1941, the state had mostly recovered from the Depression.

North Carolina contributed 362,000 men and women — more than a tenth of its population — to the armed services during World War II. They served in nearly every battle zone in Europe and the Pacific. More than 7,000 were killed. The Army base at Ft. Bragg was greatly enlarged during the conflict. Camp Lejeune and Cherry Point grew to be important Marine bases. Seymour Johnson Air Force Base also came into being. At these and other military centers in the state, more than two million soldiers were trained for combat. Among the notable industrial contributions to the war effort were the fabrics for sheets, clothing, tents and parachutes from the state's textile industry and the construction of 126 Liberty Ships by the North Carolina Ship Corporation at Wilmington.

Many North Carolinians who fought in World War II were among those called up to serve during the Korean War as well. Nearly 900 from the state were killed during this conflict.

The postwar era brought great changes to North Carolina. Textiles, furniture and tobacco products continued to be our economic mainstays, but tourism took its place as the prosperity and transportation improvements of the '50s spurred a national travel industry. Since the '20s, North Carolina had been the leading industrial state in the South, and it maintained that status after the war. Farms became larger and more mechanized, accelerating a migration from rural areas — whites moving to the cities and blacks moving out of state. Charlotte, Greensboro, Winston-Salem, Durham and Raleigh became the centers of wealth, culture, education and opportunity. Dominance in state politics shifted from rural to urban influences.

The postwar administrations of Governors W. Kerr Scott and William B. Umstead emphasized growth with bond issues approved for improvements in secondary roads, schools, port facilities, colleges and universities, prisons and mental institutions. Under Gov. Luther Hodges, the state emphasized industrial expansion, with active recruiting of businesses both in the U.S. and abroad and with tax incentives for businesses who located in the state. The concept for the Research Triangle Park was developed under Hodges.

Civil rights

Prior to the U.S. Supreme Court decision in *Brown vs. Board of Education* in 1954 that outlawed racial segregation in schools, North Carolina had operated two school systems — one for whites, one for blacks — under the "separate but equal" doctrine established by the court in the 1890s. The systems were indeed separate, but far from equal, with white schools generally having more space, better facilities and equipment and a lower teacher-pupil ratio.

The next year, the court decreed that school desegregation should move forward "with all deliberate speed." The North Carolina legislature quickly removed all references to race from the state's school laws. But it also transferred administrative powers to city and county school boards so that future desegregation suits would not be consolidated against the state, but fragmented against the numerous districts. Gov. Luther Hodges, whose calls for voluntary desegregation were not received well by blacks, named Rocky Mount businessman and politician Thomas J. Pearsall to head a panel to come up with a plan to meet the court's dictates.

"The Pearsall Plan" was enacted by the General Assembly and passed as a constitutional amendment by voters in 1956. In effect, the law allowed parents to move children from a desegregated school to another public school or even to a private school with the aid of state tuition aid. The plan remained in effect until struck down by a federal court in 1966.

Boards in Greensboro, Charlotte and Winston-Salem began admitting blacks to white schools in 1957, followed by Craven and Wayne counties in 1959, and Chapel Hill, Durham and other cities in 1960. Most of the state's districts were desegregated by 1965, often over bitter objections. In 1965, the state adopted a "freedom-of-choice" desegregation plan under which blacks and whites could petition to attend specific schools in their districts. But social resistance was such that only 15 percent of the state's black pupils chose to attend white schools. No white students chose to attend black schools.

Meanwhile Darius and Vera Swann filed suit against the Charlotte-Mecklenburg School Board in 1964 when their child was refused enrollment at an integrated school. Their suit worked slowly through the courts until in 1969, U.S. District Court Judge James B. McMillan ordered the city-county system to eliminate all racially identifiable schools and to use busing if necessary to accomplish integration.

The U.S. Supreme Court upheld McMillan's decision in 1971, and the case became a national example. Schools throughout the south began pairing black schools with suburban white schools and busing pupils between their attendance districts to achieve enrollments within approved black-white ratios.

The success of school desegregation depended a great deal on community attitudes. Generally, there were members of the hierarchy in each community that faced the inevitable with a degree of positivism that helped smooth the transition to integration. Greensboro, for example, benefitted from a Chamber of Commerce-sponsored citizens campaign to help institute the busing plan that drowned out voices of opposition. In Charlotte, whites burned McMillan in effigy and burned the law offices of Julius Chambers, the attorney for the Swanns, and it was some time before resistance was overcome.

Court-ordered busing is largely considered a failure, mainly because affluent whites were able to avoid it by moving or by sending their children to private schools. But some cities, such as Charlotte, regard it as a success because many blacks and whites realized that they could work out problems related to racial differences that had separated them since the Civil War. That realization came, some say, only because the court-ordered desegregation of schools forced them to confront racial issues instead of side-stepping them as in the past.

"Separate but equal" was also the alleged guideline for the state's dual systems of colleges and universities. But when it came to graduate school, blacks aspiring to careers other than education had to go out of state. In 1938, a Supreme Court ruling in a Missouri case, however, required states with dual systems of higher education to develop graduate programs at black schools equivalent to the white university offerings or desegregate the white schools.

Not surprisingly, North Carolina chose not to integrate, and in 1939 provided for law, pharmacy and medical graduate courses at N.C. College for Negroes in Durham and for agriculture and technology courses at A&T College in Greensboro.

In 1951, amid a changing climate in which blacks were seeking admission to graduate schools across the South, the University of North Carolina finally admitted a black to its medical school and four blacks to its school of law. But it wasn't until 1957 that it accepted three black students to its undergraduate school. And then it acted only after a federal judicial panel ordered UNC to process applications for admissions without regard to race.

Davidson and Duke admitted black students in 1961. But it took the Civil

Rights Act of 1964 and a suit against the Department of Health, Education and Welfare in 1972 to accomplish desegregation of the state university system to a degree satisfactory to civil rights groups.

Title VI of the Civil Rights Act outlawed discrimination by any agency receiving federal funds. So the Office of Civil Rights moved against states, including North Carolina, which were ordered to develop desegregation plans for their universities. But when the feds failed to enforce the order, the NAACP Legal Defense Fund filed its suit.

Finally, in 1981, the university system signed a consent decree with HEW pledging to eliminate all vestiges of segregation, boosting white enrollment at black schools to 15 percent and allocating more money and new programs for its five traditionally black schools.

None of our governors were labeled ardent segregationists as was the case in other Southern states. The National Guard was never called onto campus, nor were federal marshals used to protect black children entering public schools. But that doesn't mean that North Carolinians always capitulated peaceably to the slow but steady march of progress in school desegregation. The earliest to break the color barriers faced taunts, jeers and threats, were spit at and pelted with objects, suffered loneliness, hostility and property damage, including crosses burned in their yards.

That blacks would be allowed to sit down with their children in school was totally unacceptable to most whites. The '50s were a time in which blacks and whites drank from separate fountains and used separate restrooms. Blacks had their places in the backs of buses and in the balconies at the movie theaters. They had to go to their own restaurants and motels. They had their own churches and schools in their own side of town — often decreed in municipal code, but if not, certainly by the banks that controlled the mortgages. Whites usually associated with blacks only when the maid came to the house, or they encountered an elevator operator or shine man, generally seeing them in menial capacities. Most believed that was the way it was meant to be. Surely, the argument went, if you let them in the schools, then they'd want something else. How right they were.

Following *Brown vs. Board of Education*, the Montgomery bus boycott and the Little Rock school incident, the next most visible civil rights landmark occurred on February 1, 1960, at Woolworth's in Greensboro.

Four students from a local black college, A&T, took stools at the whites-only lunch counter downtown. They were not served, but remained peacefully at the counter until the store closed. Their protest was joined by other students — first blacks, then whites — from the city's other colleges. Within the week, the protest spread to other cities in the state, wherever there were segregated lunch counters in stores that otherwise welcomed blacks to spend their money. Their protests were met with the same kinds of reactions that accompanied school desegregation — taunts and threats, spit and eggs. In Raleigh,

41 students were arrested for protesting at Cameron Village. Two whites were arrested downtown for scuffling with picketers. After about a month, during which the sit-ins had spread to its stores in other states, Woolworth's capitulated. One by one, most lunch counters were reopened with service available to all. Today, the Woolworth's store in downtown Greensboro has closed, but a museum is being developed there to tell the state's story of the fight for civil rights.

Meanwhile, in mid-February, Dr. Martin Luther King Jr., visited with students and addressed a civil rights rally in Durham. Students, along with growing numbers of citizens, began picketing at theaters, swimming pools, restaurants, hotels and other facilities that practiced separatism. The "Freedom Ride" of 1961, the famous protest against segregated bus terminals, passed through North Carolina without major incident. The protesters were later arrested in Alabama, but achieved their goal when the ICC ordered the terminals desegregated.

Demonstrations peaked in 1963-'64 with sit-ins, picketing and marches aimed at desegregating public facilities in Greensboro, High Point, Durham, Chapel Hill and other towns across the state. Large numbers of protestors were arrested. A number of Civil Rights leaders came to the fore during this time, among them Floyd McKissick of Durham, later national director of the Congress of Racial Equality; Golden Frinks of Edenton, an organizer for King's Southern Christian Leadership Conference; Jesse Jackson, student body president at A&T; and Kelly Alexander Sr. of Charlotte, who headed the NAACP in the state. The Student Nonviolent Coordinating Committee was begun at Shaw University in 1960, and its members took part in demonstrations and in voter registration drives before and after the Voting Rights Act of 1965.

In the late '60s, non-violence gave way to more militant protests. Progress had been made in the desegregation of facilities and with voter registration. But by 1969, only one black — Henry Frye of Greensboro — had been elected to the state legislature. There was still a great disparity between the economic and social status of whites and blacks. And the pace of school desegregation was slow.

When King was assassinated in 1968, the National Guard was called out to quell unrest in several cities in the state. And it ushered in a period in which protesters and the authorities seemed more willing to use force.

Black civil rights protests became entwined with anti-war protests and labor disputes. Students sought more black-oriented courses on campus and separate governing bodies for black students. When the university system was reorganized, efforts were made to retain the identities of traditionally black schools.

Except for the efforts to desegregate the public schools and universities, which continued into the '70s and '80s, the last big dispute growing out of the civil rights movement in North Carolina came in 1972 with the arrest of the

Rev. Ben Chavis and nine others on charges of fire-bombing a white-owned grocery store and conspiring to fire on police and firemen. The store stood across the street from a church where protests were staged the year before against the Wilmington School District over closing a black school. The protests had resulted in student suspensions, arrests and fights, and the strife boiled over into the entire community. Rock-throwing incidents and shootings brought the closing of schools, and the National Guard was called in and seized the church. The school system obtained a court injunction against Chavis, Golden Frinks and others who had come to Wilmington to participate in the protests.

Those arrested in the firebombing became known as the Wilmington 10, and the case drew international attention. The 10, which included a white woman, were convicted and given prison sentences ranging from 23 to 34 years. The convictions were upheld on appeal. And pressure was brought to bear on Gov. Jim Hunt to pardon the group. After a review, however, Hunt refused pardons but did reduce a portion of the sentences.

In 1980, a federal appeals court overturned the convictions of the 10 on technical grounds.

Campus unrest

Along with the rest of the nation, North Carolinians held "Cold War" attitudes that labeled anyone with communist or socialist leanings as an enemy. On the other hand, students and educators generally felt that the opportunity to hear all points of view was a part of the learning process and came under the heading of "academic freedom."

The 1963 legislature passed a "Speaker Ban Law" at the close of the session that prevented communists, those who had taken the 5th amendment on the subject and those advocating the overthrow of the government from speaking on state-supported campuses.

Speakers with these leanings had to find places off campus to deliver their messages. At UNC in Chapel Hill, students thumbed their noses at the legislature by gathering at the rock wall separating the campus from downtown Chapel Hill. Speakers would stand off campus on the sidewalk across the wall from the students who sat on the campus grass. Publicity over these events, of course, drew much larger crowds than if the speakers had appeared on campus under normal circumstances.

Threatened with a loss of accreditation for its schools, legislators circumvented the issue and reworked the law to achieve the same effect. Finally, in 1968, after a student lawsuit, the law was declared unconstitutional.

The Vietnam War era of the late '60s saw disruptions and occasional violence at many of the state's campuses, primarily at Chapel Hill, Duke, N.C.

State and N.C. A&T. In many cases, police were called in to clear buildings that had been occupied by protesting students. The movement peaked after four students were killed at Kent State in 1970, and as the Vietnam War wound down, this period of unrest ended rather quickly.

The war itself involved the military bases of eastern North Carolina that served as training grounds and staging areas for operations against the North Vietnamese and Viet Cong. As troops left Asia, they often brought back Oriental wives and families. In addition, after the war, many Asians who fled the Communist forces settled in North Carolina.

It should also be noted that a North Carolinian, Floyd Milton Frazier of Waynesville, was the first known U.S. casualty of Vietnam. He was killed there in 1962. All told, about 1,500 residents of the state were killed in the war.

The Ku Klux Klan

Whites most hostile to advances by blacks or to leftist causes often gathered under the banner of the Ku Klux Klan, the secret society that had its roots in the Reconstruction era. Because it was secret, and because members protected one another, it was always hard to determine just how many members there were.

The Klan was organized on the local level, in Klaverns as they were called. But they were united in a loose confederation that was led by Grand Dragons on the state level who reported to a Grand Wizard, leader of all of the nation's Klans.

Without public notice, Klan members would gather in their characteristic white robes and pointed, face-concealing headpieces. At times, these were family gatherings akin to church suppers on the lawn. At other times, they were serious planning sessions against their perceived enemies. At the close of some meetings, Klan members would gather around a large wooden cross and set it afire to blaze into the night.

Typically, the Klan would threaten with notes or phone calls those people who they felt were furthering the causes they opposed. Or they would leave their calling card — the burning cross on a lawn — to deliver their message. Giant billboards in some areas of the state solicited public support for the Klan, and "KKK" grafitti would remind us all of their presence. Periodically, Klan members would march through town in their robes, as they did in Asheville as recently as 1997.

Extremist responses to the civil rights movement in the state have ranged from fights with rocks, sticks and fists to drive-by shootings and lynchings. The level of Klan involvement in any given instance could not always be determined. But in two instances, the Klan played a visible role in a fight.

In Robeson County, the Klan gathered near Maxton in 1958 to rally against a civil rights campaign by the Lumbee Indians. Conditions for the Lumbees paralleled those of blacks. Many public facilities, in fact, had three sets of water fountains and restrooms to separate whites, blacks and Indians. Determined to break up the rally, the Lumbees marched on the Klan and fired their guns into the air. The Klansmen fled across the border into South Carolina, ending their public presence in Robeson.

In November 1979, a multi-racial group under the banner of the Communist Workers Party advertised a "Death to the Klan" rally at a Greensboro housing project. A group of Klansmen and neo-Nazis drove up to the gathering of demonstrators, got out and began shooting. Five demonstrators were killed. After a lengthy trial, six Klansmen were cleared of murder charges.

Change

Over the last 20 years or so, where this history account leaves off, North Carolina has changed in many ways.

Efforts in the '50s and '60s to diversify the economy have succeeded on many fronts. We are among the Sun Belt states that have benefitted from the nation's changing economy. Where many states have lost jobs and population, North Carolina has gained. The state has more people, many having moved here from out of state to take the added jobs. Most importantly, our young people have good futures here and will not have to leave the state unless they choose to.

Many environmental issues have been resolved, but others are coming to the fore. Increased population has created demands for new developments, which in turn strain natural resources. We are struggling now with how to clean up the Neuse River, for example, which has become fouled from too much human waste and spills of hog farm wastes. Some are trying to redefine wetlands to open up new areas in the coastal plain for development.

The sons and daughters of the civil rights marchers who grew up in the era of Lyndon Johnson's "Great Society" have taken their places in the life of our state, and we have a strong black middle class and many black leaders. Still, race becomes an issue in political campaigns, and tensions can be aroused when it does.

Most of the central business districts of our cities and towns, the downtowns of the past, have become daylight-only havens for office buildings and lunchtime eateries. At night, they become deserted as workers drive home to the suburbs. White flight from the cities continues to expand formerly rural communities, where retail supercenters and their acres of parking lots have cropped up on old farmland. With some exceptions where special efforts have been made to reestablish an urban middle class, neighborhoods near the city cores continue to deteriorate with accompanying problems of joblessness, hopelessness, drug and alcohol use and crime.

Certainly we have changed politically. The elections of 1994 turned the state House over to the Republicans for the first time in this century and gave us more Republicans in Congress than Democrats.

You can read more about politics in the next chapter. And other chapters in this book will bring you up to date on other subjects.

Some historic sites to visit

Since 1936, the state has erected markers on state and federal highways across North Carolina to commemorate places and events of special historic significance.

Efforts are made to locate the signs at a turnout or where traffic slows. The wording is brief so that motorists can take in a bit of history as they travel.

The first marker was erected at Stovall in Granville County at the site of the home of John Penn, one of the state's three signers of the Declaration of Independence.

The state periodically updates its *Guide to North Carolina Highway Historical Markers,* which can be bought in book stores or from the state Division of Archives and History. The latest edition, published in 1990, lists 1,314 markers.

That's a quick way to gain some knowledge of North Carolina history. When you have more time, you might visit a place on the following list of state and national historic sites that are maintained for the public.

In general, the sites are open during normal business hours, all day Saturday and afternoons on Sunday.

Battlefields
Colonial Period
Ft. Dobbs State Historic Site. The fort was built in 1756 to protect settlers against raiding Cherokees. After the fort was attacked in 1760, raids were conducted against the natives, which eventually led to their defeat. Portions of the fort have been excavated. There is a visitors center on the grounds, which can be reached via I-40 to Statesville, north on U.S. 21 for a mile, west on SR 1930 for 1.5 miles.

Alamance Battleground. Site of the May, 1771 battle in which Gov. Tryon's army defeated the Regulators, frontiersmen who rebelled against colonial rule. The battlefield, southwest of Burlington on N.C. 62, features a visitors center and Revolutionary War-era home.

Revolutionary War
Moores Creek National Battlefield. The site of North Carolina's first Revolutionary War battle, February 27, 1776, where militiamen stopped a group of Scots marching to Wilmington to join British forces. The battlefield

is in Currie, 20 miles northwest of Wilmington on N.C. 210. Self-guided trails and a visitors center offer information about the battle.

Guilford Courthouse National Military Park. This 220-acre park of woods and fields in north Greensboro marks the site of the battle in March, 1781, that forced Cornwallis to give up his plan to conquer the South. A visitors center and museum serve to recreate the battle, and monuments and graves dot the park. Nearby, the Hoskins House in Tannenbaum Park has been restored. It is said to have been a staging ground and hospital for the British forces. Also, an old mill on N.C. 68 near Oak Ridge, which dates back to 1745, was taken over by British troops on their way to the battlefield. The mill still operates.

Civil War

Ft. Macon State Park. Built in 1834, the fort guarding Beaufort Inlet fell early during the Civil War, enabling Union forces to occupy much of eastern North Carolina. A museum is on the site off N.C. 58 on the Bogue Banks, and guided tours are offered during the summer.

Ft. Fisher National Historic Site. The fort guarding the Cape Fear River stood for most of the Civil War. But in January, 1865, 10,000 federal troops stormed the fort after a heavy naval bombardment and captured it. Take U.S. 421 south of Wilmington to the fort. A visitors center tells its story.

Bentonville State Historic Site. More than 4,000 were killed in this last gasp battle of the Civil War, the bloodiest in all North Carolina history, between forces of the South's Gen. Joseph E. Johnston and Union Gen. William T. Sherman. It happened in March, 1865, three weeks before Lee's surrender at Appomattox. The battlefield is in Newton Grove, about 25 miles west of Goldsboro. A visitors center tells about the battle, and a farmhouse that served as a field hospital has been restored on the site.

Other sites

Ft. Raleigh National Historic Site. Sir Walter Raleigh's colonists built earthen fortifications on Roanoke Island during their ill-fated attempts to establish a settlement. In 1950, archaeologists determined the location of the fort and the walls were rebuilt. A visitors center and museum are on the site at Manteo.

Elizabeth II State Historic Site. Docked across from the Manteo waterfront is a replica of a 16th century English sailing vessel of the kind that the colonists would have sailed on to reach the New World. You can tour it for a small admission fee.

Wright Brothers National Memorial. The imposing 60-foot granite monument at Kill Devil Hills commemorates the first powered flight of an aircraft. It was built by Wilbur and Orville Wright of Dayton, Ohio, who accomplished their feat in December, 1903. You can visit a museum and the actual site of the flight for a fee.

Ft.Fisher National Historic Site.

The Elizabeth II at its dock in Manteo.

The USS North Carolina Battleship Memorial. Saved from the scrap heap by North Carolinians who raised the money to buy her, the World War II battleship was refurbished and given a permanent dock in Wilmington. For a fee, visitors can tour the boat. In summers, a light show recreates WWII action.

Carl Sandburg Home National Historic Site. Connemara, the farm and home of Carl Sandburg, the poet, novelist and biographer, is operated by the federal government at Flat Rock and can be toured — the farm for free, the house for a fee. The home — originally named Rock Hill — was built before the Civil War by C.G. Memminger, first secretary of the treasury for the Confederate States of America.

North Carolina Museum of History. A treasure house of artifacts, dioramas and other displays relating to North Carolina history. It is located at 109 Jones Street in Raleigh, and is free.

Books

Barrett, John Gilchrist. *North Carolina as a Civil War Battleground, 1861-1865.* Raleigh, 1995, State Department of Archives and History.

Crow, Jeffrey J., Escott, Paul D. and Hatley, Flora J. *A History of Afro-Americans in North Carolina.* Raleigh, 1994, Division of Archives and History.

Ehle, John. *The Free Men.* (About civil rights demonstrations in Chapel Hill) New York, 1965, Harper & Row.

Gaillard, Frye. *The Dream Long Deferred.* (About the Charlotte-Mecklenburg school desegregation case) Chapel Hill, 1988, UNC Press.

Kephart, Horace. *Our Southern Highlanders.* Knoxville, 1992, University of Tennessee Press.

Lefler, Hugh Talmadge. *A Guide to the Study and Reading of North Carolina History.* Chapel Hill, 1969, UNC Press.

Lefler, Hugh Talmadge, and Newsome, Albert Ray. *The History of a Southern State, North Carolina.* Chapel Hill, 1973, UNC Press.

Lemmon, Sarah McCullough. *North Carolina's Role in the First World War.* Raleigh, 1975, State Division of Archives and History.

Lemmon, Sarah McCullough. *North Carolina's Role in World War II.* Raleigh, 1985, State Division of Archives and History.

Perdue, Theda. *Native Carolinians, The Indians of North Carolina.* Raleigh, 1988, State Division of Archives and History.

Powell, William S. *North Carolina Through Four Centuries.* Chapel Hill, 1989, UNC Press.

Thompson, Roy. *Before Liberty.* Lexington, 1976.

4

Politics

Politics in North Carolina might seem downright strange to you newcomers, especially if you're from the North.

At the beginning of the decade, Republican Jesse Helms, the state's most conservative politician in recent years, and the late Terry Sanford, one of our most liberal Democrats, represented North Carolina in the U.S. Senate at the same time.

That contradictory situation ended with the 1992 election, when Sanford became too sick to campaign and was unseated by Lauch Faircloth, another Republican conservative. That would seem to have made sense of things for once. But no.

The same voters who elected Faircloth ousted Republicans from the governor's office and elected Jim Hunt, a progressive Democrat. Then in 1998, voters ousted Faircloth for Democrat John Edwards.

In 2000, voters went Republican for President and most U.S. Congressmen and went for Democrat in state races, electing Gov. Mike Easley and a majority of legislators.

So what gives?

It seems that North Carolina has developed a true two-party system, something unheard of 30 years ago when Republicans were vastly outnumbered except in the mountain counties and who never in the 20th century had enough clout to elect anyone to statewide office.

Indeed, when Jim Holshouser was elected governor in 1972, he was the first Republican to gain statewide office since the 1890s. Helms was also first elected that year. He was the first crossover candidate — a Democrat turned Republican — to win over the state's voters since the Reconstruction era.

Holshouser and Helms benefitted from the anti-McGovern feeling of 1972 when President Richard Nixon's "Silent Majority" swamped the Democrats who were perceived as anti-war, liberal and soft on Communism.

Throughout the '70s and '80s, Republicans in the state consolidated their gains. Hunt served two terms after Holshouser. But James Martin secured the Governor's Mansion for the GOP for two terms before Hunt moved in again. Helms has never lost. But the second seat in the U.S. Senate has seesawed between Democrats and Republicans from election to election.

In 1994, Republicans captured the state House of Representatives. It was a feat they had not accomplished since exactly 100 years before. In the 1890s their rise to power was something of a fluke that was quickly undone by the Democrats. In 1998, Democrats regained the House, but Republicans remain strong.

There are several traditional themes to North Carolina politics. In the chapter on history, it was shown how Tar Heels developed a particularly deep strain of independence due to the absence of a strong government during Colonial times.

That reaction against authority — in the form of big government — helps explain the GOP capture of the state House in 1994, although the sentiment of that election seemed to have prevailed nationwide.

A better example of our independent streak may be our insistence on re-electing Helms to the U.S. Senate. To outsiders — and to many in the state — Helms has long been a symbol of the extreme right wing and has been ridiculed by those who occupy the political spectrum between middle-of-the-road and liberal. Even to those in his own party, he has been something of a loose cannon.

We know the way people feel about him, but Helms — painful for his opponents to say — has those anti-government qualities about him that most North Carolinians love. And we love to thumb our nose at the rest of the country by returning him to the Senate. Nobody is going to tell us who to elect.

Race is also a recurring theme in North Carolina politics. Prior to the Civil War, the issue was slavery. From Reconstruction to the turn of the century, it manifested itself in white supremacy campaigns and efforts to deny blacks political power. From the '50s into the '70s, the political fight was over integration. Since then, it has been over efforts to consolidate black gains in the form of affirmative action programs or the gerrymandering of congressional districts.

At times, it is difficult to distinguish the race issue from the antigovernment theme. Intervention has been such a part of civil rights history that politicians can rail against big government when deep down they know — and the voters know — that its just a cover for how they feel about blacks.

From Colonial times into the 19th century, when North Carolina was a farm state, politics was often a sectional squabble — East vs. West. The power lay in the East, with the established planters, merchants and lawyers. They were often not inclined to consider the needs of the newer settlements in the Piedmont, such as better roads or smaller counties. But they might be inclined to levy taxes statewide to pay for a Tryon Palace, for instance. Before the legislature was made more democratic, class struggles also were a theme. The 1868 Constitution abolished the last of the property and income rules for holding office.

As North Carolina began to diversify, sectional politics evolved into a rural vs. urban theme. The rural interests centered around agriculture. The urban interests involved factories and transportation, public works projects and social issues. In the last half of the 20th century, as the importance of agriculture to the economy waned, political power largely completed its shift from rural to urban.

So, there were a number of themes that have colored our political history. Often they would overlap and intertwine so that it was sometimes difficult to figure out which themes were predominant until the dust settled from this or that political struggle.

To understand North Carolina politics, it is helpful to go back to the Civil War era. In the decade prior to the beginning of war, Democrats supplanted the Whig party in the South because the Democrats took stands that favored states rights and self rule over expansion of federal power, which the Whigs favored. Democrats also in general favored the agrarian and rural interests of the South over the manufacturing and urban interests of the north, and most Democrats favored the extension of slavery into newly formed states.

The election of Lincoln, a Republican, was the final straw for Southern states, which had felt the power of statehood waning before the will of the federal government and were losing the argument on slavery. So they seceded, fought the Civil War and lost.

Under the lenient terms of President Johnson's plan for rejoining the union, all the Southern states had to do was to reject secession, abolish slavery and repudiate the war debt.

They did not have to guarantee blacks the right to vote or grant them equality. In fact, legislation such as the "Black Codes" passed in North Carolina signaled that the South had no intentions of giving blacks any political voice.

Then the radical wing of the Republican party gained control of Congress and came up with a more punitive reunification plan. It required passage of the 14th Amendment, which defined citizenship to include the freed slaves, guaranteed them civil rights and liberties and allowed federal intervention when states denied those rights.

Thus, the Republicans served notice to Southern whites that not only would they protect the rights of blacks but would override state sovereignty, if necessary, to do so.

Congress also required new constitutions in the Southern states and it set up military districts to rule the South until they were passed.

So the Republican party also became the party of political and military occupation.

Republicans organized in North Carolina in 1867. The party was made up of newly enfranchised blacks, northerners who worked in the Freedmen's bureau or "carpetbaggers" who saw opportunity in the South, and "scalawags," the southern whites who sympathized with the union during the war or who saw political opportunity in the new setup.

Because many of the old-line Democrats could not yet vote, the constitutional conventions were controlled by Republicans. So a new constitution was drawn up granting all males, blacks as well as ex-Confederates, the right to vote.

In the 1868 election, the 14th Amendment and the new constitution were passed and W.W. Holden, a Democrat-turned-Republican was elected governor.

Now, with their voting rights restored, the Democrats worked to regain power. Their goals were to discredit Holden, which did not prove difficult because of the ineptitude and corruption that characterized his administration. The Ku Klux Klan was formed to terrorize blacks and Republicans through whippings or destruction of their property. The Klan went so far as to murder the particularly powerful or defiant of their enemies. Its activity reached a peak in Alamance and Caswell counties where Republican gains were most evident in the 1868 elections.

Holden called in military force to deal with the violence. But because the Klan was such an invisible force, the effort failed. Democrats, having regained the right to vote, capitalized on Holden's failures and won back the legislature in 1870. Holden was impeached and convicted. Although the state's voters supported Republicans for governor and president in 1872, the Democrats retained control of the legislature. Then in 1876, war-time Gov. Zebulon Vance won back the governor's office for the Democrats. Voters went Democrat for their congressmen and for president as well. Across the state, the restoration of "home rule" and "white supremacy" was celebrated.

The next year, the Reconstruction period officially ended. With a Democrat in the White House, federal troops were withdrawn from the South. Republicans largely abandoned their political efforts in the South and gave up their attempts to protect blacks. But their activities during the occupation were not forgotten, and Democrats ruled state governments in North Carolina and the South for most of the rest of the 19th century.

Actually, in North Carolina, that rule extended well into the 20th century — to the Holshouser-Helms success of 1972 — except for that Republican blip of 1894-1900.

Although defeated on the state level in 1876, Republicans never went away entirely. In fact they made some of the governor's races fairly close affairs even after Reconstruction. Because Republicans controlled the White House for most of the latter 1800s, a sizeable machine existed in the state to handle the federal postal, judicial and revenue jobs. Too, although many blacks dropped out of politics because they were intimidated or because of stricter election laws, those who remained politically active were still tied to the Republicans. And in the west, where there was substantial union support during the Civil War, Republicans were strong enough to control some county governments. Republicans dominated in other pockets in the state, such as in Randolph County, where that old independent streak was expressed as anti-Democrat.

But in the last 25 years of the century, the greatest disaffected body of voters were the farmers. North Carolina's economy was being transformed as textile, tobacco and furniture factories cropped up in urban areas across the state. The lifelines of the economy were the railroads, which lobbied for tax advantages. Farmers had been modernizing as well, improving their practices to the point that production was higher than ever.

But while the factories and railroads were prospering, farmers were not. Crop prices fell lower and lower, while the costs of production — including freight rates — did not. And farmers paid a higher proportion of taxes because so much railway property was exempted. The farmers blamed the legislature and tried vainly to work within the Democratic party to change things. With Reconstruction politics still fresh in their minds, they were loathe to become Republicans.

North Carolina's farmers were not alone in their plight. Across the South and the nation, farmers were unable to influence their governments regardless of which party was in control. To gain political muscle, they formed the National Farmers' Alliance. And a North Carolinian, Leonidas L. Polk, became national president. When neither the Republicans nor the Democrats nationally would adopt the Alliance cause, many of the farmers formed the People's — or Populist — party. And about half of North Carolina's alliance members followed Polk over to the Populists in 1892.

Although Polk died on the verge of being nominated by the party for President, the Populists in the state found new leadership and remained strong. They were steeled by the attitude of the ruling Democrats, who branded them as traitors. So they joined with Republicans, and this "fusion" of parties took over the legislature in 1894 and the rest of state government in 1896.

Populist-Republican legislators enacted a number of reforms, among them the right to elect county officers. Democrats had made this an appointive process to keep blacks from gaining county offices in the east where they could muster voting majorities. Indeed, as black voters were encouraged to re-enter politics, some did win county offices. Also, some blacks were given patronage jobs by Republican Gov. D.L. Russell, and it was enough to make many white voters uneasy.

Except for ending the railroads' tax exemption, the Fusion legislature made no great change in the tax structure. But it spent more money and enlarged state government. This gave the Democrats some good campaign material. But their main efforts, as during Reconstruction, were directed at

An Appeal to the Voters of North Carolina

(A statement issued by Furnifold Simmons, state chairman of the Democrat Party, prior to the 1898 elections.)

Furnifold Simmons

The most memorable campaign ever waged in North Carolina is approaching its end. It has been a campaign of startling and momentous developments. The issues which have overshadowed all others have been the questions of honest and economical State government and WHITE SUPREMACY. ... A proud race, which has never known a master, which has never bent to the yoke of any other race, by the irresistible power of fusion laws and fusion legislation has been placed under the control or dominion of that race which ranks lowest, save one, in the human family. ...

WHITE WOMEN, of pure and Anglo-Saxon blood have been arrested on groundless charges, by Negro constables, and arraigned, tried and sentenced by negro magistrates. ... NEGRO CONGRESSMEN, NEGRO SOLICITORS, NEGRO REVENUE OFFICERS, NEGRO COLLECTORS OF CUSTOMS, NEGROES in charge of white institutions, NEGROES in charge of white schools, NEGROES holding inquests over white dead. NEGROES controlling the finances of great cities, NEGRO CONSTABLES arresting white women and white men, white convicts chained to NEGRO CONVICTS, and forced to social equality with them. ...

The battle has been fought, the victory is within our reach. North Carolina is a WHITE MAN'S STATE, and WHITE MEN will rule it, and they will crush the party of negro domination beneath a majority so overwhelming that no other party will ever again dare to establish negro rule here.

(Excerpt from *North Carolina: The History of a Southern State* by Hugh Talmadge Lefler and Albert Ray Newsome.)

whites' fears over black political gains.

Enter Furnifold M. Simmons, a Democrat who would influence state politics for the next three decades. Simmons organized the party well, and sent out speakers across the state to thump out the message of fusionist incompetence and white supremacy.

In several southeastern counties, whites formed an organization called the Red Shirts, and that is what they wore as they went about their work. As with the Klan 25 years earlier, their aim was to intimidate Republicans and blacks and to fan racial fears. Unlike the Klan, which did its work at night and in disguise, the Red Shirts would parade in daylight to the cheers of whites.

The 1898 campaign was inflammatory on each side. Simmons issued an appeal to voters, which is reprinted on page 93. It is a position that characterized most whites' feelings about blacks then. It helps to define the racial theme in North Carolina and Southern politics that prevailed well into the 20th century. It is why the Jim Crow laws were passed and why efforts to desegregate schools and lunch counters provoked such horror among Southern whites. And it explains why our largest religious denomination, the Southern Baptists, historically supported slavery and then segregation — positions not repudiated until 1994.

In 1898, the Democrats won back control of the legislature and, in 1900, the governorship. Voters also approved an amendment to the Constitution that effectively took the vote away from blacks. Republicans were pushed out of the state political picture until the 1970s, when they wrested the conservative banner from the Democrats. For the 70 years in between, North Carolina's political game was played by factions within the Democrat Party.

Conservatives, under Simmons, controlled the state for the most part into the '30s. Generally, they favored business and industry. And liberals charged they did so at the expense of farmers, workers and the poor.

Before 1915, Democrats chose their state candidates in a convention. After that, voters selected the candidates in primaries. Because the Republicans were no factor, the primaries became the most important elections for state offices.

Religion became an issue in the 1928 presidential campaign, when Democratic candidate Al Smith, a Catholic and a "wet" was rejected by voters in several Southern states, including North Carolina, who went for Herbert Hoover. It was the only time this century the state went for the Republican presidential candidate until Richard Nixon in 1968.

But conservative Democrats paid a price for abandoning Smith. The collapse of the economy that took place soon after Hoover took office and the ensuing Depression was blamed nationally on the Republicans and, in our state, on the conservatives. And the liberal branch of the state Democrats took power — and the federal patronage — along with Franklin Roosevelt in 1932.

That lesson was remembered in 1948, when conservatives in several southern states abandoned Harry Truman. The national Democratic party was beginning to espouse civil rights issues, and it was becoming apparent that Democrats would be the party of the black voter as Republicans had been in the 19th century.

Protesting "Dixiecrats" ran Strom Thurmond of South Carolina for president on a states rights ticket. Only Louisiana, Alabama, Mississippi and South Carolina went for Thurmond. North Carolina voted strongly for Truman. Many whites in the state, concerned as they may have been over Truman's civil rights drift, still considered Thurmond's abandonment of the party a traitorous act. Most were cemented by birthright to the Democrat Party. The party of their fathers and grandfathers ranked right up there with mom, the flag and apple pie.

North Carolina Democrats believed that any political fighting, whether on a national or state level, should be done within the party framework. The 1950 senatorial election was a case in point. Dr. Frank Graham, UNC president, was appointed to the U.S. Senate when his predecessor died in office. He served for less than a year. Conservative Willis Smith of Raleigh put a liberal tag on Graham and tied him to Truman's civil rights and pro-labor policies and defeated him. When you needed to remove an official, Democrats felt, you replaced him with another Democrat.

Even the liberal Adlai Stevenson, because he was a Democrat, twice carried the state over the more conservative war hero Eisenhower, although Ike came within 15,000 votes of more than a million cast for president in the state in 1956.

Rising civil rights activity was met on the state level with enough foot-dragging by Democrats in power that popular outrage was directed more at the courts — "Impeach Earl Warren" signs cropped up across the state — and the demonstrators themselves. Furthermore, the legislature shifted responsibility for integrating schools to the local level. The 1958 election results reduced the number of Republicans in the legislature from 16 to five, the lowest number in the state's history. Both U.S. Senators, Sam Ervin and B. Everett Jordan, were Democrats, as were 11 of the state's 12 congressmen. The exception was Charles R. Jonas, who represented a mountain district.

Terry Sanford, identified with a middle-of-the-road approach to school desegregation, won a hotly contested governor's race in 1960. Like John F. Kennedy, who carried the state handily over Richard Nixon, Sanford was a progressive who launched several anti-poverty programs during his administration. And while most North Carolinians seemed to be adapting to integration, Sanford became tagged as more liberal, perhaps, than the norm. Also, during his administration, the state's sales tax was extended to food. So voters rejected Richardson Preyer, Sanford's choice of successor in 1964, and elected the more moderate Dan K. Moore as governor.

After their low point of 1958, Republicans started a long comeback. Efforts were made by Democrats to gerrymander Jonas' district after the 1960 census so that a Democrat could oust him. But the effort backfired. Not only was Jonas re-elected in 1962, but because Democrats had weakened themselves by borrowing from the adjoining district, Republican James Broyhill was elected there. In 1966, Republican Jim Gardner beat Democrat Harold Cooley in the district that included Wake County, and in 1968 — although Gardner left Congress for an unsuccessful run for governor — Republicans captured a fourth seat in Congress.

The springboard for three decades of Republican progress was the civil rights thrust of presidents Kennedy and Lyndon Johnson. LBJ, a Texan, had helped Kennedy overcome religious biases and carry the South. Then North Carolina, along with the rest of the nation, voted heavily for Johnson over Barry Goldwater in an election that seemed to focus more on the prospects for war than on social issues. But many Southerners felt betrayed by the Great Society programs which expanded government's role in welfare, education and voting rights.

Resisters within the party, such as North Carolina's Sen. Ervin, were swept aside by the national Democrat machine. Many conservatives in the South, such as Jesse Helms, followed the lead of Strom Thurmond and switched parties in protest. Others looked to George Wallace, another break-away Democrat, who ran a third-party campaign for president in 1968. The national party sealed its doom, as far as the South was concerned, when it nominated the liberal Hubert Humphrey. And Democrats lost much of their moderate and liberal support over Johnson's war policies and the chaos that erupted during the Democrat convention when anti-war demonstrators clashed with police.

Richard Nixon pursued a "Southern Strategy" — garnering the support of many southern leaders by promising a go-slow approach to school desegregation efforts — and won North Carolina and five other Southern states, becoming the first Republican since Herbert Hoover to win our state's electoral votes.

Wallace also took five "Deep South" states. But it was clear that a third party candidate could not win and that the only viable alternative to the party of the "pointy-headed liberals," as Wallace called them was the Republican party. So, in 1972, North Carolina voted for Nixon again — along with most of the rest of the nation. And for the first time in the century, the state also elected Republicans Holshouser as governor and Helms as U.S. senator.

In 1976, after Watergate and the ineffectiveness of the Ford Administration, Democrats returned to power. North Carolinians elected Jimmy Carter and Jim Hunt, and only five Republicans were sent to the state House. It appeared to many Democrats that the Republican influence had peaked, that infatuation with that other party was nothing more than another historic blip, as with Reconstruction and the 1890s. But Carter's liberalism and the Iran crisis swung the state back into the GOP presidential column, where it has been ever since.

Ronald Reagan's landslide in 1980 certainly helped the GOP elect John East to the U.S. Senate, but Jim Hunt held on to the governor's job.

The clearest signal that Republicans were here to stay came, perhaps, in 1984 when Helms and Hunt, the state's two most popular politicians squared off for Helms' U.S. Senate seat.

Hunt and Helms had much in common. Both were from small towns, Hunt from Wilson and Helms from Monroe. Both had family-oriented and religious upbringings. Both were tee-totalers and devoted husbands and fathers. Both were skilled in politics.

But unlike Helms, who positioned himself on the right, Hunt had tailored a more centrist image. He developed a reputation as adaptable, skillful at shifting position within limits as political demands dictated. Helms was rigid and dogmatic, dismaying members of his own party time and again over his unwillingness to compromise. His skill lay in knowing which buttons to push to win over North Carolina voters.

Hunt was active politically in high school, then in college and law school on local and national levels. He built a grass-roots political base in each county of the state that had helped him buck the Republican political tide in 1972, when he was elected lieutenant governor, then win the governor's race in 1976, and buck the political tide again to win reelection in 1980.

Helms built his power base as a television commentator. Each week night from 1960 to 1972, Helms broadcast a five-minute editorial over WRAL-TV that covered eastern North Carolina. He attacked all of the movements of the '60s, from civil rights to anti-war. Anything to the left of his political position he labeled as liberal and un-American. Each day's editorial was picked up by radio stations and reprinted in newspapers. Eastern North Carolinians were dismayed by the turmoil in the cities and on college campuses and were receptive to Helms' words. When Helms switched his party affiliation in 1970 to Republican, the impact on North Carolina politics probably should have been given a Richter scale rating.

Helms devoted his Senate career to conservative causes — against abortion, social welfare programs and busing to achieve racial desegregation of schools, and for school prayer. He often stood alone on these issues and refused to budge for political expediency. He opposed moderate Republicans such as Gerald Ford. In the 1976 primary, Helms engineered a victory for Ronald Reagan in North Carolina that interrupted a string of Ford victories in other states. Reagan, who had been considering withdrawing, stayed the course that won him the presidency four years later, and Helms took a lot of credit for that success. Helms, with Raleigh attorney Tom Ellis, also built a phenomenal fund-raising organization called the National Congressional Club that raised millions of dollars for Helms and other conservative political candidates.

As governor, Hunt concentrated on education and social programs. A reading program for elementary grades, a minimum competency test for high school graduation and the School for Science and Math were all begun during his first administration. He appointed a black and women to his cabinet. He pushed prenatal clinics for high-risk pregnant women and day-care assistance. He spoke for ratification of the Equal Rights Amendment. If these positions put him on the liberal side of the record, the flip-side was balanced by his programs to create new industry through recruiting trips abroad with Tar Heel business leaders, to strengthen the Research Triangle Park, to encourage the budding electronics industry and to locate industries in areas of the state that had none. He also pushed crime control legislation. His popularity was such that after his first year in office, he overcame the traditional unwillingness our state had for a second term for governors. He pushed through the legislation that put a governor's succession amendment on the ballot that would enable him to run again. It was approved by the voters. Re-elected handily, Hunt pushed through a gasoline tax to finance a "Good Roads Package" and legislation cracking down on drunken driving. He continued to focus on education programs, business recruitment and crime control.

With Reagan in as president, you might think that Helms would have lost his "opposition" platform. But that didn't prove to be the case, and it seemed to weaken him politically during Reagan's first term. Helms programs, such as a bill to slash food stamp payments in half and an anti-abortion amendment, were laid aside by the Republican leadership intent on passing a tax reduction package and bolstering the military. Helms' failure to support some farm support programs angered other farm senators and nearly resulted in cuts to the tobacco support program. He lost an effort to stop the extension of the Voting Rights Act. He and Sen. East changed their votes to save a Reagan tax hike bill that included doubling the cigarette tax from eight to 16 cents a pack. (After severe criticism from home, they voted against the House-Senate tax package.) Another Helms attempt to pass anti-abortion and school prayer amendments in the Senate failed. And his extended filibuster in 1982 against Reagan's five-cents-a-gallon gas tax enraged senators because it shortened their Christmas break. They finally were able to stop his filibuster and pass the bill. The next year, Helms drew up a plan to revamp the Social Security system at the same time a Reagan-appointed commission was tackling the issue. Helms' plan garnered little support, and he eventually withdrew it.

Many political observers felt that Helms was irretrievably weakened by his quixotic adventures in the Senate and was doomed to lose his upcoming confrontation with Hunt.

Hunt had weathered a couple of small political scandals during his term which did not touch him personally. He had demonstrated a knack for sensing the political winds and shifting slightly with them. In tune with Reagan's popularity, the tone of his administration was a bit more conservative than in his early years as governor. He chaired a national commission for the Democrats which rewrote nominating rules and was seen as one of the party's rising political stars. It helped him start raising money from sources outside the state to counter Helms' Congressional Club bounty.

Hunt's and Helms' political charts seemed headed in different directions. By mid-'83, even though Hunt had not entered the race, polls showed him ahead of Helms by 20 percent. Members of the national press and Hunt's own staff believed Helms was doomed. But they underestimated Helms' visceral appeal to North Carolina voters.

In July, Helms raised the racial issue by publishing an ad in 150 small newspapers that featured a photo of Jesse Jackson meeting with Hunt and text about Jackson's plans for a voter-registration drive in North Carolina. Helms also led an unsuccessful fight in the Senate against the bill to establish the Martin Luther King holiday, which Hunt supported and the N.C. legislature was to pass. With Jerry Falwell, head of the Moral Majority, and several North Carolina leaders of the religious right, Helms started a voter-registration drive of his own. He also began a steady series of radio and television ads that attempted to link Hunt with national party factions — liberals, black activists, labor bosses and gay liberationists. By spring, 1984 — election year — Helms had pulled even with Hunt in the polls.

Things continued Helms' way as the campaign officially got under way. The N.C. Association of Educators, irked over a Hunt pay-raise freeze during recession, withheld their support for his candidacy. Helms took advantage with ads attacking Hunt's record on education and recruited a "Teachers for Helms" committee. Hunt had considered his education programs among his strengths, but was put on the defensive by Helms. Nor was Hunt helped by the national Democrat primaries, which were not fielding strong candidates against the popular Reagan. And in North Carolina, he felt he had to remain neutral with six Democrats contending for his job, including three who were closely associated with his administration. Eddie Knox, a popular former mayor of Charlotte, who lost to Rufus Edmisten in the Democratic runoff, was so embittered over Hunt's neutrality that he went over to the Helms camp amid great fanfare and took many supporters with him.

Throughout the campaign, Helms dug up inconsistencies in Hunt's record and featured them in ads that asked "Where do you stand, Jim?" For instance, Hunt had declared a Ground Zero Day for nuclear freeze proponents in 1982, then opposed the movement the next year on the grounds that nuclear strength was necessary for world peace. He had criticized Helms for raising money out of state, then turned to fund-raising on a national level himself. Helms, who proudly wore "Senator No" name tags at his campaign rallies was less vulnerable to charges of shifting position because of his history of no compromise.

But the Hunt camp did capitalize with ads on the tobacco tax vote switch and asked if Helms was an effective voice for the tobacco and other agricultural interests of the state. It also charged that Helms represented the rich in the Senate, that he was insensitive to social security recipients and that his unwillingness to be a party player alienated other senators and cost their support for programs that were in the state's interest. He also made headway with ads that ridiculed Helms' support of a right-wing El Salvador politician who opposed the Reagan-supported candidate for president, an act that embarrassed and angered his GOP colleagues.

But a Hunt TV ad that tried to link Helms to death squads supposedly supported by the Salvadoran politician brought charges of smear tactics from the Helms camp and concern among Democrats that Hunt's campaign had been lured into the gutter by Helms' own degrading ads against Hunt. The last few months of the campaign followed a pattern of charge and counter-charge, with each camp accusing the other of distortion and lies, then leveling concluding blasts against the other. The frequency of the ads produced a bewildering overall impression of an unending free-for-all. And it was an expensive free-for-all with the candidates spending almost $25 million between them, the most ever in a U.S. Senate race.

A series of three televised debates had mixed results. The first, with Helms holding back, appeared to be a victory for Hunt. The second, showing a more combative Helms, was deemed a tie. The third, with Helms attacking confidently, had Hunt on the defensive. Helms concluded the debate with the statement that the North Carolina voters' choice was clear — that Helms was a Reagan conservative and that Hunt was a liberal in the image of Walter Mondale, the Democrat candidate for president.

In the last weeks of the campaign, polls showed a growing number of undecided voters and experts said it was a reaction against the negative campaigning, a good showing by Mondale against Reagan in an early debate and a show of enthusiasm for the vice presidential candidacy of Geraldine Ferraro. A final debate had both candidates subdued, but they renewed their catfight almost immediately afterward.

But Reagan regained his stride. And even though Hunt had tried to distance himself from the Mondale candidacy, the benefits to Helms of his ties to Reagan proved unbeatable. Reagan and other GOP leaders with whom Helms had had differences appeared in the state on his behalf because he was needed to keep the Senate in Republican hands.

In the end, Reagan carried 62 percent of the state's votes. Helms' margin of victory was 52 to 48 percent. But the Republican avalanche swept away Democrats in Raleigh and in courthouses across the state, and installed as governor Jim Martin, who overcame a solid lead held by Democrat Rufus Edmisten early in the campaign. North Carolina voters demonstrated convincingly that this was no longer a one-party state.

But if Republicans felt they were whistling down Easy Street now, they got a jolt just two years later when Democrats bounced back with a vengeance. In the 1986 U.S. Senate race, Terry Sanford shook the liberal label hung on him a quarter-century earlier and beat incumbent Jim Broyhill, a Republican who had been in Congress since 1962. Broyhill had moved from the House to the Senate as Martin's appointee five months prior to the election to replace John East, who had committed suicide.

Sanford, former president of Duke University, former candidate for president, former FBI agent and lawyer, credited the victory to hard work at the grass-roots level and a strong stance on state-related issues. Political observers said that Broyhill, with his corporate Republican image, had not stirred conservative voters as Helms did. But more importantly, it looked as if the election was part of something bigger than North Carolina. Democrats had bounced back from 1984 all across the South, despite heavy campaigning by Reagan. Democrats recaptured the U.S. Senate, and other political observers suspected that the "six-year-itch" rule had been in effect — that traditionally a president suffers a loss in the elections that fall in the middle of a second term.

In any case, state GOP chairman Jack Hawke said Sanford's victory had merely stalled Republican gains in the state and that "it certainly doesn't indicate any disaster for us."

Prophetic words. But it would be eight more years before Republican dreams would be fulfilled beyond his party's expectations.

Meanwhile, Helms came up for election again in 1990, this time against black Charlotte mayor Harvey Gantt. Campaigning on education, health care and environmental issues, Gantt built up an eight-point lead in the polls in mid-October. Helms had been stuck in Washington with the budget debate and had made little headway with moderates and fence-sitters with TV ads attacking Gantt for being too liberal on abortion and gay rights.

After Congress adjourned, Helms embarked on a 10-day tour of the state and started swinging hard — and raising a familiar theme. He ran an ad showing Gantt receiving a campaign contribution from Jesse Jackson. Then he capped that with what became known as the "white hands" commercial, aimed at white fears of affirmative action plans. In it, the hands crumpled a rejection letter while a voice intoned, "You needed that job, but they had to give it to a minority because of a racial quota. Is that really fair?"

Gantt, who remembered Hunt's fate when he got into the gutter with Helms, would call Helms "divisive" instead of racist, and urged voters not to get caught up by "the sleaze." But Gantt failed to get the white vote that he needed and fell to Helms by the same 52-48 percent margin that Helms had recorded over Hunt six years before.

And speaking of Hunt, apparently all was forgiven among North Carolina voters who returned him to the governor's office in 1992. In some respects, the Republican gains of the '80s appeared to be eroding as Democrats at the state and county levels regained lost offices. But the voters did not go for Clinton. And they did not re-elect Sanford, who had become ill and could not campaign until the final days. Instead they sent Lauch Faircloth, another Democrat-turned-Republican, to the Senate with Helms.

It was two-party politics at work.

Now the stage was set for the great Republican sweep of 1994. Certainly, on the national level, failures of the Clinton presidency had emboldened Republicans, who came up with their famous "Contract with America" and the popular politician of the season in Newt Gingrich.

In the South, Clinton had provoked near-hatred among voters who had seen his health-care plan as yet another welfare, big-government scheme, and had blanched at what they considered a wishy-washy, yuppie, draft-dodging, gay-loving personality. In North Carolina, which hadn't voted for him anyway, those feelings were made worse by his stand on tobacco.

So it shouldn't have been too surprising that Republicans did well in 1994. After all, they had established themselves as a true party in the once-formidable land of Democrats. What did surprise many, however, was how deep the state Republican sweep went.

Republicans took the State House, and nearly took the Senate. They also flipped the 8-4 ratio that Democrats had held in the U.S. House. Plus, a record 42 county boards of commissioners (out of 100 counties) had Republican majorities. What's worse, Democrats moaned, success breeds success, and the Republican sweep would bring quality candidates out of the woodwork to run against them in 1996.

But the pendulum seemed to move back in elections that year. Democrats regained two of the congressional seats they'd lost in 1964. In the state Senate, they extended their majority from 26-24 to 30-20. In the state House, they narrowed the Republican majority from 68-52 to 61-59. Hopeful Republican newcomers like Richard Petty, a candidate for Secretary of State, were swept aside as Democrats won all of the Council of State offices. As usual, both Hunt and Helms won re-election.

In 1998, the Democrats regained more lost ground, with John Edwards ousting Republican Faircloth from the U.S. Senate. Democrats also padded the party's margin in the state Senate and won back the majority in the state House. On the other hand, Republicans gained a seat in the U.S. House, now holding a 7-5 edge among our congressional representatives. What's apparent is that neither party can take for granted their position with the state's voters whatever the results of the previous election. Each election year promises a real dog fight. It's a different political world from the one most North Carolina adults grew up with.

The '90s has also seen an interesting struggle over the design of North Carolina congressional districts

A rewritten Voting Rights Act of 1982 and related court rulings dictated that states with a history of discrimination redraw congressional districts to give minorities a chance to elect representatives. In its history North Carolina had sent only four blacks to Congress, all in the 19th century.

After the 1990 census, the state legislature came up with a new map that included two districts heavy with black voters. As a result, two blacks were elected to Congress in 1992: Mel Watt, of Charlotte, for the 12th District and Eva Clayton, of Warren County, for the 1st District.

It appeared that the state had done the bidding of the powers that be. But the shape of the new districts provided grounds for a suit by whites who argued that they were an unacceptable case of gerrymandering — the drawing of a district to achieve a desired political effect.

Granted, gerrymandering is nothing new — certainly it has a history in North Carolina. But neither of the new districts paid even lip service to the traditional district characteristic of compact geography.

The 1st District was top-heavy, composed of northern counties with strong black majorities, then reaching down into selected urban areas of the east.

The 12th district was even stranger looking. Some called it "the snake" as it connected black neighborhoods in the major cities of the Piedmont from Gastonia through Charlotte to Durham.

In 1993, the case made it to the U.S. Supreme Court, which sent it back to a lower court with negative comment. Sandra Day O'Connor, writing for the 5-4 majority, said that the 12th District in particular, "can be viewed only as an effort to segregate the races for purposes of voting."

In 1996, the case was back before the Supreme Court, which ruled that the 12th District was unconstitutional. It said nothing about the 1st District, but sent the case back to the lower court to determine when new districts should be drawn.

After the 1996 elections, state legislators went to work to redraw both districts and submitted new, more compact designs. But in April 1998, a three-judge panel overseeing the case, ruled that the redrawn 12th still relied too heavily on race in its makeup. It also said that congressional primaries scheduled for spring could not be held in any of the state's districts until the 12th was reworked. In June, yet another plan was submitted, reducing the proportion of black voters from 46 percent in the 1992 plan to 35 percent. This met with the court's approval, and primaries were held in September.

In 2001, the state legislature was working on a new congressional redistricting plan based on the 2000 census.

Books

Furgurson, Ernest B. *Hard Right: The Rise of Jesse Helms*. New York, 1986, W.W. Norton & Co.

Snider, William D. *Helms and Hunt: The North Carolina Senate Race, 1984*. Chapel Hill, 1985, UNC Press.

5

How the Government Works

This chapter is to acquaint you with how North Carolina government works — how it's organized, who does what.

The framework for our government's operation is, of course, the Constitution. We have had three.

The first, in 1776, was required for statehood. An accompanying Declaration of Rights outlined state government and set out the rights of the people. It set up the three typical branches of government — executive, legislative and judicial — but it gave most of the power to the General Assembly. Our history had developed in us such a profound mistrust of executive authority that governors were to be elected by the General Assembly for one-year terms. The judicial branch was left largely to function on its own. There was no provision for local government beyond the offices of sheriff, justice of the peace, coroner and constable.

The Constitution of 1868 was required before North Carolina could rejoin the Union after the Civil War. All major state officers were to be elected by the voters, a system of county government was established, property requirements for voting and for sitting in the Senate were abolished, and the governor's term was extended to four years (popular election of the governor for two-year terms had been set up by an amendment in 1835).

The third Constitution was approved by voters in 1971. This was basically a rewrite and updating of the existing document and amendments that had been passed since 1868. Anything construed as controversial was submitted to voters as amendments to the '71 Constitution, which was passed by voters along with all but one of the amendments.

Basically, scattered references to the governor and to education were consolidated; references to race were eliminated, the poll tax was dropped, and some organizational changes were authorized. A major change was the

Executive Organization Act, which combined more than 350 separate agencies, boards and commissions into 19 departments.

Since then, any changes in state government have come through amendment. Among them were amendments giving 18-year-olds the vote, approved in 1972, and amendments allowing the governor and lieutenant governor a second successive term and mandating that the state operate with a balanced budget at all times, both approved in 1977. North Carolina became the last state in the union to grant the governor veto power through an amendment passed in 1996.

Voters have rejected amendments extending the terms of the legislature from two to four years and allowing the General Assembly to issue bonds without referendum for public projects associated with private developments.

The executive branch

Council of State: Originally, the Council of State was composed of seven men elected by the General Assembly to advise the governor. Today, it is composed of the elected officers of state government: governor, lieutenant governor, secretary of state, auditor, treasurer, superintendent of public instruction, attorney general, and commissioners of agriculture, labor and insurance. The council still advises the governor, but it has a long list of specific duties ranging from allotting emergency funds and approving civil defense plans to approving parking lot and motor pool rules.

The council meets once a month in public session.

Incidentally, outside of the governor and lieutenant governor, none of the elected officers is limited to any number of consecutive terms. All are elected to four-year terms.

Governor: The state's chief executive is director of the budget, commander-in-chief of the state military, and chairman of the Council of State. He can convene the General Assembly in extra session, grant pardons and commute sentences, join interstate compacts, grant and request extraditions, and has the authority to reorganize and consolidate state agencies. At the start of each regular session of the General Assembly, the governor delivers a State of the State message. He has a number of assistants, including a legal counsel, budget officer, and press secretary. An Office of Citizen Affairs is set up to handle contact with the public.

Lieutenant Governor: First in line to succeed the governor, the lieutenant governor is a member of the Council of State, presides over the Senate and serves on a number of boards and commissions.

Secretary of State: In addition to his seat on the Council of State, the secretary is in charge of keeping the required records of state and local government and private business. He also administers oaths and sits on a number of boards and commissions.

State Auditor: This officer's duty is to audit the financial affairs of all state agencies and conduct any special financial investigations deemed necessary. The auditor conducts his business with a high degree of independence.

State Treasurer: This officer functions as the state banker, receiving and distributing all state funds. Also is the chief investment officer, the treasurer helps state and local governments manage their debts and administers the state's retirement and benefits programs. The treasurer also serves on boards and commissions that have responsibility for fiscal policy or that spend state funds.

Department of Public Instruction: The superintendent is in charge of organizing the department and administering its funds under the guidance of the state Board of Education. The superintendent also serves as secretary to the board, which adopts rules and regulations for the state's public schools. The board is made up of the lieutenant governor, the state treasurer and 11 gubernatorial appointees who are subject to confirmation by the General Assembly.

Attorney General: This officer heads the Department of Justice and the State Bureau of Investigation, and is responsible for training and setting standards for the state's law enforcement personnel, as well as representing the state in legal actions. He holds responsibilities for consumer protection and assisting local investigations when appropriate.

Department of Agriculture: The Department of Agriculture has a multitude of responsibilities related to farming and the environment. The secretary is responsible for keeping statistics on farm production, analyzing soil, controlling pesticides and protecting quality of food, meat, drugs and petroleum products, distributing surplus commodities, running the state fair and agricultural research programs.

Department of Labor: The department has a number of divisions, among them Wage and Hour, Occupational Safety and Health, Research and Statistics, and it checks fair rides and elevators, migrant housing, and mines and quarries.

Department of Insurance: The department regulates all the insurance products sold in the state and the companies and agents that sell them. It sets rates and audits insurers to monitor their solvency. In addition to insurers, the department licenses bail bondsmen and collection agencies. It also has fire and rescue training programs and certifies fire departments for insurance rating purposes.

Following are the departments headed by gubernatorial appointees.

Department of Administration: Known as the state's "business manager," the department has a host of responsibilities, including building construction and maintenance, purchases and contracts, buying and selling property, and administering programs for citizens with special needs.

Department of Correction: Controlling agency for all of the state's ninety-plus penal institutions and prisoners. It also supervises probations and parole. The secretary controls all aspects of the department except for the Paroles Commission, the sole authority for releasing offenders prior to the completion of their sentences.

Department of Crime Control and Public Safety: This department las law enforcement and crime prevention responsibilities and provides emergency services in case of disaster. The Highway Patrol and the National Guard come under its jurisdiction, as does enforcement of alcohol laws.

Department of Cultural Resources: This agency is involved with the arts, historical resources and libraries of the state. The Division of Archives and History has responsibility for the state records, the Museum of History, historic sites and historical publications. The Arts Council has the Museum of Art and the North Carolina Symphony and conducts special programs that preserve our folk arts history. The State Library also falls under the jurisdiction of the department.

Department of Commerce: This agency oversees the Employment Security Commission and other regulatory offices and promotes economic development — tourism, the film industry, downtown revitalization and industrial recruitment.

Some of the offices under its wing are the ABC Commission, which controls the sale of alcohol, the Banking Commission and the State Ports Authority. It also has charge of the Utilities Commission, which sets rates for electricity, telephone, natural gas, water and sewer companies and passenger and freight carriers. There is also a Utilities Commission Public Staff, an independent office that represents consumers before the Utilities Commission in all rate cases.

Department of Environment, Health and Natural Resources: This agency was created in 1989, combining parts of the departments of Human Resources and of Natural Resources and Community Development.

If a state agency deals in some way with water protection or with conservation of resources, it likely falls within this department. In addition, separate divisions oversee the State Zoo, the three State Aquariums and the Museum of Natural Science. Also, if an agency deals in some way with public health, it generally operates under this department. It also keeps the vital statistics of the state.

The Wildlife Resources Commission is a semi-autonomous agency within the department that manages wildlife resources, conducts restoration programs for endangered species, restocks game fish, polices boating, promotes hunter safety and issues hunting and fishing licenses.

Department of Human Resources: This department oversees agencies that serve the elderly, at-risk children, the physically and mentally disabled and those who have substance abuse problems. It operates the Governor Morehead School for the visually impaired in Raleigh and Schools for the Deaf in Morganton, Greensboro and Wilson. Its Division of Social Services administers state and federal programs for the disadvantaged.

Department of Revenue: The main responsibility of the department is to collect all of the state's taxes and to prosecute those who don't pay.

Department of Transportation: The department oversees all transportation activities of the state, including aviation, mass transit and rail, and highways and motor vehicles. It awards contracts for road construction. Its offices issue driver's licenses and sell auto tags. The department is also in charge of the 21-vessel ferry system that operates along seven coastal routes.

Office of the State Controller: The controller is the chief financial officer for the state and is responsible for managing the State Accounting System. It oversees the state's data processing and communications systems.

State Board of Elections: The board consists of five members appointed to four-year terms. No more than three can be of the same political party. It appoints all 100 county boards of elections, which consist of three members each. Election supervisors are nominated in the counties and sent to the state board for approval. The board must also approve any dismissals of supervisors.

The board oversees all elections in the 100 counties, 500-plus municipalities and 1,200 special districts, as well as handles all protests. In addition, political action committees, parties and candidates must register with the Campaign Reporting Division, which is also responsible for monitoring campaign contributions. The board has an executive secretary-director.

Office of State Personnel: This office, guided by a seven-member commission, sets personnel policy and employment guidelines for the 83,940 positions subject to the state Personnel Act.

Office of Administrative Hearings: This office solves problems of jurisdiction in state government and hears cases contesting a state agency's actions that affect a citizen's rights, duties or privileges, including licenses and monetary penalties.

The legislative branch

The Constitution gives the General Assembly (or legislature — the terms are interchangeable) the power to make laws, both civil and criminal, and sets up two houses to accomplish the task.

The Senate is composed of 50 members, the House of Representatives 120 members. Representatives from each house are elected from districts that are roughly equal in population. Thus, larger cities have several resident representatives in each house of the legislature, while many of the sparsely populated counties have none. The districts are reworked every 10 years based on the most recent census.

The General Assembly meets every two years in the legislative building in Raleigh. Representatives are elected in even-numbered years, and take office in the odd-numbered years when the session is convened. Often, the governor or the legislature itself will have a reason to hold a special session some time after the regular session has been adjourned.

To be elected to the House, a person must be a registered voter, be 21 years old on the day of the election and have lived in the district for at least one year. To be elected to the Senate, a person must be at least 25 years old on the date of election and have lived in the district for two years. Each house elects a principal clerk, a reading clerk and a sergeant-at-arms as well as its own officers.

The lieutenant governor serves as President of the Senate, and senators elect one member as President Pro Tempore to preside in the absence of the lieutenant governor. A Speaker of the House is elected by representatives to preside over that body.

Standing committees do much of the legislative work. They are formed shortly after the session convenes, with committee appointments being made by the President Pro Tem of the Senate and the Speaker of the House. Seven members from each house, including the top officer, are named to the Legislative Services Commission, which employs an administrative officer to run the operations necessary to a legislative session. Support divisions help legislators research and draft bills, keep the computers running and analyze pertinent state issues.

The judicial branch

North Carolina's multi-court system has existed in its current state since 1967. There are two trial divisions, District Court and Superior Court, and a two-level Appellate Division, the Court of Appeals (created in 1967) and the Supreme Court. An Administrative Office of the Courts helps the system function.

The Supreme Court: The state's highest court consists of a Chief Justice and six Associate Justices. All are elected for eight-year terms. Efforts to create an appointive system have failed in the legislature.

The Supreme Court, which meets in Raleigh, has no jury and makes no determination of facts in a case. It does consider whether errors have been made in legal procedures or in judicial interpretations of the law in cases that have been decided at lower levels of the court system. The court will review Appeals Court cases that involve constitutional questions, or that have produced divided decisions or stirred significant public interest.

Capital punishment or life imprisonment cases that are appealed go directly to the Supreme Court, as do appeals in Utilities Commission rate cases. The Court also handles censure and removal of judges whose cases are referred by the Judicial Standards Commission.

The Appeals Court: Twelve judges make up the Court of Appeals, also serving eight-year elected terms. The caseload is made up mostly of appeals from the trial courts, although it does hear some appeals involving state administrative agencies. Appeals are heard by three-judge panels sitting mostly in Raleigh but traveling when necessary.

Superior Court: Each of the state's 100 counties is grouped into Superior Court districts. Cases heard at this level include all felonies and all civil cases in which contested amounts exceed $10,000. When citizens are called for jury duty, the cases they hear are all in Superior Court. Judges are elected by statewide ballot for eight-year terms. The districts are divided into four divisions for the rotation of judges. Their assignments are for six months and are made by the chief justice of the Supreme Court. By law, each county must hold two weekly sessions of Superior Court each year. But almost all of the counties need more than that to handle the case load, and many counties hold court nearly every week of the year.

District Court: Counties are also grouped into District Court districts. District courts have jurisdiction over misdemeanor cases, probable cause hearings in felony cases, juvenile proceedings, involuntary commitments and domestic relations cases. District Court judges also hear civil cases where the contested amount does not exceed $10,000. Criminal cases are appealed to Superior Court, civil cases to the Court of Appeals. Judges are elected within the district for four-year terms. A chief judge, appointed by the Chief Justice, supervises the operations of the District Court.

Magistrates: Each county has a magistrate who is appointed by the senior Superior Court judge for a two-year term and who serves under the supervision of the chief District Court judge. Magistrates can deal with cases involving misdemeanor worthless checks and small claims, accept guilty pleas for certain misdemeanors, grant bail before trial in non-capital cases and issue arrest and search warrants.

District Attorneys: The state is divided into prosecutorial districts, each having a district attorney who is elected for four years by voters within the district. The district attorney represents the state in all criminal actions brought in District and Superior courts.

Clerks of Superior Court: Voters in each county elect a clerk for a four-year term. The clerk can decide special cases, such as adoptions, condemnations and foreclosures and acts as a probate judge. The clerk keeps records for the Superior Court and District Court activities in his county.

Responsibilities of the Counties: While the state funds and administers the courts, each county does have to provide and maintain a courthouse. The sheriff, or a deputy, performs the duties of bailiff and opens and closes court, assists jurors and carries out any directions of the judge. A court reporter is required for most Superior Court trials. Jurors are drawn for each session of Superior Court from voter registration lists, driver's license records, etc.

Federal Courts: U.S. District Courts have jurisdiction over cases involving federal law, bankruptcies, disputes between states and so on, and meet in Raleigh (Eastern District), Greensboro (Middle District) and Charlotte (Western District). Each district has a panel of judges, a clerk and U.S. attorney. North Carolina is covered by the U.S. 4th Circuit Court of Appeals.

The counties

North Carolina is divided into 100 counties, each with a county seat, court house, board of commissioners and a number of other elected officials to carry out its work.

The county is an administrative division of the state and has long served as the basic unit for the courts and for law enforcement. By state law, the county must do some things — such as provide school buildings — and it is allowed to do other things — such as enacting planning and zoning regulations.

According to law, a county's voters must elect a sheriff and a register of deeds. It must have a school board, a board of health, a board of social services and a board of elections. "Wet" counties must also have a board of alcoholic beverage control.

Commissioners are elected to run the county, but the manner of election varies, with some elected from districts, others at-large. Most will hire a manager to manage the county's affairs at the direction of the commissioners. Commissioners also have a legislative function and can enact ordinances that do not conflict with state law but involve community level issues that are too small for state oversight. Commissioners can express to state lawmakers through resolutions their wishes on particular issues, such as a highway plan or need for local legislation.

There are state laws governing what constitutes a quorum of commissioners and which issues — such as the budget — require a hearing before enactment. Commissioners meetings are subject to the state's open meetings law.

Voting

Any citizen who is at least 18 years old may vote in any election. Voters are registered in the county in which they reside. They may do so at the Board of Elections office at the courthouse. At that time, new registrants are assigned a precinct voting place.

Voter registration lists are purged now and then to remove names of those who haven't voted for a prescribed period of time. Generally, purging takes place if a voter misses two consecutive presidential elections and all elections in between. Voters are to be notified when their names are to be purged so they can make a case against it.

U.S. Congress

Senate: As with any state, North Carolina has two senators.

House: North Carolina has twelve representatives, having gained one seat after the 1990 census showed a population gain proportionally greater than that of the U.S. as a whole. Because population shifts within the state as well, districts are redrawn every 10 years to reflect those shifts. The redistricting that took place after 1990 was challenged successfully in court because of the oddly shaped 12th district, which opponents say was an example of "gerrymandering" or unnatural shaping of a district to benefit one political group.

Our official symbols

Like most states, North Carolina's lawmakers pause now and then from their weighty doings to honor an animal, plant or inanimate object that is somehow special to the state. The honored entity then becomes a part of the state's list of official symbols.

Most of us know that the State Bird is the cardinal and that the State Flower is the dogwood blossom. Most of us don't know our other official symbols, but we'll give you the complete list in just a minute.

First, however, because you're new to the state, we want to offer you our State Toast.

Not many of us know it by heart, but it really says something deeply felt about our state. And when we hear it given by someone such as our late native son Charles Kuralt, it can bring a welling to the throat and a mist to the eye.

So lift your mug of coffee, your glass of tea or something stronger and hear our toast:

> *Here's to the land of the long leaf pine,*
> *The summer land where the sun doth shine,*
> *Where the weak grow strong and the strong grow great,*
> *Here's to "Down Home," the Old North State!*
>
> *Here's to the land of the cotton bloom white,*
> *Where the scuppernong perfumes the breeze at night,*
> *Where the soft southern moss and jessamine mate,*
> *'Neath the murmuring pines of the Old North State!*

Here's to the land where the galax grows,
Where the rhododendron's rosette glows,
Where soars Mount Mitchell's summit great,
In the "Land of the Sky" in the Old North State!

Here's to the land where maidens are fair,
Where friends are true and cold hearts rare,
The Near land, the dear land, whatever fate
The blest land, the best land, the Old North State!

Now for a little more about our State Bird, the cardinal.

It is sometimes called the winter redbird, and the sight of the bright red male with its striking appearance and beautiful song can really brighten an otherwise gray winter day. It lives here year-round. The female cardinal is much less brilliant in color but can sing just as well.

Nests are of weed stems or grass and are built in low shrubs, or small trees, generally not four feet above the ground. Three is the usual number of eggs. Cardinals eat seeds and, occasionally, small fruits and insects.

As for our State Flower, the dogwood is one of the most prevalent trees in our state and grows from the mountains to the coast. Unfortunately, in the deep woods, the dogwoods are losing ground to a blight, particularly in the mountains. The blossoms, which come in early spring, are usually white in the wild, but a pink blossom has been created for gardeners.

Now for our other official symbols.

The State Insect is the honey bee, an industrious little critter that produces about $2 million worth of honey each year in our state and, as a pollinator, is an important part of our botanic life cycles.

The State Tree is the pine, our most common tree, which played an important role in our economy, first as a source for the naval stores industry, more recently as a source for pulp, paper products and building materials.

The State Mammal is the gray squirrel, common in most areas of the state. It is a daylight denizen of any areas with trees, from urban parks to wilderness forests. Its diet is new growth and fruits, supplemented by corn and peanuts and occasionally insects. In fall and winter, it survives mostly on acorns.

The State Salt Water Fish is the channel bass (or red drum), which lives in our coastal waters. The channel bass usually grows to 30 to 40 pounds, although they have been reported as heavy as 75 pounds.

The State Shell is the Scotch Bonnet (pronounced Bonay), a colorful and beautifully shaped shell that abounds in the state's coastal waters.

The State Precious Stone is the emerald. The largest ever found in North Carolina was 1,438 carats. Another was cut to 1,314 carats and is considered the largest and finest cut emerald in North America. Both were found at Hiddenite, near Statesville.

The State Reptile is the eastern box turtle, which thrives in moist and swampy areas of the state. It has bright markings, usually orange, and is a useful animal in that it eats insect pests.

The State Beverage is milk. North Carolina ranks among the top 20 in dairy production. There are some who might have voted for Cheerwine or Pepsi, or maybe even moonshine if the State Beverage issue had been put on the ballot.

The State Rock is granite. The largest open-face granite quarry in the world is just outside of Mt. Airy. The Wright Brothers Memorial at Kitty Hawk is among the imposing structures built from North Carolina granite.

The State Historic Boat is the shad boat developed on Roanoke Island to catch shad. This sailing vessel was built with a shallow draft for the coastal sound waters and was highly maneuverable, a help in an area where the weather changes rapidly.

The State Dog is the Plott hound. The breed was developed in the North Carolina mountains around 1750 by Jonathan Plott who used it to hunt wild boar. It is one of only four breeds known to be of American origin and is still popular for its ability to track and its loyalty.

The State Flag is four-colored: A blue vertical field, with gold scrolls above and below the initials N and C in gold separated by a white star, and two horizontal fields, red over white. On the top scroll is printed "May 20th, 1775", the date of the alleged Mecklenburg Declaration of Independence, and on the bottom scroll, "April 12th, 1776", the date of the Halifax Resolves. It was adopted in 1885.

"The Great Seal of the State of North Carolina" is printed on the State Seal along with our motto, Esse Quam Videre ("To Be Rather Than To Seem"). The seal contains the same dates as the flag. It pictures a standing Liberty with pole and cap in one hand and a scroll with the word "Constitution" in the other. Seated near her is Plenty, holding three stalks of grain and touching an overflowing cornucopia. Behind them is pictured a coastal scene with three-masted sailing ship approaching land.

The State Song is *The Old North State*, by William Gaston. Not one in a thousand North Carolinians knows this song. Most won't recall ever hearing it. Its obscurity may result from lines such this:

Tho' the scorner may sneer at and witlings defame her,
Still our hearts swell with gladness whenever we name her.

6

Our Economy

Those of us who have grown up in North Carolina sometimes have to pinch ourselves as we look around and see all the changes that have taken place in our economy in the past four decades.

Our fathers — and many of our mothers — who charged out of World War II and set up the fabulous '50s for us to reminisce about, generally worked in factories — cigarette, textile and furniture plants — or held jobs that in some way served those plants or the people who worked in them. We produced more textile and tobacco products and more furniture than any other state in the nation. Many others still worked on the farm. Among all the states, only Texas had more farms.

But our lack of diversity cost us. We were fourth from the bottom nationally in per capita income. Although we were gaining in population — this was, after all, in the middle of the Baby Boom period — more people were moving out of state than in, giving us a net loss of a lot of capable people who were seeking greater opportunities elsewhere.

The mid-'50s is a good time to look at a snapshot of our economy. The four legs of agriculture, textiles, tobacco products and furniture had held up our economic table for many years stretching back into the 19th century. But in the '50s, new supports were being fashioned. Plans were being laid for the Research Triangle Park to pool university resources and lure new industry that relied more on brain power than brawn. New interstate highways were boosting the tourist industry and mapping the routes of future economic growth.

Change, of course, was gradual. But today – nearly five decades later – we have a far more diversified economy. Furniture is still important; agriculture less so, but still a mainstay. Textiles' importance has dropped sharply with competition from overseas. Tobacco manufacturing also has declined dramatically. Banking, the health care industry, pharmaceuticals,

115

technology, transportation, travel, insurance, construction, even film-making, are among the new industries that have strengthened our economic base.

Still we have problems. Not every area of the state has shared the bounty of the new economy. And most of those who have lost jobs in textiles, tobacco and agriculture don't have the education to move into the newly opening jobs, except perhaps in the service sector where the pay is not so high.

Before looking more closely at the economy of today, it is helpful to understand our economic heritage.

Early days

The earliest settlers were mostly self-employed, making their living through subsistence farming — learned in many cases from the Indians — and fishing in the sounds and waterways where settlements first appeared. They built their own homes and hunted for meat and skins. They wove and sewed their garments.

If a settler could grow some extra corn or trap for some extra skins, he could trade for an axe, some needles or fish hooks or something else he needed but couldn't make on his own. If he was good at a craft, such as leatherwork, or somehow obtained a forge or had a boat, he could specialize in a trade and barter for goods or make some cash. It was rudimentary, but the beginnings of an economy nonetheless.

Those who did well economically or politically and amassed enough land could plant in large quantities and expand their trading opportunities to other settlements and colonies, even overseas. In fact, the agricultural system that developed in the east and was modified as it spread across the state dominated our economy until the Civil War. But more on that later.

Vast forests of pines merely got in the way of the planters at first, but by the mid-18th century North Carolina boasted a thriving naval stores industry. Turpentine, pitch and tar were products that came from the pine resin and were exported in large quantities through Wilmington. Other early wood products were barrels, planking, cypress shingles, oak bark for tanning, spars, oars and boats. Slave labor was used extensively in agriculture and in the naval stores industry. In fact, as the work was seasonal, the same slaves could be used in both.

Farther inland, where elevation changes and rocky beds made for more rapid stream flow, mills were constructed with waterwheels to harness this dependable source of power. Essential services such as blacksmith shops, stables, taverns, dry goods stores, schools and meeting houses would be established nearby. Until steam power was perfected, the first cotton mills were powered by running water.

Traveling salesmen plied the back roads of colonial North Carolina, packing pots and pans, dry goods and anything a family might need into a horse-pulled wagon and making his calls at homes far removed from the settlements.

Mining was conducted on a small scale, with copper, silver and iron ore being found here and there. Iron works were developed in Lincoln, Chatham and Orange counties,

There was even a gold rush in North Carolina. John Reed found a shiny yellow rock in Cabarrus County as he was fishing, and the family used it as a doorstop until they finally had it assayed in 1802. The Reeds started finding more nuggets and began digging holes. Word spread, and a rush was on that brought speculators from all over the world. Gold was found in a number of places — such as Gold Hill and Charlotte, which had a mine under what is Tryon Street today. Christopher Bechtler opened a private mint in Rutherfordton in 1831, which cast gold into coins and bars until 1857. A U.S. mint was established in Charlotte in 1837 which operated until the Civil War.

North Carolina had seen the beginnings of manufacturing prior to 1860. The Civil War stopped that. But it also opened the door to a new industrial revolution. It was not lost on Southerners that a diversified economy in which manufacturing had as important a role as agriculture had helped the North win the war. Also, with the end of slavery, the plantation society that had been the most productive of our agricultural institutions disappeared. Into the economic vacuum poured a number of entrepreneurs — home grown and from other Southern states — who, occasionally with the use of Northern capital, transformed North Carolina into a new state.

The able-bodied began leaving the farm *en masse* to work in the cities. As with farming, factory work was hard, and involved long hours for low pay. But unlike agriculture, the work was steady. Life was more certain. Over the next hundred years, children who grew up in towns followed their parents into the factories, and mill life became as much a part of our culture as life on the farm.

But for better or for worse, it was agriculture that was the mainstay of our economy before the Civil War, and we should look at that before tackling some of the later developments of our industrial age.

Agriculture

Corn was most important to the early farmer. It was the crop on which his family could live. It generally grew well and the yields were often such that the extra could be traded for other things the family needed. Corn could be eaten by the ear, fed to cattle, ground into flour for bread or grits, even distilled for liquor. Corn was an important export commodity by the dawn of the 18th century. Peas and beans, and to some extent, wheat also were exported.

But tobacco was the cash crop.

Tobacco grew naturally in North Carolina. In fact, Sir Walter Raleigh developed a British strain of tobacco from seeds gathered by his unsuccessful colonists. The British smoked their domestic tobacco — but only if they had to. They preferred the tobacco grown in the Spanish-American colonies, but Spain wanted a lot of money for theirs, and only the rich could afford the best.

So when John Rolfe, who married Pocohontas, started a crop at Jamestown in 1612 with seeds from the Spanish colonies, he soon had tobacco that was in great demand in Britain. The trade that resulted ensured the success of the colony, and persuaded others to migrate when they saw profits were to be made in the New World.

After about 1650, when things got to be crowded around Jamestown, and Carolina was opened to colonization, settlers began planting tobacco in the Albemarle Sound area. Because it did not have good ports, exports were nowhere near the quantities sold out of Virginia. When North Carolina's farmers became more competitive, transporting their tobacco to the northern colonies in shallow-draft vessels, Virginians began to refer to the Albemarle region as "Rogue's Harbor."

Yankee traders would load the tobacco into larger vessels and bootleg it illegally to Scotland and Holland, all to avoid paying the export taxes that England would have required had they landed at British ports.

Tobacco then was of the burley type, air-cured for five or six weeks after harvest. It was stripped from its stalks, then packed by the thousand pounds into hogsheads through which an axle was run. These barrels were rolled to market by man or animal power.

Wherever settlers cleared new ground, tobacco planting began and by the 1750s inspection warehouses were established to ensure that North Carolina was exporting a quality product.

Through the Revolutionary War, Edenton was the primary port for tobacco exports. In fact, Virginia forgot its pique and moved its tobacco through Edenton because its own ports were blockaded during the war. After the war, Wilmington became lead port.

The next major development for North Carolina tobacco came in 1839 after farmers had begun curing tobacco with heat from fires. A slave named Stephen, who worked on Abisha Slade's farm in Caswell County, fell asleep while tending fires in a curing barn. He awoke to find the fires nearly out and ran outside to a charcoal pit and fed the burning coals to the fires. The heat came up fast and the leaf dried a rich, bright-yellow color that farmers had not seen before.

When Slade got a lot more money for this "bright" leaf, others started curing their tobacco the same way and by the Civil War, it had caught on with most growers in the northern tier of counties that came to be known as the Bright Belt. At the same time, farmers were moving from direct heat to a flue-cured method that involved piping heat into a tightly closed barn from an outside furnace.

When it was found that the desired shade of leaf was best obtained from a thin, sandy soil, farmers who had previously thought their land too poor to grow crops now turned to planting tobacco. To a degree, production spread into other areas of North Carolina.

After the Civil War, markets slowly expanded for tobacco products as factories sprouted up all across the state. The new demand encouraged more tobacco to be grown. There was stiff competition between Virginia and North Carolina warehouses for the auctions that grew steadily more profitable. With the introduction of cigarette rolling machines and increased use of tobacco, the amount of tobacco grown increased dramatically. From 11 million pounds grown in 1870, North Carolina passed the 100 million-pound mark in 1895, and by the end of the century was moving ahead of Virginia in tobacco production.

Cotton was another crop that saw explosive growth during the 1800s. Eli Whitney developed the cotton gin in the 1790s, and his machine took over the time-consuming process of separating seed from fiber that had previously been done by human hands. The result on the Southern states was dramatic, as fields were put into cotton to meet the growing needs of the textile industry in the northeast and as an export product. In North Carolina, which had comparatively few slaves, the trend to growing cotton resulted in an increased slave population because more manpower was needed to pick the cotton and get it to the gin.

Cotton was grown mostly in the East, but many Piedmont farms planted the commodity as well. Measured in 500-pound bales, cotton production grew four-fold between 1840 and 1860, from about 35,000 bales to nearly 150,000. Even after the war, with slavery abolished, production quickly reached pre-war levels, and the demand of the native textile industry helped boost production to 460,000 bales by 1900.

Farmers of the period also grew corn and oats in quantity, and potatoes came to be important. But for the most part, North Carolina was a two-crop state. And most farms devoted their production to one or the other.

The deaths during the Civil War of 40,000 of the state's most able-bodied men, most of them from farms, and the freeing of the state's 350,000 slaves created a manpower shortage for farms that resulted in a number of trends in the latter part of the 19th century.

Larger farms were broken up, so that the number of farms increased and their average size became much smaller. A system of tenant farming developed with landowners allowing others to farm their land, taking a fee or, most often, a portion of the crop that was harvested. Whites and blacks became tenant farmers and put most members of the family to work. It was a livelihood, but not much of one. And it was an inefficient system that hindered farm progress.

Despite the high production levels of cotton and corn, agriculture was caught up in a national depression in the '90s that resulted from over produc-

Tobacco curing barn, staple of rural landscape for more than a century.

tion and falling prices, and an increasing disparity between production costs and the amount a farmer received for his crops. The rise of Populism in the nation and the fusion government rule in North Carolina that came about during the depression is discussed more thoroughly in chapters on history and politics.

The farm population continued to grow into the first decades of the 20th century. But continued low prices and soil depletion made farm life more difficult, and many were forced to move to the cities, which gained population even faster. The state continued to have two major crops, with cotton yielding to tobacco as the state's leading cash crop in the '20s. The Depression saw farm prices drop drastically, and many in the state lost farms as a result. But New Deal farm programs, which included loans to farmers and production controls, restored crop prices in the late '30s.

One other lasting effect of the New Deal was the extension work of N.C. State University that encouraged farmers to diversify their crops so they could live on what they grew as well as sell it. Livestock production and dairying were encouraged. Conservation practices and new forms of mechanization were taught, as were home processes such as canning that could improve a farm family's lot. Rural electrification also began during this period, and eventually brought farms into the mainstream.

But the Great Depression of the '30s started a trend that saw the state's farm population drop steadily into the mid-'50s when it began to fall dramatically. The number of farms started dwindling as well, but their average size grew for the first time in the century as some consolidation took place. Farm tenancy dropped dramatically, which was nice because it had created a social and economic drag on the farm economy. Many blacks left the rural areas and headed north where opportunities for employment seemed better. Farms were becoming more efficient through increased scale and mechanization, but labor was still needed. So, many farmers hired migrants to do the work, a system that developed its own particular host of social problems.

Cotton production peaked in the '40s, losing out to other states of the Deep South and to imports. Corn, potatoes, soybeans and peanuts became more important, as did livestock and poultry. In addition, new crop lines developed: apples in the mountains, peaches in the sandhills and truck crops in the east. But tobacco remained king.

As we reached our snapshot years of the mid-'50s, North Carolina's tobacco crop led the nation. The state still had the highest rural population and the second largest number of farms, just behind Texas.

But the trends that had affected farming over the previous quarter century combined to scramble the statistics considerably over the last five years of the '50s. By 1959, the state had lost more than 77,000 farms from the 268,000 counted in 1954. About a fifth of that was due to definition, but the real change was fairly remarkable. Farm size grew dramatically, mechanization was intense. Farming became a large-scale enterprise, and the value of farms and yields boomed. In farming, North Carolina had passed through one of those milestone periods in which we had begun to think differently about ourselves.

Still, through the '60s, tobacco reigned. In 1969, the value of the crop — nearly $600 million — was greater than all other crops combined, as it had been for the previous 30 years. The income from tobacco grew nearly six-fold during that time. But two other product categories were making some noise in 1969. Cash from hog production was just short of $120 million, a 20-fold increase from 30 years earlier. And poultry and egg sales were valued at $336 million, a 42-fold increase over the 30 years.

Tobacco weathered the '60s despite the report by the U.S. Surgeon General that tobacco could be bad for health, and has continued its growth as a cash crop since, although at a much slower pace. Problems of over production were helped through the assigning of acreage allotments, limiting the amount of land a farmer could put into tobacco.

New curing methods were less labor intensive in that they relied on gas for heat instead of hand-fed fires. The curing barn took on a new metallic look, and the old wooden barns were dismantled or given over to gravity and vines. Scientists tried to develop strains of tobacco that resisted its enemies, such as blue mold (which still is a problem, ruining much of the burley crop in 1995 in the western part of the state).

Today, tobacco is still our largest cash crop. North Carolina is still number one among all the states in its production. But that is not to say that it's still our number one farm product. The curing barn is not the only new building on the farm.

Gone too are the chicken houses and pig sties of yesterday's small farmers. The successful chicken and hog farmer of today pampers his animals in environmentally controlled buildings and serves up blends of feed worked out on a computer. The city slicker who goes into a spic-and-span, concrete floored "hog parlor" and asks, "Have you slopped the hogs yet?" is likely to draw a smile and a polite explanation of modern husbandry methods.

Thus our most valuable farm products today are broilers and hogs, both with more than $1 billion in annual sales. Only Georgia, Arkansas and Alabama raise more chickens. Only Iowa raises more hogs. Another new building on the farm is the greenhouse, with nursery products challenging tobacco, the state's other billion-dollar commodity. Only California, Florida and Texas top our greenhouse/nursery production.

Livestock and poultry producers aren't as subject to the weather as the crop farmers. But new problems are likely to arise. Animals produce waste, which has to be stored until it decomposes. In 1995, and again with Hurricane Floyd in 1999, heavy rains overburdened some of the hog waste lagoons in the eastern part of the state and caused spills that polluted neighboring creeks and rivers. The state stepped in with fines and court action. Two large producers, Smithfield and Premium Standard, have since funded $17.5 million for research at N.C. State University into alternatives for the lagoons.

As with livestock, corporations have redefined other agricultural pursuits. In the '70s, vast peaty areas of some eastern counties were bought by corporations, many of them foreign, to grow vegetables on a scale unheard of before. Farm life has become dominated by a new image – less bucolic and overalls-clad, more scientific and white-collar. We don't even call it farming anymore. It's agribusiness, if you please.

Because they produce more and do it more efficiently, the big agricultural corporations can market their product for less. The process continues to weed out the less efficient so that the number of farms continues to decline and the average size continues to grow. Over the years, some of the acreage has been put into new crops, such as pines for the timber industry or Christmas trees. Some farms now produce fish – trout, catfish, and even a hybrid fish suitable for sushi.

North Carolina still is eighth in the nation as an agricultural state. We lead the nation in turkey production and in sweet potatoes as well as tobacco. Besides hogs, we are second in Christmas trees, pickling cucumbers and trout. But we used to rank third in agriculture. The family farm that many of us who grew up in the state remember as youths doesn't exist today. It has become modernized or turned into a subdivision or grown over by a pine forest. Agriculture still is vital to our economy – in fact, the number of jobs in agribusiness grew during the 90s – the state has diversified to this degree: Where as agriculture once employed the vast majority of people in our state, it now makes up only about $1\frac{1}{2}$ percent of our labor force.

And that is truly incredible.

Textiles

In colonial days and into the 19th century, textile production in North Carolina was a cottage industry, with the processing of cotton or wool into fabrics limited mostly to what a family accomplished at home. Or, perhaps, artisans would get together and weave or quilt to meet community needs. Manufactured goods were imported.

In 1813, Michael Schenck built North Carolina's first cotton mill on the banks of the south fork of the Catawba River in Lincoln County. Joel Battle established a mill on the Tar in Edgecomb County in 1818 and George McNeil built one near Fayetteville in 1825.

But it was not until the late '30s and '40s, after an agricultural depression awoke North Carolina out of its "Rip Van Winkle" slumber, that a textile industry began to develop. Mills began to sprout everywhere. Some of the most prominent belonged to Charles Mallett of Cumberland County, Walter Leak and John Motley Morehead of Rockingham County, Edwin Michael Holt of Alamance County. The first successful steam-powered plant was built in 1837 at Salem by Francis H. Fries. But cheap fuel for boiler furnaces was always a problem, and water was the preferred power source. This spread the plants out, rather than concentrating them in one or two locations, and communities developed around the mills all across the state.

Typically, mills were built from locally raised capital but were run by machinery from England or New England, and by engineers and managers from the North. Bad times on the farm created a pool from which to recruit workers. The move from farm to town improved the lot for some, but only marginally. Slave labor was used only sparingly, for slaves were needed to pick the

Sewing room of a knitted underwear mill, early in the 20th century.

cotton for which there was now a local demand. And there was a hesitancy to teach blacks a trade. The mills of North Carolina produced mostly spun goods and woven cloth, with finished textile products the exception.

By 1860, 39 cotton mills were in production within the state. A few managed to keep going during the war. By 1870, even before Reconstruction had ended, 33 plants were in operation and production had surpassed pre-war levels. Production doubled by 1880, with 49 mills. And by the turn of the century, 212 mills were humming along. By then, however, steam was becoming the power source of choice and mills could be established in towns away from watercourses.

Many of the successful post-war plants were begun and managed by members of the families that had started factories before the war. Through marriage and off-spring, the textile "family" grew and most of the plants operating by 1900 were owned or operated by experienced North Carolinians.

Add to the names mentioned above those of Cannon in Cabarrus County, Gray in Gaston County and Erwin in Harnett County. The success of the family operations attracted some Northerners to come down, notably the Cones of Guilford County.

The textile industry prospered because raw material was close by in the cotton fields and rail transportation had improved access to markets. Labor was plentiful and cheap — workers moved into town as agriculture went through a series of depressions. Women and children were employed, in fact dominated the work force, as the men became technicians and supervisors. "Lintheads" was a name given to mill employees because of the dust and fibers they'd wear home in their hair at the end of a shift. Pay was poor, with families typically earning a subsistence wage by putting most of its members to work. Mill villages were established for the workers where they could rent homes on lots big enough to plant a garden or raise a few goats. But they usually had no running water, and privies were the rule. Typically, rent was deducted from their payslips. In some cases, workers were paid in script which could be cashed only at the company's store.

The textile industry prospered also because it was seen as an important part of the New South. In the last decades of the 19th century. North Carolina embarked on a "Cotton Mill Campaign." Every community wanted a mill because support industries grew around it and the railroad came to its doors. Daniel Augustus Tompkins campaigned for the industry through his *Charlotte Observer*, and was instrumental in establishing a School of Textiles at N.C. State. By 1915, the number of mills in operation topped 300, many adopting the latest technological breakthroughs in yarn spinning and automatic weaving machines.

World War I provided another growth spurt for the industry, and in 1923 North Carolina passed Massachusetts as the leading textile manufacturer in the nation. With Charlotte as the hub, the state's textile world stretched from the banks of the Haw and Deep rivers to the Appalachian foothills. The demand for a new kind of power source — electricity — to replace steam equipment was met by the Southern Power Co., owned by James B. Duke and his brother Ben.

Anti-trust rulings having curtailed his tobacco operations, Duke turned his attention to building a series of dams along the Catawba River to produce power. The textile industry benefitted not only from having this new source of power but also through the money that Duke invested in many of his customers' plants. The area of the state dominated by the industry also benefitted as among the earliest to be electrified. That company, now Duke Power Co., is still the state's pre-eminent power company.

By the 1920s, overproduction and a pricing system by which textile product buyers controlled prices led to an ailing textile economy, however. Most efforts to right the problems came at the expense of labor as manufacturers laid off employees or brought in new technology to eliminate jobs.

At the turn of the century, laborers had struck the mills in Greensboro, Haw River and Durham to little avail. Pressures to end child labor in the mills failed to result in any kind of legislation until the '30s. In 1919-21, strikes were called in response to wage cuts, including one in Concord in which the National Guard was called out. In some cases wage cuts were restored. In others, demands were dropped because further problems in the farm economy provided mill owners with a ready source for replacement workers. A 1929 worker protest in Marion ended with six dead and 20 wounded, when deputies opened fire on protesters.

The most infamous strike of the period took place in Gastonia, when National Textile Workers Union targeted the Loray Mill to call attention to a Southern organizing drive. The Loray plant had cut employees from 3,500 to 2,200, and workers struck over that and other issues of pay and union recognition. As the effectiveness of the strike waned, law enforcement officials moved on a tent city the union had set up to house employees booted out of their company-owned mill houses. Shots were exchanged, members of both sides were hit, with the chief of police dying from his wounds. Emotions were high for the trial of strike leaders, which was moved to Charlotte. After a mistrial, bitter vigilante squads roamed the mill town harassing former strikers. When the union tried to stage another rally, police confronted workers. In one incident, Ella Mae Wiggins, a mother of five and a union activist, was shot and killed, and a new wave of violence erupted. Five accused of killing Wiggins were acquitted, but a retrial in the killing of the chief resulted in convictions of strike leaders, and the union abandoned its Gastonia drive.

The Depression closed or drastically reduced the schedules of most textile mills. The National Recovery Act of the New Deal helped the industry rebound, but it also embraced the workers' right to collectively bargain. Union membership grew, and because the union felt that NRA was being ignored, an industry-wide general strike was called in 1934 that shut down nearly every plant in North Carolina. The strike lasted only 22 days and won little more than a federal mediation panel's promise to study workers' demands further.

Labor was not the only area in which textile companies tried to change sagging fortunes. A great deal of restructuring took place from the mid-'30s into the '50s. Many companies merged their resources, buying out competitors or purchasing companies that provided raw materials for their products.

Active in acquisitions were Cannon Mills in Cabarrus County and J.P. Stevens in Roanoke Rapids. But Burlington Industries was the leader in consolidation. Under J. Spencer Love, Burlington moved from being a producer of rayon into manufacturing of hosiery, fabric for women's undergarments, ribbon, men's suits, cotton dresses and home furnishing fabrics, and grew into the largest manufacturer of synthetic textiles in the world. In the '50s, it acquired mills that made woolen and worsted fabrics. With headquarters in Greensboro, Burlington Industries kept a large sales office in New York City and periodically revamped its operations with the latest in technology. By 1967, Burlington employed more than 80,000 at 130 plants in 15 states. The 40,000 who worked for Burlington's 78 plants in 47 North Carolina communities accounted for a fifth of all textile employment in the state

With its emphasis on rayon manufacture, Burlington was among the earliest to exploit new synthetic fibers. Throughout the century, new fibers were developed — nylon, acetate, acrylic, polyester, and spandex prominent among them. In World War II, nylon replaced silk in a number of military goods including parachutes. Blends of natural and man-made fibers became common in fabrics as new fashions required them.

In the postwar era, some North Carolina textile products became household names, often in connection with the company that produced them — Burlington Gold Cup socks, Cannon towels, Kerustan carpets from Fieldcrest, Hanes hosiery ("Just wait until we get our L'Eggs on you") and Hanes underwear. Blue Bell in Greensboro became famous as the world's largest manufacturer of denim for jeans.

Plant mergers and modernization took a toll on labor, and union activities continued after the war. But in North Carolina, union drives met with little success. An "Operation Dixie" drive to enroll Southern textile workers resulted in little gain for the TWUA. A strike closed the Harriet & Henderson Mills in Henderson for three months, and violence broke out when the company began hiring strike breakers. Eventually the governor had to intervene and the National Guard was needed to restore order. Most of the strikers were not rehired.

A decade-long campaign by the TWUA to organize J.P. Stevens workers in Roanoke Rapids resulted in a successful vote in 1974. But Stevens stalled contract negotiations and in a struggle that received nationwide attention, the union — now merged with the Amalgamated Clothing Workers — finally got a contract. But the union was not able to capitalize on the victory in its efforts elsewhere in the South, including other Stevens plants and Cannon Mills. The Roanoke Rapids struggle, incidentally, was the basis for the book, *Crystal Lee: A Woman of Inheritance,* by Henry Leifermann, which was made into the movie, *Norma Rae.*

Changes in the workplace did result from heightened concerns over brown lung, a disease from breathing cotton dust that textile workers had complained about for years. The Occupational Health and Safety Act of 1970 gave workers a new outlet for complaints which under threat of fines and court action led to improved ventilation systems and air quality.

The industry felt the pinch of rising imports in the '70s and '80s, with fabrics and apparel pouring in from the Far East and South America. By the mid-'80s 43 percent of the clothes bought in America were produced overseas. By that time, textile employment in the state had fallen to about 210,000 from its peak of nearly 300,000 in 1973 and the apparel industry to about 85,000, largely as a result of a wave of plant closings.

Weakened stocks became targets for takeovers, with Cone, Cannon and Blue Bell among speculators' prey. J.P. Stevens merged with West Point Pepperrell to become WestPoint Stevens. Cannon merged with Fieldcrest, but only after a financier borrowed to buy the company, then paid off his loan with profits after eliminating 2,000 jobs, selling the company's mill homes and sacking the pension plan. Fieldcrest is now owned by Pillowtex Corp. of Texas.

In recent years, the North America Free Trade Agreement has heightened competition from Mexico. Companies like Pillowtex and Burlington have suffered financial losses, and the trend has been to close mills in the U.S. and shift production to Mexico. The result has been a continuing loss of textile jobs for North Carolinians. By mid-2000, combined textile manufacturing and apparel employment in the state had fallen to about 180,000.

The future of textiles in our state may be uncertain. But the history of its strikes and conflicts, the uniqueness of the mill villages, our pride in the products make the industry an indelible part of our history. The scattered location of the mills helped keep us a state of small towns and, until recent times, a mostly rural people because families could keep one foot on the farm and one in the textile plant.

Tobacco manufacturing

Tobacco production is as much a part of our heritage as textile manufacturing. Its success kept a farm economy booming and contributed to the preservation of a rural heritage. While not as widespread as textile mills, tobacco factories were not concentrated either, helping to preserve an urban diversity as well. Tobacco's importance to our economy was such that the anti-smoking movement of today creates something of a dilemma for us. We suspect that smoking isn't healthy. But, man, all that tobacco heritage.

Before the Civil War, the manufacture of tobacco products took place on a limited basis, with about a hundred plants employing an average of about 15 people each. These small factories were located mostly in the northern counties of the Bright Belt from Granville County west to Davie. Products were cigars, processed tobacco for smoking in pipes or in roll-your-own cigarettes, chewing tobacco and snuff. Markets were mostly local.

The march of Northern troops through the South during the war was largely ruinous, but it did introduce Northerners to North Carolina smoking tobacco. And this served the tobacco entrepreneurs well over the next 40 years, as the national tobacco market became dominated by North Carolina products.

Within 10 years of the war's end, Durham and Winston had become the centers of tobacco production in the state.

In Durham, J.R. Green, W.T. Blackwell and Julian Carr joined to form a company that produced Bull Durham Smoking Tobacco, a product that survived well into the 20th century.

In Winston, Richard J. Reynolds moved down from Patrick County, Virginia, and became the dominant name among the several who had begun tobacco factories there. The company bearing his name became internationally famous for its Prince Albert Smoking Tobacco, and for the cigarette brands Camel, Winston and Salem.

But James B. "Buck" Duke personified the state's best rags-to-riches story. It began just after the Civil War, when Buck rode around in a wagon with his father, Washington Duke, peddling tobacco they called Pro Bono Publico (for the public good). The Dukes — father Washington and three sons — moved their operations from the farm into a Durham factory in the 1870s.

By the mid-1880s, the Dukes had begun manufacturing cigarettes, first by hand-rolling. As cigarettes became more popular, companies had to hire more and more workers, who at best could roll about 15,000 cigarettes in a 60-hour work week. A Virginian named James A. Bonsack developed the first machine and got a patent in 1884. Mechanics for Duke improved it, and soon the machine was turning out 120,000 cigarettes a day, the output of 40 workers. New machines were added, and the Duke firm soon began to dominate the market.

Buck Duke's business acumen also helped moved the family's operations to the forefront of the tobacco products industry. In 1890, Duke formed the American Tobacco Company, and by 1904 did $274 million in business, controlling about 75 percent of the nation's market, and moving into other markets overseas. He formed the British-American Tobacco Company to get a foothold on world markets.

In the face of Duke's expansion, many small companies folded or were acquired. Duke's firm came under the eye of federal authorities, who decided Duke was violating the Sherman Anti-Trust Act. By 1911, this "tobacco trust" was dissolved.

A new round of tobacco company growth and consolidation ultimately left manufacturing the domain of four towns, with R.J. Reynolds in Winston-Salem, American in Durham and Reidsville and Lorillard in Greensboro.

To North Carolinians, however, the tobacco industry was more than these factories. It also included the farms, the auctions, the warehouses, the trucking companies that moved these products, and many other businesses. From the tobacco seedling to the wrapping on a new pack of Camels, Chesterfields, or Lucky Strikes, cigarettes sustained us.

Many North Carolinians, only one or two generations removed from the farm, visited the farm as children and knew what it was like to pick tobacco, tend the curing fires, pack the golden leaves into hundred-pound bundles and ride it to market. Some had visited the tobacco auctions and heard the sing-song chants of the auctioneers.

The century had seen a huge increase in smoking, especially following World War I. Movie stars smoked, as did leaders such as Presidents Franklin D. Roosevelt and Dwight Eisenhower. Athletes endorsed cigarettes in magazines and television ads. Memorable jingles such as "I'd walk a mile for a Camel," or "Light up a Lucky, it's light up time," resounded in our brains. English teachers complained about "Winston tastes good like a (tap-tap) cigarette should." That should be "as" a cigarette should, they'd tell us.

By the mid-'50s, North Carolina dominated cigarette production as it did tobacco growing. More than half of the nation's tobacco products were made here. R.J. Reynolds was particularly strong, introducing both Winstons and Salems in the last half of the '50s and passing the American Tobacco Co. in sales in 1959. The next year, a poll showed that 58 percent of all men and 36 percent of women in the nation smoked. But that was a high mark.

The specter of health concerns hung over the industry. There was a growing suspicion that maybe smoking was not a healthy thing to do.

The Surgeon General issued a warning in 1964 that linked smoking with health problems. At first, this caused only a momentary down-blip in the steady growth of smoking. But other things followed, including a ban on television advertising and a regulation to put the Surgeon General's message on each pack. The anti-smoking message took hold, and more and more Americans quit smoking. State and local governments banned smoking in public areas. Restrictions or out-right bans snowballed even in North Carolina. The industry has settled lawsuits by states over the costs of smoking-related illnesses to state-financed health care programs. But individuals continue to sue, seeking compensation for illnesses they claim are linked to their smoking.

The companies met declining sales with varying strategies. Some, like Reynolds, diversified into other products. Others concentrated on exports. Reynolds and Liggett and Myers developed "discount" brands that short-cut part of the production process and could be sold for less.

In about 1976, Reynolds lost its position as leading manufacturer to Philip Morris. Marlboro cigarettes, made by Philip Morris, not only became the best-selling brand in the U.S., but achieved prominence worldwide. Philip Morris is a relatively new presence in North Carolina, with its manufacturing complex in Cabarrus County. In the mid-80s, Reynolds merged with Nabisco, which was in turn bought by New York financiers Kohlberg Kravis Roberts & Co., who since have taken the company public. Reynolds headquarters are still in Winston-Salem.

American closed its plants in Durham and consolidated operations in

Reidsville. American was sold in 1994 to the European firm BAT. Lorillard continues operations in Greensboro. Liggett is owned by Vector Group, producing on a small scale in Durham and with plans to produce a nicotine-free cigarette, Omni, in Roxboro.

All told, tobacco company employment has declined from about 27,000 in 1970 to about half that today.

But the legacy of the tobacco industry will, never leave us. Fortunes of the Dukes helped build Duke University. The fortunes of the Reynoldses moved Wake Forest University to Winston-Salem and gave it national prominence; the medical centers at Duke and Bowman Gray are legacies of those families, as are the Duke Endowment, the Z. Smith Reynolds and the Mary Babcock Reynolds foundations which pump millions into charitable causes.

Furniture

Like textiles, furniture was a cottage industry even when North Carolina was a colony. Prior to the Civil War, North Carolinians who didn't want homemade furniture had to order it from out-of-state or wait in line for the works of such North Carolina craftsmen as John Swisegood, of Davidson County, or Thomas Day, a free black from Caswell County.

The furniture industry didn't develop in the state until late in the 1880s, well after the textile and tobacco industries were established.

But it took hold fast, and it wasn't long into the 20th century that North Carolina furniture makers had taken their place among the nation's leaders in output.

The story begins with Ernest Ansel Snow, a lumber salesman from High Point, son of a Yankee, who liked what he saw of the South during the war and moved his family here once the war was over. Snow pooled resources with John H. Tate and Thomas F. Wrenn and began the High Point Furniture Manufacturing Company in 1888.

Although their products were crude, the plant was an immediate success. Many in the state had been unable to refurbish homesteads devastated by the war, but with improving economic conditions they now had the means to buy furniture. High Point was also well situated as an important stop on the new North Carolina Railroad. It sat amid hardwood forests that furnished raw materials, and just as with the textile and tobacco industries, found a pool of laborers who were sick of the uncertain fortunes of farm life.

The success of the plant lit a fire under High Point, and two years later six plants were going full tilt. By 1900, North Carolina boasted 44 factories, and two years later 106, some as far east as Dunn and as far west as Marion. Because transportation was vital for such heavy raw materials and products, the railroad helped determine where plants could be located. It also set up the crescent from Durham to Marion that dominates the furniture industry today.

Like textiles and tobacco, the furniture industry was home-grown with most of the capital, labor and management supplied on the local level. It was also an industry that helped keep the population spread out and helped the state retain its rural and small town character. The success of the furniture industry spawned a host of support industries that supplied wood, parts, finishes and accessories.

Attention to style and quality helped North Carolina tap national markets, and furniture built in the state was star material from Sears, Roebuck catalogues to furniture exhibitions.

From 1899 to 1929, the value of furniture products made in North Carolina had grown from $1.5 million to $54 million; the number of employees from 1,900 to 15,000, and it's payroll from $725,000 to $14.4 million. In 1925, the state ranked first in the nation in the manufacture of wooden furniture and fifth in overall furniture. Today there are about 800 companies operating in the state, employing about 75,000.

An exhibition center for regular shows to display the state's furniture was built in High Point in the '20s that evolved into the Southern Furniture Exposition Building, which in turn became the International Home Furnishings Center. Twice a year, in April and October, thousands of buyers come to High Point and surrounding towns to visit showrooms and pick up merchandise for the coming season. In the spring of 1994, show sponsors estimated that 69,000 attended, pumping $227 million into the area economy. It's no easy task to find a motel room in the furniture crescent during show dates.

As with textiles, many furniture companies were started by subscription among townspeople who had the resources to crank up a factory to meet a perceived need. But more common were private companies, many family-controlled for generations. Many also are small, filling specialized niches with their products. While small companies can suffer more in recessions, they also have some advantages. They can detect changes in fashion more quickly and change their products accordingly more easily than can larger, cumbersome companies.

Nevertheless, the merger mania has changed the face of North Carolina's furniture industry. In the mid-90s, Masco, a Michigan faucet manufacturer, became the nation's largest furniture company after acquiring Henredon and Drexel Heritage in Burke County, Universal Furniture in High Point and Lexington Furniture. Masco then turned around and sold most of its furniture operations to an investment group, LifeStyle Furniture International of High Point, which is now the nation's third largest furniture manufacturer. Number one is Furniture Brands International, of St. Louis, which owns Broyhill Furniture of Lenoir and Thomasville Furniture. Number two is La-Z-Boy, which bought LADD Industries of Greensboro in 1999.

In general, the furniture industry has suffered since about 1988, with imports and rising lumber prices squeezing profit margins. Because furniture is something that consumers can postpone buying, economic downturns can have an effect on the industry. After a couple of fairly strong years, the slowing economy began dragging down sales in mid-2000. The industry cut about 2,000 jobs in North Carolina as a result.

Research Triangle Park

Luther Hodges, who became governor when Gov. William B. Umstead died, then served a term of his own, is given much of the credit for successful efforts in the '50s to begin widening the state's economic base. The four mainstays on which the economy had rested during the 20th century were showing signs of age. As a whole, the economic base was growing, but not as fast as the rest of the nation. We were losing ground in industrial wage rates and in per capita income. Agriculture, as has been noted, was in the throes of massive change.

So, as the state wrestled with the social changes brought about by Brown vs. Board of Education, it was tackling economic problems as well. Hodges was able to build on a "Go Forward" program initiated by Gov. Kerr Scott in the late '40s that produced improvements in the state's highways and in its ports at Morehead City and Wilmington.

The legislature reworked tax laws to attract multi-state corporations and set up an ad campaign to promote the state as a new industrial haven. Hodges also led a delegation to Europe to drum up trade prospects. A *Life* magazine spread featured photos of Hodges showing off various state-made products, including one of him taking a shower in a quick-drying, synthetic suit made from North Carolina fabric.

But the most important initiative of the day was for the Research Triangle Park. Discussions among business and academic leaders produced a plan to buy land in the triangle area bounded by Raleigh, Durham and Chapel Hill and attract businesses that could take advantage of the area's educational resources.

A fund drive provided $1.5 million to buy 5,000 acres in Durham and Wake counties, and to lay out the park in segments large enough so that companies could put up their buildings and have room left over for attractive landscaping. The Research Triangle Institute, a contract research facility that employed researchers from the universities, was the first occupant of the park. That was followed by a research laboratory for the U.S. Forest Service and the Chemstrand Corp., which built a facility to develop new synthetic fibers.

When Hodges' term as governor expired, President Kennedy named him Secretary of Commerce, which gave him a national platform from which to tout the Research Triangle Park.

In the mid-60s, the National Institute of Environmental Health Sciences

Glaxo Smith Kline building in the Research Triangle Park.

laid plans for a $25 million facility on 500 acres that would employ 2,000. Its arrival attracted IBM, which employed 2,500 at a new communications system plant, the drug company Burroughs Wellcome and a research center for EPA. Over the years, companies that moved to the park or established research divisions included Ciba-Geigy, General Electric, Union Carbide, DuPont, Northern Telecom, and Glaxo (which has merged with Burroughs Wellcome and SmithKline Beecham and is known as GlaxoSmithKline). Research facilities include the Microelectronics Center of North Carolina, the Triangle Universities Computation Center and the National Humanities Center.

Today, the park has been expanded to 6,800 acres and is about two-thirds developed. New companies continue to discover the area, and a number of smaller business parks have sprung up. When site planners visit the Triangle they see traffic jams on a smaller scale than in more established urban areas. They also see a reasonable cost of living, lots of trees and open space, a good airport and high-tech communications, as well as the large university communities. A few years back, *Money* magazine selected the Triangle as the best place to live in America. All this has helped the snowball continue to grow. Of course, growth always has a price. The suburbs spread outward, overburdening towns and counties that were formerly rural and are now trying to provide services that they could scarcely have imagined 20 years ago.

The park is home to about a third of the state's employees in the "high tech" industry which towns across North Carolina sought to lure to fill the vacuum of closing textile, tobacco and furniture plants. By 2000, the high tech industry employed about 60,000 in the state and paid over $2.5 billion in wages. The collapse of the "dot.coms" in 2000 hurt the industry, but not to the degree that it did in, say, California's Silicon Valley.

Tourism

The Sandhills — Pinehurst in particular — and North Carolina's beaches and mountains have attracted tourists since the 1800s. Early travel was a pastime for the wealthy who had money for transportation, food and lodging and plenty of leisure time. In the 1920s, when families started buying cars, travel for the sake of seeing something began to draw them farther and farther from home. And a tourist industry developed. In the mid-'30s, for example, North Carolina estimated that travelers spent $36 million in the state.

The Depression, then the war limited travel. But after the war, the travel bug quickly caught on again. Just as with our other industries, the mid-'50s is a good time to look at what was happening. Postwar prosperity had given families more money and more spare time. A lot of our attention was devoted to cars and travel, and we went everywhere.

By 1950, the Great Smoky Mountains National Park, which had opened in 1939, was the most visited national park in the nation. The Blue Ridge Parkway was the most traveled road of the National Park Service. The '50s also saw the beginning of the Interstate Highway System, and North Carolina's attractions became more accessible to more people because it took less time to get there.

But the same was true for other states, and the concept of competition for tourist dollars came into being. North Carolina began billing itself as "Variety Vacationland." And it had a good product. It didn't hurt for those ads to feature a far-as-the-eye-can-see stretch of sparkling beach or a mountain vista.

By 1970, the amount of money spent by tourists in the state had risen to about $800 million.

Over the years, new specific attractions came into being, such as the battleship USS North Carolina at Wilmington, Carowinds in Charlotte, and the N.C. Zoo in Asheboro. The state expanded its own parks system to call attention to natural features that might draw interest. The ski industry developed in several mountain areas, bringing tourists there year-round.

By 1985, tourism's revenues were estimated at about $4 billion..

Communities across the state looked around to see what they could develop to attract visitors. Historic sites were renovated, and their stories researched to make an interesting package for tourists. Many communities chose a notable quality and developed a festival around the theme. In 1997, the Cherokees opened an $82 million Harrah's-operated casino on the reservation.

Now, tourism is a $12 billion industry for the state, making it just as important as some other of our economy's segments such as agriculture and manufacturing.

Movies

You can watch *Being There* or *Richie Rich* and get a good tour of the Biltmore mansion in Asheville. *Bull Durham* will take you to the old charming baseball park in Durham. *Brainstorm* has views of the Glaxo Wellcome building in Research Triangle Park.

North Carolina's mountains have been the setting for a number of movies, including *Nell, Last of the Mohicans, Dirty Dancing,* and *The Fugitive*. The spectacular train-bus wreck that freed Harrison Ford in *The Fugitive* was staged on the tracks of the Great Smoky Mountains Railroad, which has preserved the accident site and uses one of the "movie star" engines to draw tourist trains between Dillsboro and Bryson City.

Movies have been filmed in such decidedly non-Hollywood places as Burgaw (*Silver Bullet*), Hamlet (*Billy Bathgate*), Asheville (*Hannibal*) and Union and Anson counties (*The Color Purple*). *Sleeping with the Enemy, Days of Thunder, Teenage Mutant Ninja Turtles, The Original Kings of Comedy* have all featured North Carolina locations. TV's *Dawson's Creek* is filmed in Wilmington.

Today North Carolina ranks third behind California and New York as a movie state. In 2000, 25 movies and 56 television episodes were made in the state, not to mention countless TV commercials, with revenues estimated at $250 million.

The state's formal entry into the world of filmmaking came in 1980, when Gov. Hunt established the Film Office to tout the state as a movie location.

But the state wasn't totally inexperienced with films prior to that. *Thunder Road* had been made back in the '50s, starring Robert Mitchum as the mountain boy who ran moonshine and was killed in a fiery wreck as he tried to elude revenue agents. And Earl Owensby of Shelby established a local film lot in the early '70s, where he made scads of "B" movies.

Even back in the '20s in the silent film era, a fledgling industry cropped up around Saluda, with hopes — that didn't pan out — of making a Hollywood East in the mountains.

In 1984, Wilmington did become North Carolina's answer to Hollywood when Dino DeLaurentis established a film studio there. That was bought by Carolco in 1989. Although that firm later went into bankruptcy, production continues there. Studios also have been built in Charlotte, High Point and Yanceyville.

The economics of the film industry can be flighty. When a town is chosen as a film site, it can be exciting, with stars and film crew members milling about, shopping and eating out. But just a suddenly as they appear they are gone, taking their money with them.

The location of studios in the state has led to the establishment of an infrastructure of movie-making expertise. That feeling that the movie industry has become a permanent fixture in the state encouraged the N.C. School of the Arts to provide a School of Filmmaking. In 1997, the school opened a state-of-the-art complex for production and viewing of its films, including a "studio village" to help train students for jobs in the industry.

Some of our products

A few of the products made in North Carolina we've already mentioned, but there are many more that are widely known.

Pepsi-Cola is a North Carolina product. It was formulated by Caleb Bradham who ran a drugstore in New Bern. He set up bottlers and marketed his soda for a time, but eventually went bankrupt. His product, however, effervesces on.

Millions of kids have played with the "bolo-bat," a paddle with a small rubber ball attached by a long rubber band. The object was to keep swatting the ball as it snapped back from its farthest point. This toy was made by the Wham-O Corp. of High Point.

Speaking of snapping back, remember the "Snap back with Stanback" jingle? Stanback headache powders are made in Salisbury. Or you can "Take a BC Powder and come back strong." That's a Durham product. Another headache powder, Goody's, originated in Winston-Salem.

When you were a kid and had a cold, your mother may have rubbed your chest with Vicks Mentholatum, made by the Smith Richardson Co. in Greensboro, or she may have smeared your lips with Chap Stick, made in Salisbury, before sending you out in the cold.

If you've had an ulcer, you may well have gotten a prescription for your doctor for Zantac, made by Glaxo at Research Triangle Park. Glaxo recently merged with Burroughs Wellcome, which developed the AIDS drug AZT.

Not many of us could afford a Hatteras Yacht, built in High Point, but it was the most famous of North Carolina boat builders, whose industry goes way back and centers around Harker's Island in Carteret County. McLean Trucking Co. and Sea-Land were the names of companies founded by Malcolm McLean of Maxton, who revolutionized shipping the world over with his idea of moving freight in containers that could be lifted directly from ships onto tractor-trailers.

Some newcomers to the state find it economical to buy a mobile home — or manufactured home, as the industry prefers to call it — and Oakwood of Greensboro is the nation's largest builder. All told, the state is the second largest manufacturer of mobile homes in the nation and ranks first in sales.

Two of North Carolina's banks took advantage of deregulation in the '80s to expand beyond our borders. NCNB became NationsBank, moved into Florida and Texas, then merged with Bank of America in California. It kept that name, with headquarters in Charlotte, to become the nation's fourth largest bank. First Union, our second largest bank, spread into Florida, Pennsylvania and New Jersey before running into financial problems when the economy slowed. It plans to merge with Wachovia, our third largest bank, based in Winston-Salem. It would retain the Wachovia name with headquarters in Charlotte. Statewide, First Union employed 22,500 in the state and Wachovia 8,770 in the fall of 2000. A number of jobs would be cut in the merger. Bank of America employs about 15,000 in the state.

But our biggest employer is Delhaize America Inc., a holding company for Food Lion and Kash N' Karry supermarkets, based in Salisbury. It employs more than 36,000 across the state, according to *Business North Carolina.*

Centers of commerce

Those who have grown up in North Carolina have come to associate our cities with certain businesses.

Charlotte, we think of as a trade center. It was established as a crossroads commercial center, in fact, and over the years became headquarters for a lot of companies that needed a central point for their Carolinas territories. Because it nearly straddled the line separating North and South Carolina, Charlotte became a mecca for those displaced by declining rural or small-town enterprises. Banking and insurance are among its driving forces, and it's the largest stop between Richmond and Atlanta. Recently, sports has become a driving force, with pro basketball and football franchises certain to provide coattails for other enterprises, including downtown renewal efforts.

Greensboro developed on the strength of textiles, insurance and other manufacturing. Other driving forces were education — Greensboro has five colleges — and its position as a crossroads. Winston-Salem was built on a strong Moravian work foundation and had three main legs — tobacco, textiles and banking. High Point was built by furniture. The three towns make up what is known as the Piedmont Triad, with a regional airport uniting them. Their location has also proved convenient for a number of large trucking firms.

Raleigh was founded as the state capital and has derived its growth mainly from government. It also has a number of colleges and universities and has served as a magnet for people in eastern North Carolina who desired to move to the city.

Durham was a tobacco and textile town and site of Duke University which has contributed a great deal to its character, including the medical complex. It is also home to the N.C. Mutual Life Insurance Co., the largest black-owned business in the state, founded in 1898.

Chapel Hill has always been driven by the university. It also is a huge medical center.

Raleigh, Durham and Chapel Hill are now linked as the Research Triangle, which has brought a great deal of growth to all three cities.

Wilmington, close to two of our most popular beaches, has been a tourist capital of the coast. But it is also our most important port. Asheville has grown as the point of destination for mountain travelers.

The military has contributed to the growth of a number of our cities, including Fayetteville, Goldsboro and Jacksonville.

Our other important towns, as we have seen, owe their growth mostly to agriculture, textiles and furniture. In the 19th century, they either had an industry established that the railroads felt necessary to serve or they developed as a result of the railroad's presence. In the 20th century, the interstate highway system tended to serve those same towns, and they became even stronger.

Today, the state's most vibrant cities and counties are spread along the interstate highway corridors. The farther an area is removed from an interstate, the less likely it is to be doing well economically.

But that may change to a degree with a new era of sophisticated communications. As the metropolitan areas become saturated, those who have mastered the ability to work on computers can link their product or service to mainstream America by telecommunications may ultimately help spread the wealth by populating the rural regions off the beaten path.

Books

Blythe, Legette. *William Henry Belk/Merchant of the South.* 1950. Chapel Hill, UNC Press.

Brooks, Jerome E. *Green Leaf and Gold: Tobacco in North Carolina.* 1975. Raleigh, Division of Archives and History.

Burrough, Bryan and Helyar, John. *Barbarians at the Gate/The Fall of RJR Nabisco* 1990. New York, Harper & Row.

Glass, Brent D. *The Textile Industry in North Carolina/ A History.* 1992. Raleigh, Division of Archives and History.

7

Sports

Pardon us if we bask a little in the glory that our athletes have brought us in the new millennium.

We have honors aplenty showering our college basketball teams, our golfers and our stock car racers – the three sports we're wild about.

But it was a track star, Marion Jones, that has garnered the global attention, winning three gold and two bronze medals in the 2000 Olympics in Sydney. Although born in California, the fact that she made a name for herself here – she was on the UNC women's championship basketball team of 1994, and now lives in Chapel Hill – helps us claim her as one of our own. She remains the top sprinter in the world.

Mike Krzyzewski, Coach K to us who struggle with his name, led his Duke Blue Devils to a third NCAA championship in 2001 and was named to the Basketball Hall of Fame. For 20 years, he has developed winning teams with an even temperament, without scandal and with players who graduate. Shane Battier, a member of the NCAA championship team, was college Player of the Year.

Matt Doherty was college Coach of the Year in his first season with the UNC Tar Heels. The team was ranked No. 1 during the season, but faltered in the NCAA tournament. Doherty, a member of the 1982 championship team, replaced Bill Guthridge, who took the team to the Final Four twice in his three years. Guthridge, had taken over from Dean Smith, the winningest basketball coach in college history.

Coach of the Year in the NBA was Larry Brown, who played at Chapel Hill in the early '60s. He led the Philadelphia 76ers to the NBA finals.

Candy Hannemann, of Duke, won the NCAA Women's Championship in Golf.

And speaking of golf, the Pine Needles Lodge and Golf Club in Southern Pines hosted the 2001 U.S. Women's Open. 100,000 tramped the fairways and a national TV audience watched as Karrie Webb ran away with the title. The golf club is owned by Peggy Kirk Bell, a star with the LPGA in the '50s, who played out of Pinehurst.

In stock car racing, tragedy has overshadowed all else, taking two prominent North Carolinians.

140

Dale Earnhardt, of Kannapolis, was killed when he crashed during the last lap of the Daytona 500 in February, 2001. Known as the Intimidator for his aggressive driving tactics, his death shocked the South like none other since Elvis'.

In May 2000, Adam Petty was killed in a crash during practice at New Hampshire International Raceway. Petty, 19, was the 4th generation of our most famous racing family. His death came while the Pettys, of Level Cross were still mourning the passing of Lee Petty, one of the early drivers of NASCAR history, who begat Richard, who begat Kyle, who begat Adam.

Racing is a dangerous sport. But the fact that tragedy struck our two preeminent families – Earnhardt's father raced, now his son does as well – seemed unbelievable.

Fans had always argued over who was the greatest driver ever, Earnhardt or Richard Petty. King Richard, they called him. He drove his "Petty Blue," number 43 car to 200 racing victories. By the time Earnhardt had established himself, speeds had become so high that NASCAR was forced to restrict the power of the engines. Earnhardt proved himself to be the best under these more equalized conditions. Although he didn't have as many victories, he won seven championships, the same number as Petty.

There is little argument, however, over who was the best basketball player ever.

Michael Jordan played basketball at Laney High School in Wilmington, at the University of North Carolina and in Chicago with the Bulls. He wore number 23, and even past his prime was still the biggest draw in the NBA. He would drive for the basket in long, airborne glides of seemingly impossible distance and duration. In flight, he twisted his body around opposing players and churned his legs to gain distance. Whether graceful or ungainly, these drives inevitably ended in a dunk or in the flip of the ball that swished, banked or rolled around the rim, dropping through for a score.

Michael and Richard, Marion and Coach K. represent the best of North Carolina. They are not prima donnas, but are easy to smile, approachable and seem to have a sincere enjoyment of their fans. Between them, Michael and Richard seem to have endorsed nearly every product you can buy in a mall, supermarket or hardware store.

One of the safest bets in North Carolina is that no matter what kind of group you find yourself in, knowledge of basketball or stock car racing will give you a common ground on which to converse. But we follow other sports as well.

We've touched on golf.

Minor League baseball brings folks out on summer nights all across the state. The movie *Bull Durham*, filmed in Durham, celebrated our allegiance to the game.

Interest in football is seasonal and most of us get caught up in the thrill of college games in autumn. But we rarely crack the Top Ten as with basketball. Pro sports center around Charlotte, with the Charlotte Hornets of the NBA, the Charlotte Sting of the WNBA, the Carolina Panthers of the NFL. The state's only National Hockey League franchise is the Carolina Hurricanes of Raleigh.

Basketball

With the exception of the new NBA franchise in Charlotte and the occasional rise of a small college team to prominence, the story of basketball in North Carolina has taken place along Tobacco Road — that stretch of highway that separates Wake Forest, N.C. State, Duke and UNC and traveled by wonderful and legendary teams for decades.

It is college basketball that we follow here. We're not like Indiana, where every hamlet lives and breathes high school basketball. And, outside of Charlotte, most of us don't have enough experience with the pros to discuss it at any length. But college basketball is all we really need. A chapter of our state history should involve the struggles on the court among these four great universities and their battles with outsiders. The ebb and flow of each school's basketball fortunes, the continuous entrance and exit of truly great players, the scads of tournament, Sweet Sixteen, Final Four appearances and our eight NCAA championships — have been great entertainment.

You will notice that even the most industrious North Carolinians will become distracted in the spring when the ACC tournament starts. And they don't get back into things fully until their particular college team has been eliminated in the NCAAs. The level of that distraction always surprises newcomers to the state, so be forewarned.

Our basketball history must also include the smaller colleges, such as UNC-Charlotte, A&T in Greensboro, Winston-Salem State, Guilford College, High Point College and Davidson, each of which has produced championship teams and Hall-of-Fame players and coaches.

For the record, the first college basketball game in the state took place in 1906 at Guilford College with the Quakers beating Wake Forest 26-19. By 1911, teams had been formed at each of the Big Four schools. In the 1920s, they became members of the Southern Conference and when their teams were good enough, played in (and won their share of) season-ending tournaments in Atlanta, then in Raleigh.

But our preoccupation with the game begins in 1946, when Everett Case, who had been a successful high school coach in Indiana, became head coach at N.C. State and began building a strong basketball tradition. He recruited Indiana players, who became known as the "Hoosier Hotshots" and introduced the fast break, which made the game more exciting than the old game dominated by two-hand set shots and low scores.

Case's teams were an immediate hit. At one point, students and fans literally broke down the door of the small, 3,500-seat campus gym, forcing cancellation of a game. Games were moved downtown where a few more seats were available. The conference tournament had to be moved to Duke, which could seat 8,000. Finally, in 1949, Reynolds Coliseum opened with 12,000 seats. The

Wolfpack was moving into the big league of college basketball.

With the birth of the Dixie Classic in 1949, Case raised the rest of the Tobacco Road schools into national prominence. The first of the holiday tournaments, the Dixie Classic lasted three days and pitted the Big Four teams against four top teams from around the country that were chosen by Case.

The first tournament, which saw Georgia Tech, Rhode Island State and Penn State invited to play, drew more than 52,000 fans. It was won by N.C. State, which took seven of the 12 Dixie Classics played. Southern hospitality did not extend to the Reynolds gym floor. Overall, the Big Four's record against the outside schools was 59-33, with State's record against its guests 21-4.

The most celebrated tournament was held in 1958 when Cincinnati, with Oscar Robertson, came in ranked No. 1 in the nation. UNC was ranked No. 3, State No. 6 and Michigan State No. 9. Cincinnati was beaten twice, by State and UNC, and State won it all with a victory over Michigan State.

In 1932, the Southeastern Conference had been carved out of the Southern Conference by schools that tended to emphasize football over basketball. Then in 1953, the Atlantic Coast Conference was formed by the Big Four schools and four others who disagreed with the direction of the Southern Conference.

Case's dominance of southern basketball in the first postwar decade is easy to document. His teams won the Southern Conference tournament six years straight from his first season in Raleigh in 1947 through 1952. After Wake Forest beat State by one point in the 1953 SC tournament, Case's teams came back to win the first three ACC tournaments, 1954-56, and again in 1959.

Case's influence raised the level of play among the Big Four teams to the point that eventually they eclipsed him. Carolina brought in Frank McGuire, who recruited out of New York City. Duke hired Vic Bubas, a former player and coach for Case. Wake Forest hired Bones McKinney, a former UNC and NBA star and a colorful Baptist preacher. Probably the best way to absorb post-Case basketball history is to study it school by school.

But first a mention should be made of the point-shaving scandal that hit State and Carolina in 1961 and resulted in the death of the Dixie Classic. The NCAA had issued one-year probations for basketball recruiting violations against State (1954) and UNC (1961) and a four-year probation against State for a football violation in 1956. So, officials of the state university system were already worrying about sports when a national gambling investigation that focused on New York City stretched down into North Carolina. Case had asked the State Bureau of Investigation to look into a couple of games he thought suspicious. Three students at State were found to be involved. Two were implicated at North Carolina, including Doug Moe, a future NBA player and coach, who was suspended from school not because he participated in the point shaving, but because he knew what was going on and didn't come clean. University officials countered by reducing the schedule, eliminating the Dixie Classic,

Frank McGuire, former head coach at the University of North Carolina at Chapel Hill, with successor Dean Smith at his side.

and limiting out-of-state basketball scholarships. Although these restrictions were eventually relaxed, the tournament was never revived, and it weakened the heart of Tobacco Road basketball for a time.

But the patient recovered. And the only stress on the basketball heart today is the tremendous excitement that fans get by being in one of the Big Four gyms — or one of our cities' coliseums — for a good game. Nothing matching that excitement exists in our state, except maybe for sitting in front of the TV to watch the game. Here's that promised school-by-school breakdown that will be invaluable to you once you've asked a North Carolinian, "Where did you go to college?"

Carolina

Of course they played basketball at Chapel Hill before 1957, but nobody remembers much about it. There was an All-American and national player of the year back in the '30s named George Glamack. UNC won the Southern Conference championship several times in the '20s and '30s, and in 1924 was 26-0. That was before a national tournament, so any claims to a national title then were just that — claims.

On the other hand, anyone who saw it could never forget that first televised NCAA final between UNC and Kansas, featuring Wilt "The Stilt"

Chamberlain, when the Tar Heels won in triple overtime to complete a 32-0 season. That championship was official.

Frank McGuire was in his fourth season at UNC. He had been hired after leading St. Johns to the championship game in 1952, where they had been beaten, ironically, by Kansas which, incidentally, had a reserve guard named Dean Smith.

The '57 team was led by senior Lenny Rosenbluth, a New Yorker, who was college player of the year.

There were a number of close calls during the season — down four points with 30 seconds to go against Maryland in College Park, for example, then winning in two overtimes. The team fared well in the media centers, beating NYU in Madison Square Garden, and Dartmouth and Holy Cross in the Boston Gardens. Of course, they swept the Dixie Classic, the regular season and the ACC tournament. After winning the regional NCAA games fairly handily, the Tar Heels went three overtimes with Michigan State to reach the finals.

Carolina went into the tournament ranked No. 1 in the nation, with Kansas ranked second. McGuire's strategy was to contain Chamberlain with a triangle of players. The ploy worked, limiting the seven-footer to just 13 shots. Again it took three overtimes, but the Tar Heels won 54-53.

McGuire left in 1961 to coach in the NBA — at Philadelphia where Chamberlain was his star — and later returned to college coaching at the University of South Carolina.

The head coaching job at UNC was given to one of his assistants, Dean Smith.

Smith, who retired in 1997 as the nation's winningest basketball coach ever, began his career slowly. Under the scandal-limited schedule, his first team went 8-9. His early stars were Larry Brown, a holdover from the McGuire team, and Billy Cunningham. Both went on to play pro ball and to coach, as have scads of Smith's players over the years. The next year was a good one, with high profile victories over Kentucky and Notre Dame. But the record fell to 12 and 12 the next year and then 6-6 through the schedule of 1964-'65. The Tar Heels returned from an away-game loss to Wake Forest to find a student mob waiting and Smith's effigy hanging from Woollen Gym.

Smith weathered the pressure and within a couple of years was in the Final Four of the NCAA tournament with Bobby Lewis and Larry Miller, his first real recruited stars. Carolina lost to Dayton in the semifinals. But next year, 1968, the Tar Heels reached the finals with Charley Scott, Smith's first black player, and Eddie Fogler added to the mix. But this was the Lew Alcindor (Kareem Abdul-Jabbar) era and UCLA had begun its string of NCAA championships. Carolina lost 78-55. The next year, minus Miller, the Tar Heels added Rusty Clark at center and Dick Grubar and went to the Final Four again, losing to Purdue in the semifinals.

With Robert McAdoo, Bill Chamberlain and George Karl, Smith's Tar

Heels made it back to the Final Four in 1972, but lost to Florida State in the semifinals.

Despite injuries, the Tar Heels of 1977 used last-minute heroics time and again to beat Purdue, Notre Dame, Kentucky and Nevada-Las Vegas, before losing to Al McGuire's Marquette in the final game. Stars of that team were Phil Ford, Mike O'Koren, Tommy LaGarde and Walter Davis.

Smith returned to the Final Four in 1981 with James Worthy, Sam Perkins and Al Wood his stars. After beating Virginia in the semifinals, the Tar Heels lost 63-50 to Bob Knight's Indiana and his star Isaiah Thomas.

In 20 years, Smith had become a coach of national renown and was able to attract player after player of All-American calibre to UNC, many of whom had played in North Carolina high schools. Having a depth of good players, he was able to substitute freely, to keep his starters fresh. Each season he remolded the team according to the cast. He preached role-playing, selflessness and senior leadership. His teams ran, were constantly in motion on offense, constantly passing in search of the open man. When a player scored off an assist, he would point at the passer on the way back down court. In the days before a shot clock, Smith became famous for the Four Corners, a slow-down game — hated by opponents, and some Carolina fans as well — that required his best ball-handler to dribble around and pass to one of his teammates in a corner, who might throw it back immediately or who might just hold onto it until an opponent came out and challenged him. If a team overplayed, it often left a man open for an easy basket underneath.

But despite his position as one of the nation's pre-eminent coaches, with six trips to the Final Four and three losses in the championship game, Smith was stigmatized with a "can't-win-the-big-one" reputation.

That ended in 1982 in New Orleans, when Michael Jordan joined Worthy and Perkins, Jimmy Black and Matt Doherty in the starting five. Carolina entered the Final Four with a record of 30-2, the losses to Wake Forest and Virginia. The Tar Heels beat Houston in the semi-finals, then met Georgetown – with stars Patrick Ewing and Eric "Sleepy" Floyd from Gastonia – in the championship game.

It was a close game all the way, neither team gaining more than a five-point lead. With less than a minute left, Georgetown scored for a 62-61 lead. With 32 seconds left, Smith called time out. Worthy and Perkins were heavily guarded, and when the ball was played in, it spent time outside — then Black passed to Jordan, who jumped and shot. Swish! And Georgetown had the ball, now a point down with 15 seconds left. Down the floor they came, with Worthy trailing the play. Fred Brown was dribbling the ball for the Hoyas and as Worthy moved into his peripheral vision, Brown threw the ball to him. That was it! But no, it wasn't. Worthy was fouled, missed his shots, and Floyd had time for one more desperation shot before time ran out. He missed. And *that* was it. The Tar Heels were the NCAA champs, and Dean Smith had finally won "the big one."

Eight years passed before Carolina got to the Final Four again.

In 1991, Smith lost to Kansas in the semifinals. Kansas was coached by his former assistant, Roy Williams.

Then in 1993, another championship. Smith had Eric Montross, Derrick Phelps, Donald Williams, George Lynch and Brian Reese as his starting five. The Tar Heels beat Arkansas and Cincinnati in the regionals to reach the Final Four, which had come around again to New Orleans. In the semifinal game, Smith got back at Kansas and Roy Williams, sending them packing 78-68. After answering Kansas' first basket, the Tar Heels never trailed.

The championship game was something else. Michigan had beaten Kentucky to win a return to the finals, having lost the title game to Duke the previous year. Michigan, led by Chris Webber, built a ten-point lead in the first half that was erased by a North Carolina spurt. At the half, UNC led 42-36 and built the lead to eight early in the second half. That was their largest margin, however, as Michigan scrapped back to lead by four. Carolina regained control and led by one with Pat Sullivan on the foul line shooting one and one with 20 seconds left. He hit the first, missed the second. The ball was rebounded by Webber (who Carolina fans think should have been called for traveling) who raced down the court and, well defended in the corner, signaled timeout. What a blunder. Michigan had used all its timeouts, and was called for a technical foul. Williams hit the two technical shots and two more when he was fouled after the inbounds play. Carolina had won another for Smith 77-71. If you really want to rile a Tar Heel fan, just say that both of Smith's NCAA championships were decided by opponents' bonehead plays. But be prepared to duck.

In 1995, Jerry Stackhouse and Rasheed Wallace led the Heels into the Final Four with a victory over Kentucky in the East regionals. But the Tar Heels couldn't get past Arkansas, which had beaten Duke for the title the year before.

Then in 1997, Smith went to the Final Four for the last time, with a team led by Antawn Jamison, Vince Carter and Shammond Williams. After a slow start, Carolina had launched a string of victories, enabling Smith to pass Adolf Rupp as the winningest coach in college basketball history. Arizona beat Carolina in the semi-finals, and before the next season began — with 36 years and 879 victories under his belt — Smith announced his retirement.

Long-time assistant Bill Guthridge was named to replace Smith. The Jamison-Carter-Williams team returned to the Final Four in 1998, only to be beaten by Utah in the semi-finals. Florida knocked the Tar Heels out in the semi-finals of the 2000 tournament. The team, led by Ed Cota, Brendan Haywood, Jason Capel and Joseph Forte, bowed 71-59.

Guthridge retired after three seasons, and Matt Doherty, who was making a name for himself as head coach at Notre Dame, won the job. In his first season, Doherty led the team to a 26-7 record, a No. 1 ranking during the season and the Sweet 16 in the NCAA tournament and was named college Coach of the Year by the Associated Press.

N.C. State

The 1959 Wolfpack gave Everett Case his last ACC championship. He coached until the beginning of the 1964-65 season when his health forced him to turn the job over to Press Maravich. Case died in 1966, and left part of his estate to former players. When Maravich left after two years to follow his son, Pistol Pete, to LSU, Norman Sloan began a term as head coach that carried through 1980.

Sloan had been a player on Case's first team at N.C. State, but played football as an upper classman. Nevertheless, he swallowed a lot of the Case formula that combined, energy, intensity and a positive attitude. Sloan had coached basketball at the Citadel and the University of Florida. He began slowly at State, Eddie Biedenbach his only inherited star. In his first ACC tournament, he threw a stall at third-ranked Duke in the semifinals and came up with a 12-10 win. Within three years, he had begun attracting the kind of players he wanted to play a more simplified give-and-go, one-on-one offense and, on defense, full court, man-to-man pressure. In 1970, he recruited Tom Burleson of Avery County, who stood seven feet, four inches tall. The next year came David Thompson of Gaston County, Monte Towe and Tim Stoddard. The 1973 team went 27-0, but because it was on probation couldn't go to the NCAA tournament.

The stage was set for 1974, one of the most thrilling season finishes ever for all North Carolina basketball fans, no matter for whom they normally pulled. State entered the ACC tournament ranked No. 1 in the nation and had lost only once — to UCLA, the powerhouse of college basketball, by 84-66 early in the season. Maryland, ranked No. 4, was the opponent in the ACC final. These were the days when, after the regular season was over, the lose-one, go-home rule applied. Only one conference team went to the NCAAs. Either team would have represented the conference well that year. But in what many regard as the greatest ACC game ever played, the Wolfpack won 103-100 in a fast-tempo game of heroic match-ups that was decided with six seconds left in overtime when Towe sank two foul shots.

As luck would have it, State was able to play the NCAA tournament in North Carolina — the regionals in Raleigh and the finals in Greensboro. But any reading of the brackets showed the inevitable. As certain as death and taxes, the Wolfpack would have to play UCLA again to get to the final game. Indeed, they sailed through the regionals, beating Top 10 teams Providence and Pittsburgh. Fans got a scare in the Pitt game when David Thompson went high for a rebound, glanced off another player and hit the floor head first. He lay still and was carried off the floor to the hospital, where it was found he had a mild concussion. He returned to Reynolds Coliseum before the game ended, waved to the crowd and was answered with a thunderous cheer.

The following Saturday afternoon, Thompson was in Greensboro with

Towe, Stoddard, Burleson and Moe Rivers, a junior college transfer who had become a starter. Warming up on the other end of the Coliseum floor were Bill Walton, Jamal Wilkes and the rest of Coach John Wooden's dynastic UCLA team, which had won the NCAA championship eight years in a row and would win it again the following year.

All day the excitement built among basketball fans, and everybody in the state, it seemed, got caught up in it. Even the governor was writing a column in the Greensboro paper. Because it was in Greensboro, more North Carolinians than ever found a way into the Final Four. Those who couldn't planned their entire day around game time on the tube, and the food and liquor stores were packed. We were the subject of national attention. This was David versus Goliath, the legendary wizards of basketball entering the Tobacco Road lair of the Wolfpack, hope ("We can beat these guys") overlaying despair ("There's no way we can beat these guys") and back to hope ("If David can … maybe …").

UCLA led early, but the Wolfpack came back to lead late in the game. They they were tied. It came down to a final shot by Stoddard — all breathing stopped — which glanced off the side of the rim. Overtime. The mixed feelings of hope and doom intensified. It was clear that State could play with these guys, but they'd had their chance to win and didn't. They continued to play it close and, tied, Burleson faked Walton for the final shot in overtime, which bounced off the back of the rim. Oh, this was cruel. Two chances blown. Now in the second overtime, UCLA scooted out to a seven-point bulge, and, well, that seemed to do it. But again, hope. An exciting comeback put State ahead 76-75 as time was running out. A foul and Towe was on the line for two. He made them both, and UCLA was beaten.

The championship game was anti-climactic, with State beating Marquette 76-64. Coach Al McGuire was called for two technicals, and the Pack led by as much as 16 points. Nearly 16,000 fans were in the Coliseum to see that game, as another 42 million watched on TV.

So N.C. State became the national champs in 1974, but there was no question that being able to play in the state before friendly crowds helped the Wolfpack pull it off. This was not the case in 1983. State had to win this NCAA championship entirely on the road.

It was not supposed to be their year. Carolina was the defending champion, and with Jordan and Perkins returning, most basketball sages felt they had a good shot at repeating. Nobody even thought of State. After all, Dereck Whittenberg, their star, had broken his foot and had been out most of the season.

But Coach Jim Valvano said the misfortune to their star taught other players — Thurl Bailey, Lorenzo Charles, Sidney Lowe, Terry Gannon and Cozell McQueen — a lot about their own games. No longer able to rely on Whittenberg, they began to shoulder more responsibility and gained confidence. When Whittenberg returned toward the end of the season, State began beating those teams they had lost to earlier in the year.

Because of its record, State probably would not have been chosen for the tournament field, but the winner of the ACC tournament still gets a spot. And that's how State made it, beating Wake Forest and UNC to gain the finals against Virginia. The Cavaliers, with Ralph Sampson and Othell Wilson, had beaten State seven straight times. But the Wolfpack won by three points for the ACC title and a berth in the NCAAs.

First to fall in the early round games at Corvallis Ore., was Pepperdine in double overtime, then Nevada-Las Vegas, who had the country's best record (28-2) and a 12-point lead with 10 minutes left. But State won by a point to make the regional finals in Ogden, Utah the next weekend.

After a fairly easy win (75-56) against Utah, State faced Virginia again. It was Sampson's last shot at an NCAA championship, and the Cavaliers went up by 10 points. But State came back and the last two minutes were back and forth. Charles made two free throws with 23 seconds left for a 63-62 State win. It was yet another squeaker and State went to the Final Four in Albuquerque as the Cinderella favorite among many of the nation's fans. Not only were they winning impossibly close games, but Valvano's incessant joking and optimistic chatter got him lots of network air time.

In the semifinal, State beat Georgia (which had ousted UNC) 67-60. Houston was the opponent for the championship. Akeem Olajuwon led the Cougars, who finished the season ranked first in the nation and who were noted for dunking the basketball — hence, their nickname, Phi Slamma Jamma. Against Louisville in the semifinals, Houston had 13 dunks.

As in 1974, it seemed an impossible task for State. Valvano planned to slow the game down and to clog the air space around the basket to try and stop the Cougars. At halftime State was up by eight. But Houston came back, scored the first 10 points of the second half and built a six-point lead with three minutes left. But with Whittenberg hitting clutch shots and with Houston missing from the free-throw line, State pulled even with a minute left. Again Houston missed a free-throw, and State had 40 seconds to play for a final shot. Time almost ran out before Whittenberg shot desperately. It was short. But underneath, Lorenzo Charles jumped, caught the ball and stuffed it into the basket. N.C. State, which had limited Olajuwon and the Cougars to one dunk during the game had used Houston's own weapon to win. Valvano later became athletic director at State, then was stricken with cancer in the early '90s. He died in 1993.

State advanced to the Midwest Regional finals in 1986 and has made the tournament several times since. The head coach is Herb Sendak.

The Wolfpack plays in a new 22,000-plus seat Entertainment and Sports Arena that it shares with the National Hockey League franchise, the Carolina Hurricanes.

Duke

In the pre-Everett Case era, Duke won several Southern Conference championships under coaches Eddie Cameron and Gerry Gerard. Cameron — later Duke's athletic director — was also active in conference basketball matters, including being first chairman of the ACC Basketball Committee.

In the early '50s, the program produced its first superstar in Dick Groat, who was named national player of the year in 1952. His No. 10 jersey has been retired. Groat achieved fame in baseball, being named MVP of the National League in 1960, the year the Pirates beat the Yankees in the World Series.

Duke's rise to national prominence came in 1959 with the hiring of Vic Bubas, who played under Case at N.C. State and was an assistant coach there. Bubas immediately recruited Art Heyman, of Rockville Center, N.Y. and the next year, Jeff Mullins of Lexington, Ky.

Bubas won the ACC tournament his first year, 1960, then again in 1963 when Heyman was a senior and Mullins a junior. With Jay Buckley, another blue-chip player, Duke advanced to the Final Four. In the semifinal against Loyola, a poor shooting performance in the first half put Duke 17 points down. A second-half comeback closed the gap, but Loyola spurted again to win 94 to 75. Heyman, a three-year All-American, was named player of the year.

In 1964, Buckley and Mullins led Duke back to the Final Four. In the semifinals the Blue Devils beat Michigan 91-80, and were one game away from an NCAA championship. The team that stood in their way, however, was UCLA under John Wooden. In a 98-83 UCLA victory, which saw Duke commit 29 turnovers, UCLA began its domination of the college basketball world, which resulted in 10 NCAA championships over the next 12 seasons.

In 1965, Duke was upset by N.C. State in the ACC tournament finals and didn't get into the NCAA tournament. Only the tournament victor made it in those days. But the Blue Devils were back in 1966. Again they made the Final Four, this time ranked No. 2 in the nation. Duke had a strong five, with Jack Marin and Bob Reidy as forwards, Mike Lewis at center, and Bob Verga and Steve Vacendak as guards. But in the semifinals, they faced No. 1 Kentucky. And the week before, team leader Verga had spent time in the hospital with strep throat. He had a sub-par game, and Kentucky squeaked by at 83-79.

Bubas retired as coach in 1969, and filled a couple of administrative positions at Duke before becoming the first commissioner of the Sun Belt Conference. He was followed by Bucky Waters, Neil McGeachy and Bill Foster.

In 1978, his fourth year as coach, Foster took Duke back to the Final Four with a team led by Gene Banks, Mike Gminski and Jim Spanarkel, each of whom were All-Americans at some point during their careers. This was something of a surprise team because it had finished 2-10 in the ACC the year before. In the semifinals, Duke held off a Notre Dame comeback 90-86, but lost to Kentucky 94-88 in the championship game as Wildcat Hank Givens scored

41 points. Foster left Duke in 1980 to become head coach at South Carolina.

His replacement was Mike Krzyzewski, who coached at Army. He started slowly but within three years brought Duke back to prominence. He has led Duke to three NCAA National Championships and nine Final Fours. He has done it with real students who actually graduate, many with academic honors. He has been somebody's coach of the year 7 times, was The Sporting News' Sportsman of the Year in 1992, and in 2001 was named to the Basketball Hall of Fame.

The only real problem with Krzyzewski is his name. It's not one North Carolinian's are used to. We try to say Ker-ziz-oo-ski or jus Ker-zoo-ski. It's actually pronounced Shu-shef-ski, but for some reason that's beyond us. At last someone solved by the problem by dubbing him "Coach K," and we were all thankful.

Coach K played at Army under Bobby Knight, then served in the military for five years before joining Knight as an assistant graduate coach at Indiana. He coached at Army for five years before coming to Duke.

In 1986, in Coach K's first trip to the Final Four, Duke was led by Johnny Dawkins (Naismith player of the year), Mark Alarie, Jay Bilas and David Henderson. After beating Kansas 71-67 in the semifinals in Dallas, Duke lost to Louisville 72-69 in the championship game.

A completely different five brought Duke back to the Final Four two years later in Kansas City. Danny Ferry, Billy King, Quin Snyder, Robert Brickey and Kevin Strickland could not overcome Kansas' home court advantage and lost 66-59 in the semifinal. The Jayhawks were led by Danny Manning, national player of the year, who played at Page High School in Greensboro, and were coached by Larry Brown, formerly of UNC. They beat Oklahoma that year for the NCAA title.

The next year it was Ferry who was player of the year. He, Snyder and Brickey were joined by Christian Laettner and Phil Henderson. In Seattle, despite Ferry's 34 points, Duke lost to Seton Hall 95-78 in the semifinals.

In 1990, the team lost Ferry and Snyder, but added freshman point guard Bobby Hurley and Alaa Abdelnaby to the starting five. In the Final Four in Denver, Duke beat Arkansas 97-83, but could not stay with explosive Nevada-Las Vegas who won 103-73.

It was table-turning time in 1991, with the Final Four teams gathering in Indianapolis. Brickey, Abdelnaby and Henderson were lost to graduation. But Duke added Grant Hill, Greg Koubeck and Thomas Hill as starters. UNLV had four of five starters returning from its championship team, including future Charlotte Hornets star Larry Johnson, and entered the semifinal game against Duke undefeated. UNLV led by two at the half, but Duke, led by Laettner's 28 and sub Brian Davis' 15, came back to upset the Running Rebels 79-77.

In the finals, it was Kansas again — this time coached by former UNC assistant Roy Williams. Laettner was 12-for-12 from the free-throw line and led scoring with 18. Guard Bill McCaffrey came off the bench to score 16, and Duke avenged its 1988 loss to Kansas by beating the Jayhawks 72-65 for the championship. Hurley played all 80 minutes of the final games and had 16 assists.

Not since UCLA took seven straight NCAA titles in the '60s and '70s had a team won back-to-back championships. Duke was favored to do it, however, as sports writers ranked the Blue Devils No. 1 all through the '91-'92 season. Antonio Lang replaced Koubeck in the starting rotation, and by the Final Four games in Minneapolis, Duke had Cherokee Parks as a well-developed substitute along with Davis. In the semifinal game, Coach K defeated his one-time mentor Bobby Knight, 81-78 after being down by five at the half. Hurley led with 26 points, including six three-pointers.

In the final, Duke broke open a close game in the second half to outscore Michigan 71-51. Duke's final record was 34-2, its only losses to UNC and Wake Forest. Nearly everyone who chooses a player of the year picked Laettner.

Duke was back in the Final Four in 1994, with Chris Collins and Jeff Capel joining Parks, Lang and All-American Grant Hill. After beating Florida 70-65 in the semifinals in Charlotte, Duke lost to Arkansas 76-72 in the championship.

In 1998-99, Duke had the first-ever perfect ACC season (19-0) with Elton Brand, Trajan Langdon, William Avery, Chris Carrawell and Shane Battier as starters. After beating Michigan State, 68-62, in the semifinals, Duke lost to Connecticut, 77-74.

Coach K won his 3rd NCAA championship in 2001, with Shane Battier, the NCAA player of the year, and All-American Jason Williams leading the charge. Halfway into the season, inside man Carlos Boozer broke his foot, and fans – including Duke alumnus sportswriter John Feinstein – counted Duke out of the Final Four. But they were wrong.

With Boozer healthy, and ranked No. 1 in the nation going into the tournament, Duke stormed through the field to the semi-finals in Minneapolis to meet Maryland, which had beaten Duke in Cameron during the season. At Maryland, Duke had made up a 10-point deficit in the last minute to win in overtime, and this tournament game reflected that, with Duke falling behind 22 points in the first half, then winning 95-84. In the finals, Duke beat Arizona 82-72.

Wake Forest

The Demon Deacons have been to the Final Four only once — in 1962. But it still has a long and colorful basketball history.

There was that first collegiate game played in the state, in 1906, with Wake losing to Guilford.

Wake also played in the first NCAA tournament game, in 1939. The

Deacons had lost in the Southern Conference tournament and had figured the season over. But the NCAA chose Wake as the best team in the district, one of eight in the nation, and the Deacons traveled to Philadelphia for the tournament. They were coached by Murray Greason, and their star player was Jim Waller, from Kentucky, who had developed a hook shot. In the opening game, against Ohio State, Wake built a six-point halftime lead. But with 12 minutes left, Waller fouled out, and Ohio State pulled out the victory.

Greason coached Wake Forest from 1934 to 1957, and is still the school's winningest coach with 228 victories. His high point came in 1953 when the Deacons won the Southern Conference tournament championship, beating N.C. State 71-70. The Wolfpack, under Everett Case, had won the tournament for the previous six years. Wake Forest was led by Dickie Hemrick, an All-American from Jonesville, who scored an ACC record 2,587 points in his four years.

Greason became assistant athletic director and turned over head coaching duties to Bones McKinney, a basketball fixture in the state for many years. McKinney had played for Durham High, which won 69 straight games, then for N.C. State, then for UNC after World War II had interrupted his college career. He was an all-pro player at Washington in the NBA, then coached briefly there and at Boston, then enrolled in the Baptist seminary at Wake Forest in 1952 and joined Greason's staff. Tall, thin and angular, McKinney was almost as much fun to watch as the game as he jerked and gyrated with emotion. He was also fun to listen to — a good storyteller who never ran out of jokes.

McKinney had a string of winning teams between 1960 and 1964. But his best showing was in 1962 when Wake Forest won the ACC Tournament for the second year in a row and advanced to the Final Four. The team that year was led by forward Len Chappel and guard Billy Packer, now a TV basketball commentator, with Bob Woolard, Frank Christie and Dave Wiedeman also starters. Wake lost to Ohio State in the semifinals, but beat UCLA in the consolation game.

McKinney left after the 1965 season and was followed by Jack Murdock, then Jack McCloskey whose high point was an 18-9 season in 1969. Wake Forest did not return to the NCAA tournament until 1977 under Carl Tacy, who lost to Marquette in the regional finals. Had they won, they would have joined UNC and UNC Charlotte in the Final Four. Tacy returned his teams to the tournament in 1981, 1982 and 1983. Tacy also won four of the Big Four tournaments, an ACC record.

The Big Four tournament lasted from 1970-1980 and pitted the four Tobacco Road schools against each other. Skip Brown, Frank Johnson and Alvis Rogers starred for Tacy during their years of success in this tournament, which was played in Greensboro. The coaches never liked it, preferring to play their season's extra games outside of the conference. It was dropped after the NCAA expanded its tournament field, and losses incurred in the tough Big Four games could work against a team "on the bubble."

Tacy left after 1985, and Wake Forest went into a rebuilding phase under Bob Staak. The high point of the late '80s was the play of Tyrone "Muggsy" Bogues, a five-foot-three crowd pleaser who was a terrific ball handler and defensive player. Bogues went on to a pro career with the Charlotte Hornets.

Dave Odom became head coach in 1990 and led Wake Forest to a couple of ACC championships in the '90s with future NBA stars Randolph Childress and Tim Duncan. Each season saw Wake in either the NCAA tournament or the National Invitational Tournament. Odom left after the 2001 season for South Carolina, and Wake hired Skip Prosser of Xavier as head coach.

Beyond the Big Four

Davidson: The Wildcats' basketball history goes back to 1909, and at one time the state's Big Five included Davidson. That was before the ACC was formed. Davidson was a power in the Southern Conference, and still is. But it was under Lefty Driesell, head coach from 1960 to 1969, that Davidson was in the national spotlight. Dreisell compiled a 176-62 record while at Davidson. He built 20-plus winning seasons with Terry Holland and Fred Hetzel, but couldn't win the Southern Conference tournament to get into the NCAA tournament.

Finally in 1968 and 1969, Dreisell's teams made it in. Both times, they played for the East Regional championship and a trip to the Final Four. Both times they were beaten by UNC. The day after Charlie Scott scored with three seconds left to beat him in the '69 regionals, Dreisell announced that he was leaving to coach Maryland.

UNC-Charlotte: The 49ers from Charlotte had two years in the limelight when Kinston native Cedric "Cornbread" Maxwell led UNCC to NIT runnerup in 1976 and into the Final Four the next year. We just missed a UNC-Chapel Hill vs. UNC-Charlotte final game as Marquette scored in the last second to win. That was the year Marquette had to beat three of our teams — Wake Forest, UNCC and UNC to win the title.

Guilford College: With future pro stars Lloyd (World) Free and M.L. Carr, Guilford College won the NAIA Tournament in Kansas City in 1973, beating Maryland Eastern Shore 99-96. Three years earlier, Guilford had made it to the championship game, but had lost to Kentucky State. Other North Carolina runners-up in the tournament were Western Carolina in 1963 and Campbell in 1977.

UNC women: With less than a second left and down two points to Louisiana Tech, UNC won possession on a jump ball and called timeout to set up a final play. The pass came in to forward Charlotte Smith, who took a shot from behind the three-point line — and hit! In any game this would have been a great ending. But this happened to be the championship game of the 1994 NCAA women's tournament. The Tar Heels thus became the first ACC women's team to win it all. It should also be pointed out that Smith is the niece of former N.C. State star David Thompson.

Carolina Cougars: Over a five-year span, 1969-1974, this ABA franchise pulled together a number of former area stars, including Billy Cunningham, Larry Miller, Bob Verga, Art Heyman, Gene Littles (High Point College) and Joe Caldwell. Bones McKinney was the team's first coach, followed by Larry Brown, who took the team to the ABA finals, losing in seven games to Kentucky. The team played in Greensboro, Charlotte and Raleigh, but declining attendance forced the franchise to move to St. Louis.

Charlotte Hornets: Born in 1988 as a National Basketball Association expansion franchise, the Hornets last made the playoffs in 2001, when they advanced to the second round. The Hornets have made noises about leaving Charlotte because of the small size of "The Hive," the Coliseum where they play. A popular guard Bobby Phills, was killed in a car accident after practice in mid-season in 2000.

Charlotte Sting: Charlotte's member of the Women's National Basketball Franchise began play in 1996. The team, with many former ACC standouts on the roster, is coached by former Olympian Ann Donovan.

N.C. State Women: During the 25 years she has coached the N.C. State women's basketball team, Kay Yow has built a nationally prominent program. With more than 600 victories at N.C. State and Elon, she ranks fifth on the NCAA's all-time victories list. Perennially ranked among the nation's elite, her team made the Final Four of the NCAA women's championships for the first time in 1998. The team lost to Louisiana Tech in the semi-finals.

Black coaches, players: John McClendon, coach at North Carolina College (now NC Central University), dominated basketball in the black college leagues of the '40s, winning the first CIAA tournament in 1946. Clarence "Bighouse" Gaines, of Winston-Salem State University, and Cal Irvin of A&T dominated in the '50s and '60s, into the era when traditionally white colleges began recruiting blacks. Gaines, over a career that spanned five decades, had an 828-446 record. Each school produced NBA standouts: Sam Jones of the Celtics from North Carolina College; Al Attles of the Golden State Warriors from A&T, and Cleo Hill of the St. Louis Hawks from Winston-Salem State. Two other future NBA stars, Walt Bellamy of New Bern and Lou Hudson of Greensboro, played at Big Ten universities because of racial barriers in the South. Henry Logan, in 1964, became the first black player to receive a basketball scholarship to a North Carolina college. He played for Western Carolina, and was the first black to play at a predominantly white school in the Southeast. In the late '80s and '90s, A&T has been a regular in the NCAA tournament.

Stock Car Racing

If you're a newcomer to North Carolina and really want to fit in, buy yourself a pickup, go down to your local NASCAR collectibles store, get a decal with a number on it and stick it to the back window.

You might choose 88. That's Dale Jarrett's number. He's from Conover and won the Winston Cup championship in 1999. Or maybe you'll pick No. 18, the number of the car driven by Bobby Labonte, who won the cup in 2000. He's from Texas, but he drives for Joe Gibbs, of Cooleemee, the former Washington Redskins coach who now builds race cars in a shop north of Charlotte.

Out driving, you'll see a number of windows with a sticker that says, "In Memory of No. 3." This was Dale Earnhardt's number. Earnhardt, of Kannapolis, was a 7-time NASCAR champion who was killed in a crash at the Daytona 500 in February, 2001. After his death, many fans lost interest in racing for awhile. Others transferred their allegiance to Dale Earnhardt Jr., No. 8. He won the summer race in Daytona, the first there since his father's death.

Wherever you go in the state, you can break the ice quickly with a good knowledge of racing. You may not know a camshaft from a valve lifter, but they'll treat you with respect in the auto parts store if you know who won the last race and how. And if you can visit the Petty Museum at Level Cross or take some time off to attend a race, maybe even spend the night in the infield of the Charlotte Motor Speedway, then the stories you'll be able to tell can open many doors.

Stock car racing is a uniquely Southern sport, and much of its heritage is North Carolina-based. Just about everyone agrees that its origins are intertwined with the bootleg whisky industry that flourished in the South, mostly in the mountains, in the '30s, '40s and '50s. Young mountain boys would haul this "moonshine" from the family stills to outlets in the Piedmont. The product was carried in cars that were "souped up" so the bootlegger could outrun the law if necessary.

In their spare time, these "good ol' boys" and others who liked cars would get together and race wherever they could find a convenient place. Now and then someone would try to organize things to the point of selling tickets and offering a purse to the winner.

The most successful of these promoters was Bill France, a Virginian, who organized races at Daytona Beach in the late '30s, then picked up the pace after World War II at tracks around the South. In 1948, he and a couple of others interested in racing organized the National Association for Stock Car Auto Racing, or NASCAR, as we still know it today. The first race organized by the new outfit was at the Daytona Beach course and was won by a man named Red Byron.

In 1949, France decided to stage a race between cars that could be found

Winston Cup racing at Charlotte Motor Speedway.

on the showroom floors of dealerships where people went to buy their new cars. The war was four years over. Car production was in full swing, and people were able to afford them. France held his race at a small dirt track in Charlotte. It was won by a Kansan named Jim Roper, who drove a Lincoln. The race drew 13,000 paying customers and thus was born the Grand National division of NASCAR, later to be known as the Winston Cup.

Today, small tracks dot the rural landscape, and local garages and drivers field cars in a variety of divisions. Even the best-known drivers of today compete in a number of racing categories. But while the Winston Cup cars of today resemble the showroom model in shape only, this is still the division that has paid the big money and drawn the big crowds to the superspeedways since that first race in 1949.

The first big stock car track was built at Darlington in 1950. The Southern 500, held there each Labor Day, is known as the granddaddy of all stock car races, and no driver feels complete until he's won it.

Superspeedways have since been built at Daytona, Charlotte, Atlanta, Rockingham, N.C., Talledega, Ala., and Fort Worth, Texas. Grand National racing also spread outside of the south, with tracks in California, Delaware, New York, Pennsylvania, Vermont and Michigan. The Brickyard 400, run on the Indianapolis Motor Speedway, is a prestigious race for a NASCAR driver to win.

The most memorable early drivers were the most colorful. Virginians Joe Weatherly and Curtis Turner, a former bootlegger, were hell-raising, hard-drinking buddies who dominated racing in the '50s. Weatherly died in a race at Riverside, California, in 1964. Turner, a wheeler-dealer who actually built the Charlotte Motor Speedway, then lost it, was killed in his airplane when it crashed in Pennyvania in 1970.

North Carolina contributed several drivers to this early pantheon, including Junior Johnson of Wilkes County, a bootlegger-turned-driver who was written up by avant-garde journalist Tom Wolfe in the early '70s in an article for *Esquire* entitled "The Last American Hero is Junior Johnson. Yes!" Hollywood then picked up the baton and mangled Johnson's story in the movie, *The Last American Hero.* Johnson survived his racing days to become a car builder and owner.

Some other names that thrilled NASCAR fans in the early days were Fred Lorenzen, Lee Roy Yarborough, Tim Flock and Fireball Roberts.

Roberts, a Floridian, abandoned his engineering studies to become a successful driver. But in 1964, at the World 600 in Charlotte, he was involved in a wreck with Johnson and Ned Jarrett, and suffered serious burns when gas from his ruptured fuel tank caught fire. He died six weeks later. Both the wreck and his death were front-page news, and it led Goodyear to develop a rubber safety liner for fuel tanks.

Jarrett's is one of a number of father-son racing families. Now a race announcer, his son Dale is a top NASCAR driver. A couple of years ago, Ned was at the mike in an exciting finish at the Daytona 500 that Dale won over Earnhardt, something the father-son duo repeated in the 1996 race. Buck Baker was a successful driver from the early years, whose son Buddy followed in his tire tracks. Sterling Marlin, who won in 1994 and 1995 at Daytona, was the son of long-time NASCAR driver Coo-Coo Marlin. Dale Earnhardt, Jr. is now making his mark as a driver.

But the most famous family dynasty in racing belongs to the Petty clan of Level Cross.

Lee Petty began racing at age 35 in 1947, and was top driver three times during the '50s. He was also consistently voted most popular driver by the fans. Petty was able to combine a winning personality with his deep competitive drive. He won the first Daytona 500 in 1959, but never won at Darlington. A good example of his competitiveness came in Atlanta, also in 1959, when he crossed the finish line behind his son Richard. It would have been Richard's first NASCAR victory, but Lee protested and was declared the winner after a recheck of the scoring cards.

Lee retired his No. 42 car during the 1962 season. He had won 54 races, a NASCAR record. By that time Richard, in No. 43, had also learned how to win. He got his first in a 100-miler at Charlotte in 1960, and by the end of the '62 season, had taken the checkered flag 14 times.

Richard passed Lee in number of victories during the spring of 1967. That was a storybook year in which Petty won 27 of 48 races, finished second in seven more and at one stretch won 10 straight. He became known as King Richard, and his fame spread beyond the confines of the race crowd and rural America.

In 1971, he won 21 of 46 races and became the first driver to pass the $1 million mark in earnings.

On and off throughout the '60s, the nation's automobile factories would sponsor cars and drivers because there seemed to be a correlation between track wins and showroom sales. Factory engineers worked with the race crews to build faster and faster cars. NASCAR officials judged whether or not certain modifications were allowable under the rules and, when they were ruled against, sometimes the auto makers would pull out.

Through 1972, Petty drove a Plymouth and was sponsored for much of that time by the Chrysler Corp. Whenever he changed cars — in 1969, he went with Ford — it made big news. The Pettys also turned racing into a big business and it was an extended family affair. Petty Enterprises included not only Lee and Richard, but brother Maurice and cousin Dale Inman, who built the cars. Petty was also the first driver to achieve that quality of hero worship that Madison Avenue liked in a spokesman for consumer products. When Chrysler pulled out of racing for good, Petty hooked up with STP and began endorsing their products. He also endorsed everything from headache powders to auto parts, and started a chain of car washes.

A number of big-name drivers of the day raced with Petty Enterprises at some time in their career, including Bobby Myers, Tiny Lund, Jim Paschal, Marvin Panch, Dick Brooks, the Bakers and Morgan Shepherd.

Petty dominated racing for two decades. He won 200 races, the last in 1984, although he continued to race until 1992. He won the Daytona 500 seven times and was seven times the national driving champion. The *Petty Story: No. 43*, was the movie version of his life. He had fan clubs all over the world and appeared on the cover of the *New York Times Magazine*.

It is convenient to use Petty as a means of acquainting newcomers to the love affair between NASCAR racing and the South. But that doesn't mean he was the only talented driver of those decades. Others were also highly successful. They were from different states and drove different cars, won lots of races and all had their followings as well. Cale Yarborough, of South Carolina, A.J. Foyt, a converted Indy car racer, and Benny Parsons of Ellerbe come to mind. Some developed fierce rivalries with Petty. Among them was Freddy Lorenzen, who broke into racing about the same time and was another young lion going up against the legends of the '50s. Lorenzen drove a Ford and had his share of wins when he quit racing in 1967.

Bobby Allison, from Alabama, had a fierce rivalry with Petty in the '70s that saw them often fighting each other to the finish line, now and then banging into each other in the process.

David Pearson of South Carolina is the second winningest NASCAR driver with 105 victories. That Petty finished second to Pearson in nearly a third of those races provides evidence of the intensity of that rivalry. In 1976, Petty and Pearson crashed in the final turn at Daytona, and while Petty spun out onto the infield Pearson limped across the finish line at 20 m.p.h.

Since 1970, R.J. Reynolds has awarded the Winston Cup to each season's NASCAR champion. Points are awarded throughout the season for winning races, for finishing high, for leading laps and so forth. The arrangement was perfect for the cigarette manufacturer, which had been banned from advertising on television.

In the late '70s, new faces started to appear in the winner's circle. But the Winston Cup stayed in the hands of the second generation of racers, Yarborough having won it three years running, when Darrell Waltrip gave Petty a run for the championship in 1979. For a variety of reasons, Petty had been winless the year before. Waltrip, a brash and cocky driver out of Tennessee, built a large lead over Petty late in the season, and appeared certain to win the title. But Petty started winning and stormed back to within two points going into the last race at Ontario, California. He finished fifth in the lead pack. But Waltrip was a lap down, and Petty won the Winston Cup for his final championship.

Petty's 200th victory came in 1984 at Daytona in the July 4 Firecracker 400 when he edged Cale Yarborough to the start-finish line after a wreck and the race ended under a caution flag. President Reagan was in the press box for that one and, although Petty drove through the 1992 season, he never visited the winner's circle again.

Besides Waltrip, who shook off his 1979 disappointment to win three of the next five Winston Cup championships, a number of other new drivers began to make their presence felt. Among them were Bill Elliott, out of North Georgia, Terry Labonte, a Texan who now races out of High Point, Mark Martin from Arkansas, Harry Gant of Asheville, Geoff Bodine of Julian, Rusty Wallace of Concord and Ricky Rudd of Cornelius.

But the most influential among them was Dale Earnhardt, who won Rookie-of-the-Year honors the year of the Waltrip-Petty shootout, then won the Winston Cup championship himself the next year. Earnhardt, of Kannapolis, was son of a champion Sportsman circuit driver, Ralph Earnhardt, and quickly became known as "The Intimidator" for his aggressive driving tactics. Time after time, Earnhardt's car would bump an opponent's in his way, often sending his opponent or both of them spinning or into the wall, sometimes taking out other drivers who were following close behind. Victimized drivers would rant and rave and give Earnhardt or the press an earful. Fans would get mad too. NASCAR penalized him several times. But Earnhardt generally shrugged.

After winning his first championship in 1980, Earnhardt had a long dry spell until his second Winston Cup in 1986. By then he had hooked up with Richard Childress, a former driver turned car owner. Childress landed sponsors in Wrangler, then GM Goodwrench, that helped him start turning Chevrolets into winning race cars. He put together a garage team that has pretty much stayed together, something unusual in a day when good mechanics and engine-builders were tempted to jump for higher pay.

Until 1998, the only prize that had eluded Earnhardt was a victory in the Daytona 500. Just about every year, it seemed, he was in the race at the end. But something always happened. He ran out of gas, had problems in the pits, was involved in accidents. Time after time he placed second, unable to get around the top-finishing car. In 1989, he was way out front on the last lap, when he ran over some debris on the track, blew out a tire and hit the wall. At the 1996 Daytona 500, Earnhardt ran true to form, as he spent the last lap unsuccessfully trying to get around winner Dale Jarrett. Then in 1998, Earnhardt took first place 60 laps from the finish and held the lead — while his fans held their breath — to the end.

So, it was the ultimate irony that Earnhardt was killed on the last lap of the Daytona 500, even as Michael Waltrip crossed the finish line in one of Earnhardt's cars. Controversy followed Earnhardt's death. NASCAR claimed that his seat belt had failed, but a rescue squad member said it was intact when he arrived at the crash site. A Florida newspaper sued to gain access to the autopsy photos, but the state of Florida had them sealed. Doctors generally agreed, however, that death was caused by a basal skull fracture and significant injuries to the base of the brain.

Head injuries were also ruled as the cause of death of Adam Petty, who crashed at the Loudon, N.H. speedway in May, 2000, and Kenny Irwin, who died in July, 2000 at Loudon. Both died in practice lap crashes when their accelerators stuck and carried their race cars into the wall. A head injury also killed Tony Roper, a truck racer, at the Texas speedway in October, 2000.

The deaths have led many of the drivers to begin wearing a head and neck support system, known as HANS, a collar that snaps to the back of the helmet and is designed to protect against the head snapping forward and producing the kind of head injuries that killed these drivers.

Despite tragedy, racing goes on. A week after Earnhardt's death, the drivers were back on the track at Rockingham, competing in a 400-mile race won by Steve Park. A new generation of stars is finding the winner's circle. Jeff Gordon, of Indiana, who won three championships in four years, was back in the hunt for the points title in the summer of 2001 after a drought made his fans wonder. Bobby Hamilton, Tony Stewart, Jeff Burton, Kevin Harvick and Elliott Sadler are among the new names making waves.

By far, most of the teams that compete for the Winston Cup have their garages in a triangle from Charlotte to Hickory to High Point. Possibly because of the influence of the Lowe's Motor Speedway, the Charlotte area has always been a hot bed of racing. Today, in the small towns that dot the Lake Norman area, many of NASCAR's top teams and drivers prepare for racing Sunday.

Golf

Behind basketball and stock car racing, golf is next in North Carolina's sports hierarchy.

You'd be surprised at how many people play golf. It's not just a game for the wealthy. Not only do men and women sneak away from offices to go out and play a round, they slip away from auto repair garages and farm chores as well. You'll also see a lot of workers from the third shift out there on the course.

We are proud of our championship courses — the famed No. 2 Course at Pinehurst, Forest Oaks outside of Greensboro, and Tanglewood near Winston-Salem. But we have our little nine-hole courses too, tucked in among a city's neighborhoods or laid out across an old pasture where small-town folks can gather to play. In North Carolina, a least, golf is a more democratic sport than the tournament broadcasts portray.

But we do trace our golf history's beginnings to wealth. The first courses, built in the 1890s, were at country clubs.

The grandfather of golf in our state was a wealthy businessman, James Walker Tufts, who moved down from Massachusetts in 1895 to retire in

Golfers approach a green on the famed No. 2 golf course at Pinehurst.

Pinehurst in the Moore County sandhills. Not content to be idle, he saw the potential of the pleasant winter climate for a resort, bought 5,000 acres, built a nine-hole course and bade his fellow Yankees to come on down.

With the birds, the golfers flocked south. And within five years, Tufts was able to hire Scottish golf course designer Donald Ross, who built the famous Pinehurst Course No. 2. It opened in 1907. By that time, however, Pinehurst was already hosting North-South amateur tournaments for men and women and a North-South pro tournament for men.

Pinehurst continued to dominate golf into the 1940s, with Denny Shute winning the Professional Golf Association championship there in 1936.

But other locales in the state were picking up the pace, with championship courses in Raleigh, Charlotte, Durham and Asheville. In 1938, the Greater Greensboro Open was launched at the Starmount Forest club. It was won by Sam Snead, who went on to win eight GGO titles in all. Ben Hogan won the GGO in 1940, and Byron Nelson won it in 1942 and 1945.

By the time the GGO was established, there were more than 80 courses in the state, a third of them public. More opportunities to participate, coupled with the chance to see professional talent helped the sport grow.

And a few local heroes developed. For instance, Tony Manero, club pro at Sedgefield in Greensboro, won the U.S. Open in 1936.

Golf was also one of the few sports open to women. Estelle Lawson Page, of Chapel Hill, developed into one of the best female golfers in the world. She won the 1937 National Amateur women's championship and seven of the North-South amateur titles in the 1930s and '40s.

Beginning in the '50s, a number of golf stars developed here. Arnold Palmer drew early notice as a student at Wake Forest. When he joined the professional tour, he took golf to new heights of popularity. "Arnie's Army" was always the largest throng on the course, and where he moved the crowd followed. He may have been from Pennsylvania, but his college experience made him one of us. What's more, he still has a Cadillac dealership in Charlotte. A number of other Wake Forest grads, taught by golf coach Jesse Haddock, joined the pro tour, among them Lanny Wadkins, Curtis Strange, Joe and John Inman and Jay Haas. His brother, Jerry Haas, is now golf coach at Wake. John Inman is coach at UNC. Pro golfer Scott Hoch also played at Wake Forest, and Davis Love at UNC. Duke graduated Mike Souchak and Art Wall.

Tar Heel natives making the grade include Vance Heafner, whose father Clayton of Charlotte played in the '40s and '50s, Chip Beck of Fayetteville, Jim Thorpe of Roxboro and Mark O'Meara of Goldsboro, winner of the Masters and British Opens in 1998. Charlie Sifford of Charlotte was the first black to win a PGA tournament. Raymond Floyd, of Fayetteville, has won more than 20 PGA tournaments, including two PGA championships, the Masters and the U.S. Open.

We also had some great amateurs — Billie Joe Patton, Bill Harvey, Dale Morey and Harvey Ward. Brenda Corrie-Kuehn, a Fletcher amateur, led the American team to a Curtis Cup victory in 1998 over the European team by going 4-0 in her matches and by sinking the tournament's winning putt.

Some stars of the female circuit also have played through North Carolina, including Peggy Kirk Bell, who played the LPGA tour out of Pinehurst in the '50s, Carol Mann, who attended Woman's College in Greensboro in the late '50s, and Donna White of Kinston.

The GGO moved first from Starmount to Sedgefield, then to Forest Oaks, and top players on the tour have come to compete at Greensboro since 1938 except for a brief interlude during World War II. Pro events also have been held at Pinehurst (The World Open), at Wilmington (The Azalea Open) and at Charlotte (The Kemper Open). We saw all of the game's greats — except for one. Jack Nicklaus in his prime did not play the GGO because it fell on the week before the Masters. When his competitors were fighting for the purse in Greensboro, Nicklaus was practicing in Augusta.

But we came out to the GGO anyway. There was more than Jack to see. And many of us have hacked our way around some of the hallowed courses. Golf is in our blood and, if you play, its a good way to get to know North Carolinians.

Football

For many of us, football occupies those lost weekends in fall that precede the basketball season. That doesn't mean there aren't football fans among us. There certainly are. In fact, we all become football fans occasionally when our high school, our college or, now, our pro team gets hot. We have some heated rivalries that have produced outstanding games, teams and individuals.

But unlike as in basketball, stellar seasons among our football teams are the exception rather than the rule. We'll generally fill up the stadium even in an off-year, but the hottest ticket in town it's not.

For Big Four football fans, the annual drubbing seemed to take place in Clemson, where they named their stadium Death Valley, or in College Park, Maryland. But even those teams seem to have slipped back into mediocrity. We thought things might improve when we let Georgia Tech join the conference. That was a football school, right? We would have to improve to compete now, wouldn't we? But no, it was Tech that seemed to slip back to our level. Now it's Florida State, perennial candidate for No. 1 in the nation. Will the Seminoles save us?

But enough whining. Let's get to the glory.

In the first intercollegiate game in the state, Wake Forest beat North Carolina 6-4. This was at the State Fair in 1888, and the rules were made up as the game went on. On Thanksgiving of that year, in the first game played under accepted intercollegiate rules, Trinity (later Duke) pounded North Carolina 16-0.

NC A&M (now N.C. State) also fielded a team early on, as did Davidson, Elon and Guilford, Shaw, Livingstone and A&T.

The game sputtered along amid controversies that still surround college sports, including issues of eligibility and professionalism, athletics versus academics and the physical toll on players. At one time or another, all of the Big Four schools dropped football. There were a couple of good seasons for A&M and UNC before World War I. But it wasn't until the '20s that the game hit its stride.

The forward pass had opened up the game before the war and made football more interesting. Radio broadcasts and news coverage increased its popularity. Improved automobiles and roads helped more people get to games, and they became big social events. Of course, it was also prestigious for your college team to win, and the alumni interference in the game rose with the sports popularity.

UNC had brothers Bill and Bob Fetzer as coaches for several years, who had a couple of single-loss seasons in the '20s. Coach Chuck Collins (1926-33), went 9-1 in 1929 with "The Team of a Million Backs." Carl Snavely took over in

1934, and had a winning season with UNC's first All-American George Barclay. The next year, Snavely was 8-0 and a Rose Bowl contender until Duke popped the Heels 25-0. Snavely left after that season when UNC President Frank Graham tried unsuccessfully to de-emphasize football.

In 1920, Duke (known as Trinity until 1924) fielded its first team in 25 years, but had only limited success until hiring Wallace Wade as head coach in 1931. Wade coached for 11 seasons and built Duke into a national power. In 1933, with All-American lineman Fred Crawford, Duke was undefeated and headed for the Rose Bowl until losing its last game to Georgia. The "Iron Duke" team of 1938, with future All-American George McAfee, was 10-0 and had not given up a single point all season when it went into the Rose Bowl against Southern Cal. Duke led 3-0 going into the final minute, but Southern Cal scored a touchdown to beat Duke 7-3. Duke earned another trip to the Rose Bowl with an unbeaten season in 1941. After the Japanese bombed Pearl Harbor, the game was moved to Durham, where Duke was beaten by Oregon State 20-16.

That Rose Bowl was played in Duke Stadium, which was built in 1929. Kenan Stadium was built at UNC two years earlier. The two schools were the powerhouses of football in the state in the period between the wars. The intense rivalry that exists between the two schools to this day goes back to the football played in the Roaring '20s.

State and Wake Forest fielded teams during the period, but were largely unsuccessful with a couple of exceptions. State went 9-1 in 1927 under Coach Gus Tebell and All-American back Jack McDowall. Wake Forest's best was a 7-2 season in 1924.

Among small colleges, A&T went 7-0 in 1927, and Catawba was undefeated in 1930.

Two players from Duke, George McAfee and Clarence (Ace) Parker, became NFL standouts. McAfee starred with the Chicago Bears; Parker was named Most Valuable Player in 1940 and is in the football Hall of Fame.

After the war, Carl Snavely returned to UNC and compiled a 32-9-2 record over the next four years, including losses in the Sugar Bowl in 1946 and 1948 and the Cotton Bowl in 1949. The big reason for his success, in the regular seasons anyway, was Charlie (Choo-Choo) Justice of Asheville. Justice was an All-American who could run, pass, punt and return kicks. He finished second in the Heisman Trophy balloting in 1948 and 1949. He went onto a pro career, but it was not as distinguished as his college football years.

Carolina football foundered for the next 20 years or so with a couple of exceptions. Jim Tatum, in the late '50s, appeared to be building a strong program, but died in 1959. His successor, Jim Hickey, had one good year in 1963 with future NFL stars Ken Willard and Chris Hanburger helping him to a 9-2 season, including a Gator Bowl victory over the Air Force.

In the '70s, the Tar Heels went to six bowls with coach Bill Dooley. The highlight of his tenure came in 1972 when the team went 10-1, then beat Texas Tech in the Sun Bowl. In the '80s, the team was coached by Dick Crum, who also took the team to six bowls. He went 10-1 in 1980 and, helped by future NFL great Lawrence Taylor, beat Texas in the Bluebonnet Bowl.

UNC, not known for quarterbacks, has a history of 1,000-yard-per-season running backs. The reign began with Don McCauley, who ran for 1,720 yards in 1970, and continued into the '90s with Leon Johnson.

After ten seasons and after leading Carolina to a 10-1 record in 1997, Coach Mack Brown resigned to become head coach at Texas. His assistant Carl Torbush, led the Tar Heels to a Gator Bowl victory and was given the head job. After three lackluster seasons, he was replaced by John Bunting, a former all-ACC player for UNC who coached in the pros.

Duke, N.C. State and Wake Forest each produced a quarterback in the '50s that went on to fame and fortune in the NFL.

Duke's was Sonny Jurgenson, Class of '57. Make no mistake, he was a fine college quarterback, but didn't hit his stride until entering the pros, when he starred for the Eagles, then the Redskins and was voted into the pro football Hall of Fame. Jurgenson came to Duke a year after Bill Murray became head coach. Murray replaced Wade who, after the war, had been unable to return Duke to the national rankings and left to become commissioner of the Southern Conference.

Murray led the Blue Devils to outright or shared conference titles from 1952 to 1955 and 1960-62. Among the All-Americans he coached was Mike McGee, who won the Outland Trophy as the nation's best lineman in 1959. Murray left in 1965 to become head of the American Football Coaches Association, and was replaced by Tom Harp, then McGee, then Red Wilson, then Steve Sloan. Steve Spurrier took over in 1987, and the next year Duke went 7-3-1 for their first winning season since 1962.

Individuals spiced up the lean years, among them Ben Bennett, ACC player of the year in 1983, who passed for 9,614 yards in his career, then an NCAA record, and quarterback Anthony Dilweg, also ACC player of the year, who played for the Green Bay Packers.

Duke was co-ACC champ in 1989 and went to the All-American Bowl, where they were beaten by Texas Tech. Clarkston Hines, a wide receiver, was a concensus All-American that year. In 1995, first-year coach Fred Goldsmith led Duke to an 8-4 record and trip the Hall of Fame Bowl. But Duke's record sagged, and in 1999, Coach Carl Franks was brought in. In 2000, Duke hit bottom with an 0-11 record.

N.C. State's contribution to the world of star quarterbacks was Roman Gabriel, ACC player of the year in 1960 and 1961, who later played with the Los Angeles Rams and Philadelphia Eagles and was the NFL's Most Valuable Player in 1969. At State, he played under Earle Edwards, who had a fairly successful coaching career from 1954 to 1970.

Actually, State started off the postwar era well, with an 8-2 season under coach Beattie Feathers. The Wolfpack went to their first bowl game ever that year, the Gator Bowl, but lost to Oklahoma. After that, however, the program floundered until Edwards came along.

Edwards' best teams were in 1957, when All-American halfback Dick Christy led the Wolfpack to a 7-1-2 record and ACC championship; in 1963, when State was 8-2 and conference co-champion but lost in the Liberty Bowl; and in 1967, when State won its first bowl game, over Georgia in the Liberty Bowl, also after an 8-2 season. During Edwards' tenure, Carter-Finley Stadium was finished, and the Wolfpack had a modern home to replace Riddick Field.

Lou Holtz, who now coaches South Carolina, got Wolfpack fans' hearts beating madly when he took the team to four straight bowls from 1972 to 1975. Bo Rein kept football at State at a high level with bowl appearances in 1977 and 1978 and an ACC championship in 1979. Stars during his reign were running back Ted Brown and Outland Trophy winner Jim Richter, both of whom had great pro careers. Rein left to coach LSU and was killed during a recruiting trip in a bizarre airplane accident. For some reason, Rein lost consciousness while flying his plane which, apparently while on automatic pilot, crossed North Carolina then plunged into the Atlantic Ocean when it ran out of gas.

After lean years under Monty Kiffin and Tom Reed, State returned to prominence under Dick Sheridan with an 8-2-1 record and trip to the Peach Bowl in 1986. Quarterback Eric Kramer, who played for the Chicago Bears, was ACC Player of the Year. Sheridan retired in 1992 and was replaced by Mike O'Cain. In 2000, State hired Chuck Amato, an assistant at Florida State, who led the Pack to an 8-4 record, including a 38-30 come-from-way-behind win over Minnesota in the Micronpc.com Bowl.

Wake Forest's famed quarterback was Norman Snead, who played professionally for the Redskins and the Eagles after graduating in 1961. His performance at Wake topped the individual heroics that Demon Deacon fans have learned to look for in lieu of glory teams.

The postwar era started off well with Douglas (Peahead) Walker leading the 1945 Deacs to the Gator Bowl, where they beat South Carolina. They lost to Baylor in the Dixie Bowl in 1948, then lost Walker over a salary dispute in 1950. For the next three decades, Wake fans had a number of players to brag about, including Snead and other quarterbacks John Mackovic, Jay Venuto and Mike Elkins, and running backs Billy Barnes, Brian Piccolo, Larry Hopkins and James McDougald.

Hopkins led the 1970 team, playing in the new Groves Stadium, to an ACC championship. In 1979, Venuto and McDougald, coached by Mackovic, took the Deacons to the Tangerine Bowl after an 8-3 season. Wake had a fairly successful run under Bill Dooley, who took over as head coach in the late '80s. In 2001, coach Jim Caldwell was replaced by Jim Grobe, who built Ohio University's program into a perennial conference contender.

East Carolina moved up in the football ranks in the early '60s, when Clarence Stasavich was hired away from Lenoir Rhyne. He produced three straight 9-1 seasons, each capped by bowl victories.

The '70s were a good decade for the Pirates under coaches Sonny Randle and Pat Dye. Ed Emory and Art Baker had mixed success through the 1980s. Then Bill Lewis built a successful program that culminated in a 1992 Peach Bowl victory over N.C. State. Steve Logan replaced Lewis and has taken the Pirates to six bowls since 1994. East Carolina plays in Conference USA.

The state's small colleges have now and then risen to national attention as well. Lenoir Rhyne, under Stasavich, was NAIA runner-up in 1959 and 1962, and won the championship in 1960. Red Wilson coached Elon to NAIA finals losses in 1973 and 1978. Under Jerry Tolley, Elon won the NAIA crown in 1980 and 1981. Western Carolina was runner-up in the NCAA-1AA finals in 1983, as was Appalachian State in 1987.

Others not already mentioned who excelled in the pro ranks from North Carolina include Bill George, a Hall of Fame lineman for the Bears who played at Wake Forest; Mike Quick, wide receiver for the Eagles, and lineman Darrel Dess from N.C. State; linebackers Mike Curtis and Bob Matheson of Duke; linemen John Baker and Doug Wilkerson of N.C. Central, Jethro Pugh of Elizabeth City State, and J.D. Smith of A&T.

Active players include from East Carolina: New Orleans quarterback Jeff Blake and Detroit punter John Jett; from UNC: San Diego tight end Freddie Jones, Green Bay fullback William Henderson, Carolina guard Kevin Donnalley and cornerback Jimmy Hitchcock, New England defensive tackle Riddick Parker, Buffalo linebacker Keith Newman and Cincinnati linebacker Bryan Simmons; from Duke: Denver guard Lennie Friedman; from Wake Forest, Baltimore defensive end Michael McCrary, St. Louis receiver Ricky Proehl and Denver tight end Desmond Clark; from N.C. State: receivers Torry Holt of St. Louis and Alvis Whitted of Jacksonville and Pittsburgh cornerback Dewayne Washington; from Appalachian State, Dallas linebacker Dexter Coakley and Tampa Bay punter Mark Royals; from Western Carolina, Seattle cornerback Willie Williams and Carolina fullback Brad Hoover; from Winston-Salem State: Carolina running back Richard Huntley.

Pros from North Carolina who went to college elsewhere include Carl Eller of Winston-Salem, who played for Minnesota, Heath Shuler, of Bryson City who played quarterback for New Orleans, and Brad Johnson of Asheville, in 2001 a backup quarterback for Tampa Bay.

Several of our most poignant sports stories have involved football.

Steve Streater of Sylva, who had starred for the Tar Heels, flew back to Raleigh-Durham in 1982 from a trip to Washington where he signed a pro contract with the Redskins. He was driving home from the airport when he wrecked his car and injured his spine, becoming a quadriplegic.

Bob Waters coached at Western Carolina for 20 years, compiling a 116-94-

6 record. In 1983, he was Southern Conference coach of the year, taking the Catamounts to the NCAA Division I-AA championship finals. Two years later, he learned he had Lou Gehrig's disease, but continued to coach. His team was second in the conference in 1986, a year in which he lost use of his arms. The disease progressed, and in 1989 he died at 50.

Brian Piccolo, of Fort Lauderdale, was a star fullback for Wake Forest in the early '60s. In 1964, he led the nation with 1,044 yards rushing and 111 points. In his fifth season with the Chicago Bears, Piccolo was diagnosed with cancer. Radiation treatments and several operations failed, and he died the next year. Piccolo had an effusive personality, and he met his end with humor and courage. His life inspired several books and a movie, *Brian's Song.*

Baseball

At the beginning of the century, baseball was a popular sport without much organization. It was played at colleges and in neighborhoods throughout the state. But efforts to establish viable professional teams were largely unsuccessful before World War I. Teams and leagues were begun, then folded and the most interesting part of that baseball history can be told in a few anecdotes.

The first involves Jim Thorpe, the legendary Indian athlete from Pennsylvania who pitched and played first base with Rocky Mount and Fayetteville in the Eastern Carolina Association in 1909-1910. After Thorpe won the decathlon at the 1912 Olympics, word leaked out about this North Carolina experience as a professional ball player, and he was forced to return his gold medal and give up his amateur status.

Ernie Shore, of East Bend, was one of the earliest major league stars from North Carolina. He won 65 and lost 42 as a pitcher, and is the only pitcher to throw a no-hitter in relief. In 1917 with the Red Sox, Shore relieved Babe Ruth against the Senators. Ruth had walked the lead-off batter, argued with the umpire and been ejected from the game. Now, with Shore pitching, the runner tried to steal second but was thrown out. Then Shore retired the next 26 batters, and he was credited with a no-hitter.

Shore later became sheriff of Forsyth County. His fame lasted locally into the latter decades of the 20th century because the ball field in Winston-Salem was named for him, and his picture and a little rundown on his career were included in each program.

Speaking of Babe Ruth, he is said to have hit his first home run in North Carolina, specifically in Fayetteville in March, 1914. A state historical marker has been erected to commemorate the event.

After the First World War, interest in baseball picked up everywhere. In North Carolina, the Piedmont League dominated the sport through the 1920s, with teams in Greensboro, Durham, Raleigh, Winston-Salem, and High Point.

Occasionally, one team would fold or one would be added, and at times, the league included teams from Asheville, Charlotte, Henderson, Rocky Mount, Salisbury and Wilmington. But it thrived, as did the Eastern Carolina League, the South Atlantic League, the Virginia League and the Southern League, all of which included North Carolina teams.

William G. Bramham, a Durham lawyer, presided over several of these leagues, and his capable administration brought him national attention. When the Depression brought hard times to minor league baseball, it was Bramham, as president of the National Association of Professional Baseball Leagues, who helped bring it back.

By the late '30s, a number of new leagues were in operation that included teams from cities and towns all across the state. Night games enabled more people to come to the ball park. This was an era, too, when many communities fielded teams to play the nine from the burg down the road. Textile mills had their own teams, and sandlot games would involve boys of every age. This resulted in a lot of good baseball. Players got in plenty of practice. Would-be professionals and those recently washed out of the pros would play for the town and mill teams. And interest ran high.

Many of the stars of the day are unknown to us now — Dan Boone, Lloyd Smith, Carr Smith, Cliff Bolton. But a number of others made the majors. The best of them were Hank Greenberg for Detroit, who played in Raleigh; Johnny Mize of the Cardinals who played in Greensboro, and Johnny Vander Meer of the Reds and Charles Grimm of the Cubs, both of whom played in Durham.

Among the North Carolina sons who went to the majors were the Farrell brothers of Greensboro — pitcher Wes and catcher Rick, who made the Hall of Fame; Luke Appling of High Point, and Tom Zachary of Graham, who won 185 games in the majors, but is best remembered for serving up the pitch that Babe Ruth whacked for his 60th home run in 1927. Buck Leonard of Rocky Mount was a star first-baseman in the Negro Leagues, and is a member of the Hall of Fame at Cooperstown.

Baseball's revival was put on hold during World War II, but as players were released from the services, the sport came roaring back. Over the next decade or so, 49 teams played in eight leagues in places large and small.

Again, many of the stars of those days are remembered mainly among the fans who are still around who saw them play: hitters Pud Miller at Hickory, and Floyd Yount of Newton-Conover; pitchers Horace Benton of Rocky Mount and Alton Brown of Roanoke Rapids; and home run hitter Leo "Muscle" Shoals of Reidsville.

But several who played here in the '40s and '50s made the big leagues including Al Rosen and Eddie Matthews, who played at Thomasville, Harvey Haddix and Ray Jablonski at Winston-Salem, Hoyt Wilhelm at Mooresville, Johnny Mize, Greensboro and Johnny Pesky, Rocky Mount.

Top players from North Carolina in the post-war decade were Enos

(Country) Slaughter of Roxboro, a Hall-of-Famer, Forrest "Smokey" Burgess from Caroleen, Billy Goodman of Concord, Johnny Temple of Lexington and Whitey Lockman of Lowell.

TV and the rise in popularity of other sports, basketball in particular, in North Carolina contributed to the decline in interest in minor league baseball. By the late '50s, most of the leagues and teams that had their heyday in the earlier post-war years had disappeared. The strongest league to survive was the Carolina League, which had teams in the Piedmont. Charlotte teams, owned by the Crockett family, consistently played in Class AA leagues. And the Western Carolina League held on. Loyal fans got to see the likes of Curt Flood, who played for High Point-Thomasville, Carl Yastrzemski (Raleigh), Joe Morgan and Mickey Lolich (Durham), Mel Stottlemyre (Greensboro), Rod Carew (Wilson), Lee May and Tony Perez (Rocky Mount), Sparky Lyle and George Scott (Winston-Salem), Harmon Killebrew and Tony Oliva (Charlotte), Willie Stargell (Asheville), Bobby Bonds (Lexington), Gene Tenace (Shelby) and Richie Zisk (Gastonia).

In the '70s, North Carolina became known as a birthplace of pitchers. Hoyt Wilhelm of Huntersville, a reliever who threw the knuckleball, ended his career in the early '70s and was elected to the Hall of Fame. Jim "Catfish" Hunter, of Hertford, pitched for the Oakland As and the New York Yankees en route to the Hall of Fame. The Perry Brothers, Gaylord and Jim, from Williamston, both won the Cy Young award during their careers. Gaylord, who befuddled batters and umpires with his spitball, won 314 games. Other pitchers who made their mark were Mike Caldwell of Tarboro, Tony Cloninger of Lincolnton, Jim Bibby of Franklinton and Ted Abernathy of Stanley.

The 1975 World Series between the Red Sox and the Cincinnati Reds is credited with reviving interest in baseball, and entrepreneurs responded to the game's new-found popularity. In towns across the state old stadium seats were dusted off and town councils were prodded into renovations. New teams with new names and new affiliations reappeared in the old ballparks and the fans turned out again.

Durham was perhaps the most successful team in the new revival. The homey old park near downtown Durham was spiffed up, and the team was tied into the Braves farm system. It wasn't long before players like Brett Butler who starred in Durham were appearing in Braves games on television. It was a pipeline to America's Team, and it was exciting. The Bulls nickname recalled the Bull Durham smoking tobacco that made the town's name a household word across the nation. And it was the title of the Kevin Costner film, a story of minor league baseball, that was filmed in and around Durham and particularly at the ballpark. Durham had been leading the nation in attendance at the Class A level, and after the film came out in 1988, broke the Class A all-time attendance record with 270,000 paying fans.

Durham's Bulls now play in a new stadium and are a Triple-A affiliate of the Tampa Bay Devil Rays. The Bulls and the Charlotte Knights, an affiliate of the Chicago White Sox, play in the International League. Fans there can see their local stars jump to the big leagues at any time. The Carolina Mudcats, out of Zebulon, play baseball in the AA Southern League. At the A level, North Carolina has the Winston-Salem Warthogs and the Kinston Indians in the Carolina League. Also at the A level, the South Atlantic League has five teams – the Greensboro Bats, the Asheville Tourists, the Hickory Crawdads, the Kannapolis Intimidators and the Wilmington Waves.

Many players have gone on to the majors after playing for North Carolina teams, including Cal Ripken Jr. (Charlotte), Sammy Sosa (Gastonia and Charlotte), Fred McGriff (Kinston), Ivan Rodriguez and Juan Gonzales (Gastonia and Charlotte), David Wells (Kinston), Derek Jeter, Jorge Posada, Andy Pettitte and Mariano Rivera (Greensboro), and Chipper Jones, Andruw Jones, Javier Lopez, and Kevin Millwood (of Gastonia) and David Justice (Durham.

North Carolina natives in the Big Leagues include Trot Nixon of Durham, James Baldwin of Southern Pines, Ray Durham of Charlotte, Brian Moehler of Rockingham, Wes Helms of Gastonia, Brent Butler of Laurinburg, Mark Grace of Winston-Salem and Sterling Hitchcock of Fayetteville. Add to that two managers who won divisional titles in the '80s: Roger Craig of Durham with the San Francisco Giants and Hal Lanier of Denton with the Houston Astros.

It should be noted that North Carolina also is the home of the worst team in professional baseball history, the 1951 Rocks of Granite Falls in Catawba County. The Rocks lost 96 games while winning only 14. In their desperation to turn around their fortunes, they became the first professional team in the South to use black players.

Track and Field

A few names stand out in track and field, a sport that generally does not pre-occupy our minds until a record is broken or the Olympics beckon.

As mentioned at the beginning of this chapter, Marion Jones has established herself as the top female sprinter in the world. A former star at UNC, she now makes her home in Chapel Hill. At the 200 Olympics in Sidney, Jones won gold medals in the 100-meter, 200-meter and 4x400-meter relay, and bronze medals in the long jump and 4x 100-meter relay.

Leroy Walker of North Carolina Central University in Durham has coached many college stars and Olympics medalists over the years, and was head coach of the successful men's team of the 1976 Olympics. Walker and Duke coach Al Buehler have organized a number of national and international meets for Durham.

Jim Beatty, of Charlotte and UNC, was the first to break the four-minute indoor mile, with a 3:58.9 performance in Los Angeles in 1962. Tony Waldrop of Columbus and UNC broke the indoor mile record in 1974 with a 3:55 time.

Dave Sime of Duke was regarded as the world's fastest human when he set a 20-second mark for the 220-yard dash in 1955.

Lee Calhoun, of North Carolina Central was a gold medalist in the 110-meter high hurdles at the 1956 and 1960 Olympics.

Kathy McMillan of Raeford placed second in the long jump at the 1976 Olympics.

Pro sports

Carolina Panthers: After playing their first season in Clemson, S.C., the Panthers moved into brand new Erickson Stadium in downtown Charlotte for the 1996 season. And what a season, Under Coach Dom Capers, the team made the playoffs and beat Dallas in the semifinals of the National Conference championship. It was a great game and it seemed like everyone in the state watched it. Even though the Panthers lost to the Packers in the finals, we felt like we had a team we could pull for. Former San Francisco coach George Seifert came on in the 1999, but times lately have been lean.

Carolina Hurricanes: The Hartford Whalers moved south and changed their name to give North Carolina a National Hockey League franchise. The team played its first year in Greensboro, then moved to Raleigh, sharing an arena with the N.C. State basketball team. The team made the playoffs in 2001, losing to the New Jersey Devils in the first round.

Books

Barrier, Smith. *On Tobacco Road/ Basketball in North Carolina.* 1983. New York, Leisure Press.

Bledsoe, Jerry. *The World's Number One, All-Time Great Stock Car Racing Book.* 1975. Garden City, N.Y., Doubleday.

Browning, Wilt. *The Rocks/ The True Story of the Worst Team in Baseball History.* Asheboro, Down Home Press.

Vehorn, Frank. *The Intimidator/ The Dale Earnhardt Story/ An Unauthorized Biography.* 1991. Asheboro, Down Home Press.

Vehorn, Frank. *A Farewell to the King/ A Personal Look Back at the Career of Richard Petty, Stock Car Racing's Winningest and Most Popular Driver.* 1992. Asheboro, Down Home Press.

8

Travel and Leisure

Those of us who grew up in Piedmont North Carolina considered ourselves fortunate. We lived halfway between the beach and the mountains, and it seems as if our family vacations were split about evenly between the two.

This was back in the '50s, when two-lane highways were the rule, and those highways took you right through the middle of every little town. It took all day to get to the beach, with much of the time spent fuming over the slow car at the head of the long line of traffic. Same with the mountain trips. And to top things off, dad always seemed to get caught behind a semi on those winding, uphill climbs.

The typical beach vacation of the day was spent at a cottage or motel as close to the ocean as possible where you swam until you were sunburned, then went off to the pavilion to play miniature golf or pinball. Maybe dad went off to fish and, if you had a kitchen, maybe mom cooked his catch for supper. More likely he didn't catch much and you had to go find a sit-down restaurant. There were no McDonald's in those days.

Every other year, it seemed, we went to the mountains. That was different from the beach. We would establish a base of operations — a cabin at Fontana Village, say — and take day trips from there. Looking at scenery was the prime objective — from Clingman's Dome in the Great Smoky Mountains National Park, from Mt. Mitchell, from lookout points along the Blue Ridge Parkway. Occasionally, we would spice things up with a trip to the Cherokee reservation to have our pictures taken with an Indian in headdress or buy a rubber tomahawk. Or we'd take a ride on Tweetsie, a narrow gauge train with a steam locomotive that operated on three miles of track near Blowing Rock.

Then sometimes we stayed near home. There didn't seem to be a lot to do in the Piedmont. We could camp in the state parks at Hanging Rock or Pilot Mountain, or we would go out to a municipal lake or park and picnic and swim.

176

That was about it, back in the '50s. There was nothing to do, and we said that a lot.

But then things started happening.

North Carolina started advertising itself as the "Variety Vacationland," and "The Goodliest Land" and urged tourists to see our state "From the Mountains to the Sea." They did come, and tourism became a very big business for North Carolina.

When they saw the tourists coming, entrepreneurs created more things for them to do — not just miniature golf courses or souvenir stands, but big things:

A drydock at Wilmington for the decommissioned battleship *North Carolina* where now, during season, a light show tells the story of a World War II battle.

Carowinds theme park near Charlotte (now *there* was something for the Piedmont tourist).

Ski resorts at Beech Mountain, Wolf Laurel and Cataloochee that extended the mountain tourist life beyond the October leaf season.

Lake Norman, all 32,000 acres of it, built by Duke Power to store water for its power generating needs. It is our largest body of fresh water, and people throughout the Piedmont flock to it to boat, camp and fish.

Other entrepreneurs thought up new kinds of excitement:

Rafting on swift mountain rivers, a sport that has become so popular that stretches of the Nantahala River are as crowded now as those old one-lane highways.

Hangliding, a daredevil activity that involves a foot-powered takeoff from some high spot while hanging onto a set of fabric wings. This is popular at Grandfather Mountain and at Jockey's Ridge, near Kitty Hawk, appropriately in sight of the Wright Brothers Monument that celebrates manned flight.

Jet-skiing and windsurfing — new ways to get around bodies of water. Jet-skiing is getting so popular that accidents have become more numerous in recent years, especially at Lake Norman.

The federal government did its part by moving right along on the interstate highway system. It also built "Appalachian corridors," four-lane highways into the far reaches of the mountains. And it made the Cape Hatteras and Cape Lookout National Seashores more hospitable to tourists. The state improved the ferry service along the Outer Banks, built the N.C. Zoo near Asheboro and set up parks across the state on land that was donated or bought.

And every little town on the map, it seems, has found a reason to celebrate. Festivals every weekend. We've always had some, such as the Azalea Festival in Wilmington, the Fiddlers Convention at Union Grove and the Highland Games at Grandfather Mountain. Now we have Mule Day at Benson, Livermush Country in Shelby and the Southeast Old Threshers Reunion, in Denton.

Today there is plenty to do — too much, in fact. And here, we can tell you about it only in a general sense. But we'll try to bring you up to the minimum-required level of knowledge and tell you where to go for more information.

But the basics for getting information are these:

Tourist information centers are everywhere. Where the interstates bring you into the state, N.C. Welcome Centers have scads of brochures, and are manned during day hours with hosts who are trained to answer your questions. Individual chambers or tourism authorities also operate information centers. Keep your eyes open for signs leading you there.

If you want information for advance planning, call the Chamber of Commerce at places along your route. They'll be glad to send you brochures or printouts on the area.

The state's Travel and Tourism Division has several publications to help with travel plans. Two of the best are the *N.C. Travel Guide* and the *North Carolina Calendar of Events*. To contact this office, call 1-800- VISIT NC, or send a letter to 430 North Salisbury St., Raleigh, N.C. 27603.

Other material is also abundant. Nearly every major attraction and many of the smaller ones publish informational brochures. These are stuffed into racks at welcome centers, airports, restaurants, motels and major tourist attractions. The Chambers publish guides with overviews to specific areas, as well. Tourist-oriented magazines and newspapers, many of them free, can give you ideas about places to go and things to do. And for more detail, books on every conceivable travel subject can be found at any good book store.

You're holding one in your hand, and it's about to give you some travel highlights about North Carolina, beginning with the mountains.

The Mountains

When the leaves are on the trees — roughly from April through October — that's the primary season for mountain tourism.

Four-lane highways are scarce — Interstates 40 and 26, the Great Smoky Mountains Expressway between Canton and Almond, U.S. 441 from Dillsboro to the Georgia line, and some short stretches between major travel points. Otherwise, you must travel winding mountain roads. In fact, it's sometimes faster to come down out of the mountains and climb back up than it is to follow the spine of the Blue Ridge from one point to the other.

There's plenty to do — hiking, camping, boating, rafting and canoeing, fishing, climbing, tubing, biking, horseback riding and so on. The Appalachians are famous for their crafts and music, and there are opportunities for seeing both. One of the best things to do is to find a high spot and view the scenery. Or you can visit one of the ever increasing number of tourist attractions. The latest is gambling on the Cherokee Indian Reservation, where a casino with electronic gaming machines has opened.

In the spring and early summer, it can be wet. More rain falls in parts of the southern Appalachians than anywhere else in the U.S. except the Pacific Northwest, and the spring months are the wettest. The mountains are generally cooler than in the flatlands — the higher the elevation, the cooler — and nights can get downright chilly. So, be prepared with a jacket or sweater.

The farther into summer, the more crowded it gets. Summer traffic peaks from July to late August. There are plenty of motels, inns, lodges and bed-and-breakfasts for those who want a roof over their heads and plenty of campgrounds for others. But in the peak time and on any weekend during season, it's best to reserve a place.

During the summer, visibility can also become a problem. When the mountains fill up with cars, and the air becomes stagnant, the smog can severely reduce your scenic views. But then a storm can come through and wash it all away and everything seems bright and clean again.

By far the most wonderful time to visit the mountains is during fall leaf season. The tree-packed hills are always beautiful, but when the leaves change ... well, it's just difficult to describe without using cliches such as "riot of color" or "every hue in the rainbow" and so on. The change lasts for two to three weeks in October, peaking around the third weekend. The trouble is, everyone knows about the leaf season, and it is by far the most crowded time of the year in the mountains. You just have to allow for that and, with a little exploring off the beaten track, you can find the less crowded spots.

That leads us into late fall and winter. We've already mentioned how the ski slopes bring in winter tourists. But late fall and early spring and even the moderate days of winter can be ideal for hiking and camping. With the leaves off of the trees, more can be seen. And with fewer people and cars, you can hear and feel the wilderness.

Now for some specifics:

Great Smoky Mountains National Park

Of all the parks in the National Parks System, this is the most visited. And there's only one main road — Newfound Gap Road that connects the entrances at Cherokee on the North Carolina side and Gatlinburg in Tennessee. So, in peak travel season, it can take far longer than the hour-and-a-half that it normally takes to make the trip.

The views are terrific. There are 16 peaks above 6,000 feet. Trails for hiking and horseback riding lace the half-million acres of the park. You can also camp, fish and — at Deep Creek, near Bryson City — rent a tube and ride it merrily down the swift-flowing stream.

There are a few backroads, but not many. The main side trips are to Clingman's Dome, the highest point in the park, where a climb to an observation tower gets you the best view in the Smokies, and Cades Cove, on the Tennessee side, a recreated pioneer community that you can tour by car or on

Linn Cove Viaduct on the Blue Ridge Parkway at Grandfather Mountain.

foot.

The best way to get around is to get a map at one of the park entrances. And if you fish, or camp along a hiking trail, you'll need a special permit. And please, pick up your trash, don't pick the flowers and, above all, don't feed the bears.

Blue Ridge Parkway

This wonderful scenic route connects the Shenandoah National Park in Virginia and the Great Smokies National Park. More than half of it rides along the North Carolina section of the Blue Ridge.

Because its course is northeast-southwest, you don't have to drive deep into the mountains to get to the Parkway. Even if you live in the urban Piedmont you can make a day trip to the mountains that can include stretches of the Parkway.

Nobody takes the Parkway as the best way to get from point A to point B. The speed limit is 45 miles per hour and sight-seers can make the going even slower. Its more a place just to go to. There are interchanges at most major highway crossings, and even a short trip can give you magnificent scenic views and pulloffs where there are picnic areas, nature trails or benches to just sit and contemplate.

In fact, the whole drive is soothing. The Parkway is lined with woods and split rail fences, well tended grassy roadsides, meadows of flowers and farmland scenes. It was laid out to avoid urban areas, although there is encroachment here and there as the cities of Asheville and Roanoke, in Virginia, move out to meet it.

Some of the best views are at Grandfather Mountain, Linville Gorge, Devil's Courthouse and Waterrock Knob. Some of the best places to visit are Doughton Park, Moses Cone Park, Julian Price Park, Crabtree Meadows, Craggy Gardens and Mount Pisgah.

At the Cone Park visitors center and in the Folk Art Center in Asheville, the finest crafts of the mountaineers — members of the Southern Highlands Handicrafts Guild — can be bought.

The parkway is maintained by the National Park Service, and there is no charge to travel it. The best way to begin to know it is to get a map or guide. These are available at the Parkway visitors centers.

Hiking

Well maintained hiking trails exist in all parts of the state, from the short nature walks in municipal parks and gardens to the Mountains-to-the-Sea Trail now under development that would connect Clingman's Dome to Whalebone Junction by way of new and existing trails.

But the most scenic and challenging hikes are in the mountains. Here, after all, is the famed Appalachian Trail, and the Great Smokies park, the Joyce Kilmer Forest-Slickrock Wilderness Area, Linville Gorge and Shining Rock, all of which are laced with trails of varying difficulty.

They all have their ups and downs and therein lies the challenge. We don't have to explain up. Some of the trails are so up that you want to start shedding some of the equipment that you once thought so vital. Some are so down that it can put a strain on the knees as you fight the gravity that wants to bring you down too fast and too awkwardly.

But you don't have to be a seasoned veteran to enjoy hiking in the mountains. There are plenty of trails rated easy to moderate that provide opportunities for family hikes. Many of the hikes along the Parkway or around the visitors' centers are like this. In Graham County, the Kilmer Forest, named for poet Joyce Kilmer, who wrote "Trees," has an easy and placid two-mile loop through virgin woods. From Clingman's Dome, the Forney Ridge Trail takes you less than two miles out and 500 feet down to Andrews Bald for a beautiful view of the Smokies and Fontana Lake.

In general, however, you do need to be in shape for mountain hiking. And you need to plan — your equipment, food and water, where to stay overnight. Equipment needs, for example, can change pretty quickly because of the changeable weather. Rain gear can come in really handy in this wet area. Drops in temperature can bring on the danger of hypothermia, so extra clothing is advisable. Food is self-explanatory. Trail water, however, should be purified by boiling or tablets even if its from a source near a shelter. And speaking of shel-

Connestee Falls, 110 feet high, near Brevard

ters, along the Appalachian Trail, they are free but occupied on a first-come, first-served basis. Quite often they are full during season, and you'll need to camp outside. In the Great Smokies park, reservations for shelters are required.

One last thing about hiking. Unless you are a true woodsman and very familiar with your area, it's best to stay on the trails. Most are well marked and easy to follow (except in Linville Gorge, where you should take a topographical map for an extra measure of comfort). Once you get off the trail you increase your likelihood of getting lost, coming upon a cliff or meeting a wild animal (such as a poisonous snake). People get lost every year in the mountain wilderness. People also fall off of ledges or get swept over waterfalls to their deaths each year because they venture off the paths or beyond the rails at scenic viewpoints.

River riding

One of the more interesting ways of seeing the mountains is by river. This can be leisurely; or it can be exciting and death defying, depending on the stretch of river you choose to travel.

Some you shouldn't choose at all because they may go over waterfalls or wash over dams. If you're trying a river for the first time, you obviously need to study maps and talk with someone who knows what to expect along the way.

There are placid stretches of river in the mountains. The Wild and Scenic New River, in the northernmost stretches of the Blue Ridge, is a prime example. Throughout the mountains, you can find long, placid stretches with maybe a mild rapid or two that can make for a leisurely canoe or raft trip.

"Whitewater" canoeing, or rafting, or kayaking is one of the thrill sports that have become popular in the past couple of decades. The stretch of the Nantahala River at Wesser in Swain County is jammed with rafts during the summer months. Tourists pay for a trip on a bus upstream, then climb into rafts with professional guides for a wild ride back to the parking area.

Mining for gems

What could be more fun than to dip your hands into some mud, splat it into a pan with a screen on the bottom, whirl it around and see what emerges as the sand and dirt are sifted away. Thousands of people do this each year at a number of mines that are located around Franklin, where the corundum yields crystals containing rubies and sapphires.

Basically, you buy the mud in buckets at a dollar or two a shot, and sit at a sluice where a constant flow of water helps you separate the treasures from the muck. Some of the mines dig their mud on site. Others truck it in. Some "salt" their muck, so that you'll find something interesting. Others don't. Usually the stones you find range from the semi-precious, such as garnets, to the worthless but colorful quartz crystals or small chips of precious stones. But now and then, somebody finds a real gem, and sometimes it's so good that they make the news.

Fishing

Barely do North Carolina children get the pacifiers out of their mouths before they want to go fishing. (Remember, that last scene of the Andy Griffith show has Andy and Opie walking happily off to the old fishing hole.) A tremendous variety of fish live in the state's waters. Visions of fish on the line tugging and whipping this way and that, and of fish sizzling mouth-wateringly on the plate has inspired us to great heights of invention in our efforts to land them.

In the mountains, the visions are of trout. Brook, rainbow and brown trout inhabit our mountain waters. The brook trout, which prefer the cooler waters of higher elevations, are also known as speckled trout or "specs" to the mountaineers and have been the historic mainstay of mountain trout fishing. When logging practices around the turn of the century put stress on their habitat, the larger rainbows were brought in and, with the browns, dominate streams at lower levels.

Trout, of course, reproduce on their own. But in order to keep the streams well supplied, government wildlife agencies restock the waters under their jurisdiction.

More than 2,100 miles of trout streams are accessible to the public. Trout can also be caught in the mountain lakes. The purists prefer to fly fish the streams, and volumes of how-to books and literature have been written about trout fishing.

But when a good fishing spot is found or when someone trusts another fisherman enough to take him to his spot, mum's the word. You can read all the fishing books you want but the truly best holes won't be written up. You'll just have to find them yourself or build a friendship with a knowledgeable fisherman. The real insiders keep an eye out for the fish restocking trucks and know where they're going. And they catch their limit pretty quickly as they cast among the newly enlarged population of trout.

Trout fishing requires a special license, in addition to a regular fishing license. Because regulations can vary from year to year and from place to place, it is always good to check with the state Wildlife Commission or one of the licensing outlets in the mountains before setting off.

Attractions

The relative coolness of the mountains during summer has attracted tourists since before the Civil War, when torturous stage coach rides would bring them up. Afterwards, when the railroad reached into the hills, the tourist industry flourished. Some of the more wealthy built summer homes in our mountains that still stand as lodges or bed and breakfasts. But the grandest — Biltmore Estate in Asheville — is an attraction unto itself. The 250-room home

The Biltmore House in Asheville.

was built by George Vanderbilt — actually he hired 1,000 men to build it and it took them five years — in the 1890s. His 125,000-acre yard was later given to the government and became a part of the first national forest. The Cradle of Forestry museum near the Blue Ridge Parkway tells that story. Biltmore Estate, with its unique architecture, gardens, lawns and views, is the most visited attraction in the state.

A typical mountain vacation might also include the Mile-High Swinging Bridge at Grandfather Mountain, Chimney Rock, which has a scenic view that includes Lake Lure, or Mt. Mitchell, the highest peak (6,684 feet) east of the Mississippi. Farther south, the Great Smoky Mountains Railway provides scenic tours between Dillsboro and the Nantahala River Gorge.

In Cherokee, look beyond the main drag and its stores for the real story of the Cherokee. *Unto These Hills*, is an outdoor drama staged nightly in an ampitheatre that has a beautiful view of the mountains. The drama conveys the sense of injustice of the removal of Cherokees from their land. There is also a good museum on the Cherokees. And now, of course, there is gambling. Harrah's operates a casino for the tribe, whose members share in the profits. The casino, housing electronic gaming machines, opened in 1997 and has proven so popular that an expansion is planned.

The Coast

The coast is the land of beginnings.

Our history as an English speaking nation began at Roanoke Island with Sir Walter Raleigh's abortive attempts at colonization. The earliest towns of our colonial period sit by the sounds and rivers.

At Kitty Hawk, Wilbur and Orville Wright flew the first powered aircraft from its dunes.

And here the food chain begins with micro-organisms teeming in the waving rushes of the shallow salt waters. Indeed, on a shoreline such as this, the evolutionists say, a sea creature made its way on to dry land a few eons back and began the organic adaptations that led through apehood to man.

But when North Carolinians think of the coast, we don't think much about history, or marine ecology or evolution. We think about good times — family trips to family-oriented beaches, fishing off the pier or from shallow-draught boats in the sounds, beach walks with first loves on starry nights, ferry rides and climbing the steps of old lighthouses, great seafood meals at restaurants overlooking the Intracoastal Waterway, the north-south highway of the big boats.

There are a couple of ways to see the coast. One is to get a place for a week and explore the surrounding areas. The other is to spend more time in the car, stopping here and there to sample what you spot from the road or in a travel guide.

There are plenty of places to do the former — Roanoke Island, Morehead City or Beaufort, Wilmington, are excellent bases for coastal exploration.

For a road trip, just pick a starting point, a finishing point and go.

A trip from Corolla on the northern Currituck County end of the banks to Calabash in southernmost Brunswick County can consume a week of fairly leisurely travel and allow time for sidetrips.

You actually have to drive up to Corolla from the Kitty Hawk area, then double back down the banks. Your route takes you over the Bonner Bridge at Oregon Inlet, then south through the Cape Hatteras National Seashore to Hatteras, where you catch a ferry over to Ocracoke Island.

Another ferry takes you from Ocracoke to Cedar Island, where U.S. 70 winds you through the fishing villages of Carteret County to Beaufort and Morehead City. The you can take a mainland route or go across the bridge to Atlantic Beach, travel Bogue Banks and return to the mainland over another bridge. Then you can go up to Jacksonville and catch U.S. 17, which will take you through Wilmington and down to Calabash, or you can take a number of detours that visit the banks then rejoin the main road until you finish the trip.

If you have history on your mind, you could choose a route that links our earliest towns: Elizabeth City, Edenton, Bath and little Washington, New Bern, Jacksonville and Wilmington.

Neither of these is a high-speed trip, but that's not the point is it? Most of the roads are two-lane and you generally have to wait for the ferries, which in themselves can be fairly lengthy trips.

As in the mountains, travel in season can be especially slow. The season generally runs from Easter to Labor Day, and if you can go during the off-season you'll have the run of the place.

The beaches

The nice thing about the beach is its simplicity. As complex as the mountains are, the beach seems about as basic as you can get. Ocean, sand, sun and breeze. You can lie there in the sun, tanning your body, while the tides beat in the background of your consciousness. Pulse of the earth. How peaceful. Why, some hypnotists like to play a seashore tape as they put you under.

Of course that all changes during a storm. The beach becomes a violent battleground. The waves crash in, the dunes flatten. Trees and vegetation bend with the force. If the storm is strong enough and from the right direction, it can eat into the sand, carrying hundreds of yards of beach out to sea. It can open inlets, close others. Trapped water can rise in the sounds, then rush across the banks when released by the winds.

After a storm is one of the best times to walk on the beach. There is a sense of newness to this eternal landscape. Shells and driftwood are washed ashore. Often an old shipwreck is exposed. Treasure hunters with their metal detectors scour the sands, hoping to find lost items that have been brought closer to the surface.

We have no shortage of pristine beach in North Carolina. The Cape Hatteras National Seashore extends for 72 miles across parts of Bodie, Hatteras and Ocracoke islands. The Cape Lookout National Seashore stretches for another 55 miles over Portsmouth Island and the Core Banks and Shackleford Island. You can drive the length of Hatteras, but to get to the Cape Lookout park, you must take a ferry from Atlantic, Williston or Harker's Island. A ferry ride is also necessary to get to Hammock's Island State Park off the coast at Swansboro. The challenge of getting to these isolated beaches is rewarded by the solitude and the unspoiled natural surroundings.

Nor do we have a shortage of highly developed strand, especially at Atlantic, Carolina and Wrightsville beaches. Sometimes that beach is hard to find behind the motels, restaurants, bars, game rooms and shops that cater to the tourists. These beaches are meccas for singles, and many of us as youths spent lost weekends in their hedonistic pits. But more often we considered these beaches too overrun with servicemen and would go to Myrtle Beach or Ocean Drive to dance the shag and meet the opposite sex.

Most typical of the North Carolina coast are the family beaches, where the construction is not quite as dense, where the dunes and beach roads are lined with single family homes on pilings and where the shore is readily accessible. These beaches dominate the banks outside the parks, outside the three urban beach areas, and outside of the privately owned islands such as Bald Head and Figure Eight. The family beaches are great compromises. They're not the wilderness of the national seashores, but they have plenty of pockets of escape and solitude. They don't have the excitement of the city beaches, but in most areas those are usually close enough so that if you want to spend a day there you can. The kids have a few things to do, such as go to the game room, but there's plenty of room for invention. And there's likely to be a not-so-crowded fishing pier nearby.

The ferries

It's hard for many of us to go to the coast and not think about taking one of the ferries. There's a bit of romance to a ferry. If the weather's nice, you can get out and lean on the rail and watch the seagulls. Locals use the ferries, and it gives you an opportunity to hear their "hoi-toiders" brogue. Unless you have a boat yourself, the ferry is the only way to get to Ocracoke Island.

The ferries run by the State of North Carolina connect Southport and Ft. Fisher, Minnesott and Cherry Branch, Aurora and Bayview, Cedar Island and Ocracoke, Swan Quarter and Ocracoke, Hatteras and Ocracoke and Currituck and Knotts Island.

The ferries operate year-round, but with reduced schedule during the off-season. The trips range from 20 minutes for the Minnesott-Cherry Branch run across the Neuse River to 2 1/2 hours for the Ocracoke-Swan Quarter run. Fares of $10 per car are charged for the ferries connecting Ocracoke with Cedar Island and Swan Quarter and $3 per car for the Ft. Fisher-Southport run.

Ferry schedules are listed on the North Carolina State Highway map that is available free at any Welcome Center. Reservations are recommended for the Ocracoke ferries and can be made in person at the terminals or by telephone.

The lighthouses

If you need a reason to travel, why not collect lighthouses?

We have eight lighthouses, all but two of them operational. They're very photogenic and one of them — at Hatteras — you can climb. Most are fairly accessible, although several are off the beaten path.

From north to south, here's the rundown:

Currituck Beach Lighthouse is at Corolla, about 40 miles north of Whalebone Junction. This is an automated lighthouse, 150-feet-tall, constructed of unpainted red brick. It was built in 1875.

Bodie Island Lighthouse is also 150 feet high, built in 1872 on the north side of Oregon Inlet. The existing lighthouse, distinguished by its alternating horizontal bands of black and white, replaced a lighthouse blown up during the Civil War. That lighthouse, in turn, had replaced an 1848 structure that was so poorly built that it leaned and the light wouldn't work. This light is not open to the public, but the National Park Service operates a visitor's center and museum in the old keeper's house.

Cape Hatteras Lighthouse is our most famous, completed in 1870, the tallest lighthouse in America at 208 feet. The current structure replaced an earlier one that was first built in 1803, elevated in 1853 and damaged during the Civil War. At times in its history, beach erosion has threatened the lighthouse foundation and prompted efforts to preserve it. This lighthouse is open to the public. You can climb up to its observation deck and see way up and down the coast. It is distinguished by its black and white spiral bands.

Ocracoke Lighthouse was built in 1823 to replace one that had been hit by lightning and burned five years before. It is the oldest active lighthouse in the state, with an automated low-intensity light. Its exterior is whitewashed cement and it stands 76 feet high.

Cape Lookout Lighthouse was built in 1859 to 150 feet, replacing a shorter one that was often shrouded in ground mist. The height became the standard for the later lighthouses built to the north on our coast line. Because they were similar, each was painted with a distinctive pattern. The Cape Lookout tower is painted with black and white diamonds. This lighthouse is on the Core Banks of the Cape Lookout National Seashore, which can only be reached by ferries from docks in Carteret County.

Old Baldy Lighthouse sits near the marina of the Bald Head Island resort. It is our oldest lighthouse, but no longer operable. It was built in 1818 to replace an older structure, and lit the way for ships heading into the Cape Fear River.

Price's Creek Lighthouse sits on private property near Southport, but can be seen from the Ft. Fisher ferry. It was built in 1850 as one in a system of lights to mark the way up the Cape Fear from Oak Island to Wilmington. It is not operable but has been restored by the chemical company which owns the property.

Oak Island Lighthouse, on the opposite bank of the Cape Fear from Bald Head Island, was activated in 1958 and is the most powerful lighthouse in America. It is 169 feet tall and has three bands — black at the top, white in the middle and gray at the bottom. The lighthouse is at the U.S. Coast Guard station on Caswell Beach, but is not open to the public.

In addition to these lighthouses, light towers mark treacherous waters at Frying Pan Shoals, 20 miles off the mouth of the Cape Fear, and Diamond Shoals, 13 miles offshore from Cape Hatteras. If you just have to add these to your collection, you'll have to charter a boat to see them.

Fishing

There are many ways to pull fish from the salt waters. You can float a small boat and fish the sounds, rivers and streams that feed them, or cast your lines

Cape Hatteras Lighthouse.

Fishing from the pier, a popular pastime all along the coast.

from the beach, take your bait bucket out on a pier or a jetty or charter a boat to take you out to the Gulf Stream.

Fishing is a year-round activity in North Carolina's coastal waters, although it's best in the non-winter months. Drum and bluefish make surf fishing exciting in spring and fall. In the rivers are spotted sea trout, largemouth bass, chain pickerel, catfish and gar. Prowling the sounds or offshore waters are mackerel, flounder, tarpon and tuna. And there are the old reliables of pompano, gray trout, whiting, croaker, spots and mullet.

Between Kitty Hawk and Ocean Isle, there are 30 or so piers along the North Carolina coast. Most are open from March or April to November or December, although some are open year-round.

Charter boat operators can be found all along the coast, particularly at Hatteras, Morehead City, and Carolina Beach.

The kinds of fish that inhabit our salt waters and their environments are so varied that it can take a lot of on-the-job research to become a good fisherman. Coastal fishermen may be a little less secretive about their methods than the mountain trout fishermen, but still it can be difficult. There are a few books that can help, but by and large you'll have to learn through trial and error.

While no license is required for salt-water fishing for now, there are length limits on some fish as well as limits on the number you can catch. As these may vary from season to season, you can check with wildlife officials, tackle shops and piers for up-to-date regulations.

Attractions

The Lost Colony, the nation's first outdoor drama was written by our native son Paul Green, a Pulitzer Prize-winning playwright. The play has been staged in an amphitheater at the Ft. Raleigh National Historic Site in Manteo since before World War II. The show is held nightly except Sunday, with tickets costing $10 for adults, half that for children.

The historic site itself offers tours during summer that give an idea of what it was like for the colonists who attempted to get a foothold in the New World for England. Nearby, the Elizabeth II State Historic Site provides mooring for a replica of a sailing ship of 16th century England.

Not far from Manteo, at Kill Devil Hills, is the Wright Brothers National Memorial, a 60-foot tall granite monument to the first powered flight in 1903, which took place nearby. A visitor's center tells the story and is open year-round. Jockey's Ridge is a giant dune in the same range that you can climb for a scenic view. Hang-gliding courses are offered in the area, and it's a good place to get an introduction to the sport.

The North Carolina Aquarium has three facilities on the coast. All feature the fish, turtles, alligators and other species found in North Carolina's salt waters in vivid recreated habitats. The Aquarium facilities are at Manteo, Pine Knoll Shores west of Atlantic Beach and at Ft. Fisher.

Hang-gliding from Jockey's Ridge.

The forts themselves are interesting to visit. In addition to Ft. Raleigh, the federal government operates a historic site at Ft. Fisher at the mouth of the Cape Fear on Kure Beach. The state has a park at Ft. Macon, east of Atlantic Beach at Beaufort Inlet. Both forts were captured by Union forces during the Civil War. Ft. Macon's fall early in the war led to the occupation of much of eastern North Carolina. The taking of Ft. Fisher in 1865 led to the fall of Wilmington.

Ocracoke is an attraction in itself. The island was an important colonial port. Edward Teach, better known as Blackbeard the pirate, used Ocracoke as a base for his thieving fleet until he was captured by the royal navy and beheaded in 1718. Ocracoke is a quaint village built around Silver Lake and is absent the nightspots and condos that you'll find elsewhere on the coast. Other towns on the coast known more for their picturesque charm than tourist hub-bub are Beaufort and Oriental. Beaufort has a Maritime Museum worth seeing. Oriental is a sailing center.

Historic districts have been restored in several coastal towns that prospered in colonial days. Among these are the waterfronts of Elizabeth City, Murfreesboro, Bath, Edenton and New Bern, all important colonial ports. Bath was the colony's first port. Edenton was a center of Patriot activity before the Revolutionary War. New Bern became the colony's capital and Gov. Tryon built his capitol there, restored now as Tryon Palace. The state's oldest house is in Hertford. Known as the Newbold-White House it was built around 1685. Most of these places feature walking tours, museums and buildings open to the public. In some cases, full access to the facilities may be limited to tourist season.

The granddaddy of the historic districts is in Wilmington. It covers 200 blocks and can be a tourist destination in itself. Museums, restored homes, river cruises, horse-drawn carriage rides and subtropical gardens can fill more than one or two days. The Battleship *North Carolina,* docked near downtown, is open year-round. A sound and light show in tourist season tells the story of the battleship during World War II. Wilmington is our largest deep-water port and has become a movie-making center. It's an interesting boom town. And the completion of Interstate 40 a few years back has made a trip there a lot faster than it used to be.

The coast is full of motels, inns and bed-and-breakfasts. Usually there are enough to go around. But reservations are always a good idea during season wherever you plan to go. The National Park Service operates several campgrounds on the Outer Banks. Reservations may be required, but usually campground policy is first-come, first-served.

The Piedmont

The Piedmont — a combination of the French words for foot and mountain — is that vast area that lies roughly between Interstate 95 and the Blue Ridge. Most of us North Carolinians live and work here, particularly in the Piedmont's "Crescent" which is the urban corridor between Charlotte and Raleigh.

The Piedmont has never been much of a destination of choice for vacationers. When outsiders visit, it's generally on a business trip. If it's a pleasure trip, it's more likely to be for an event, such as a college basketball game, a golf tournament, a stock car race or maybe the Stonybrook steeplechase.

Now you might think we're saying that the Piedmont is a nice place to live, but you wouldn't want to visit here. No, not at all. There are plenty of places to visit in the Piedmont. The State Zoo and Carowinds are obvious family choices. The lakes too. But beyond that, if you're the kind of traveler who demands a lot of attractions, you'll just have to be a little creative.

We who live in the Piedmont certainly like our situation. There's plenty for the sports-minded to do, be it boating, fishing, golf or spectator sports. There are lots of state parks and rivers. And there's lots of scenery.

You just have to get outside of the city and off of the interstate highways to enjoy it. Once you do, you'll find our pastoral scenes match up with anyone else's. And when you think about it, the cities take up just so much space. In the Piedmont, there's a whole lot more rural landscape than urban to admire.

Pinehurst

The exception to the no-vacation-destination-in-the-Piedmont rule is Pinehurst, which has been a resort area for the well-to-do since the 1890s.

Pinehurst started simply as a hotel with pleasant grounds but quickly adopted golf as one of its main reasons for being. Northerners took to the resort, and its success and fame grew along with the quantity and quality of its golf courses. Today there are seven courses within the resort itself. But within a short drive are nearly 30 more.

Although it can be nippy in winter and sweltering in summer, you can find the courses crowded at just about any time of year.

But if you go looking for the Golf Hall of Fame in Pinehurst, you're going to be disappointed. An interesting feature of the area for some time, the hall was moved a couple of years ago to Ponte Vedra, Florida.

Pinehurst is an upscale resort, and most of its hotels, restaurants, and shopping districts have prices that reflect the clientele. Still, if you shop around, you can come up with tour packages that include golf for a more mid-scale budget.

In April, the Stonybrook Steeplechase attracts people from all around the area to watch the horse races and the tailgate parties, which often feature the best silver, linen and succulent food that the highbrows can summon up.

The lakes

For many within the state, the lakes of the Piedmont provide the perfect weekend getaway.

In many driveways, you'll see well maintained motorboats on trailers ready to be hitched to the backs of cars on Friday afternoons.

Some of the campgrounds at the larger lakes provide water and sewer hookups, and it is not uncommon for some of our urban dwellers to park their campers there permanently. These folks may come out to the lake every pretty weekend and spend their vacations there as well. Who can blame them? A lot of Americans have to drive a long way to fish, water ski, swim and sail.

But you don't have to have a permanent trailer site to enjoy our lakes. The state operates recreation areas at several of our larger lakes in the Piedmont, including Kerr Lake, Jordan Lake and Falls of the Neuse Lake. In addition, state parks are located on Lake Norman, Lake James and Lake Tillery. All of the parks and recreation areas have swimming areas and put-in ramps for watercraft. Most have campgrounds as well.

In addition, most of the lakes have private ramps and camping facilities. Where the economics are right, private marinas rent and store boats. Bait and tackle shops are also plentiful.

In the Piedmont, it's the lake fishing that predominates, with small- and large-mouth bass, stripers, crappie, various kinds of perch and sunfishes and,

A pair of rhinos at the North Carolina Zoological Park.

in the cooler lakes close to the mountains, walleyed pike, that are the favorites catches.

N.C. Zoological Park

If you find yourself near Asheboro with some time to spare, the N.C. Zoological Park is a great place to fill it. You can spend a couple of hours there or a couple of days.

Since 1971, the zoo's designers have been building habitats for animals that are as near as possible to their natural surroundings, using moats and boulders as barriers where possible instead of fences Construction began on the 1,400-acre Purgatory Mountain in 1971 and is ongoing.

So far, African and North American sections have been opened, with indoor and outdoor exhibits for each. The stars of the zoo are the R.J. Reynolds Aviary, which houses birds and tropical plants from around the world, and the African Pavilion, a nine-story building with recreated homes for about 200 species. The North American section features a Sonora Desert exhibit with habitats for reptiles, rodents and other plants and animals of the desert. The chimps, which frolic in a large, park-like environment in the African section, are real crowd pleasers, as are the seals and polar bears which have their own areas. Large outdoor ranges allow African and North American animals to roam freely. You can ride a tram to see it all, and spend as much time at each exhibit as you like. Tickets are $5 for adults and $3 for children. Additional donations are welcome, as new exhibits and animals depend a great deal on the private funds that are raised.

Seagrove pottery shops

Just a few miles south of the zoo is Seagrove, on the western edge of the largest concentration of potters in the world. The area, covering parts of Randolph, Moore and Lee counties overlies a blue-veined clay that attracted potters to the area in the mid-1700s.

The area is home to the world-famous Jugtown and more than 60 other potters. Some are eighth and ninth generation potters; others are just starting out. The Seagrove Pottery Museum is a good place to start any visit to the area.

At the museum, you can see the best of the work produced in the area and pick up a map that will show you where all the potteries are located. Any day but Sunday, when the museum and potteries are closed, is a good time to visit the area.

For more on the pottery heritage of the area, see the chapter on Arts and Entertainment.

Carowinds

This 83-acre theme park, owned by Paramount, offers a good selection of roller coaster and other thrill rides and a lot of other attractions. The park is ten miles south of Charlotte, with much of it organized around the food and entertainment styles special to the Carolinas.

The park is open weekends only from mid-March through early June and from mid-August into mid-October. From mid-June to mid-August, the park is open daily. Concerts are held on a regular basis.

Attractions

The urban areas of the Piedmont offer most all of the things that cities are expected to muster, such as museums, art galleries, musical events and sports.

The three major areas are the Triangle, which brings together the Raleigh-Durham and Chapel Hill areas; the Triad of Greensboro, High Point and Winston-Salem, and Charlotte.

The Triangle combines government, three major universities and the Research Triangle Park. The combination makes this the intellectual capital of the state, and the cultural offerings of the area meet expectations. Raleigh has notable art, history and natural history museums and the North Carolina Symphony. Chapel Hill has the Playmakers Theater and the planetarium. Durham has the Museum of Life and Science and the American Dance Festival.

In the spring and fall, you can tour the Governor's Mansion, which is next to the restored Oakwood residential district. Durham and Chapel Hill both have notable gardens, the Sarah Duke gardens at Duke University and the N.C.

Botanical Gardens south of Chapel Hill.

An interesting museum north of Durham is at James B. Duke's birthplace. It tells the story of tobacco manufacturing in the area and of Duke himself, the tobacco magnate who brought us electricity and set up the university that bears his name.

The Triad links Greensboro, Winston-Salem and High Point. Greensboro and Winston-Salem have symphony orchestras, art museums and so on. Greensboro — actually Guilford College, on its western fringe — hosts the Eastern Music Festival each summer. Winston-Salem is the home of the N.C. School of the Arts. High Point has a doll museum and a six-week Shakespeare Festival.

Greensboro also has a National Military Park where Gen. Nathaniel Greene inflicted heavy casualties on British Gen. Cornwallis during the Revolutionary War and forced him back to Wilmington and eventual defeat at Yorktown.

Old Salem, the hub of the early Moravian settlement that grew into Winston-Salem, has been restored and offers interesting history and food.

Charlotte also has a symphony and opera, art museums and Discovery Place, a hands-on museum for children.

The Queen City is becoming known more and more for sports, with the NBA Hornets, the WNBA Sting and the NFL Panthers bringing pro basketball and football to the area. An imposing new football stadium was built near downtown for the football team.

All told, Charlotte is the most interesting town in the state architecturally. Some of the buildings, such as the Nations Bank building are worth a look inside just to see the exquisite interiors that all of those bank charges and loan interest can finance.

But Charlotte is also full of gardens and wildlife sanctuaries if you know where to look.

There are lots of surprises in store for the patient Piedmont traveler. Off the beaten path, many of the little towns have fixed up their historic districts, parks or gardens. Interesting homes have been restored, such as the Koerner House in Kernersville and Blandwood in Greensboro.

On the weekends from spring to autumn, you might stumble on to a festival of some kind. Just about every town has come up with one to celebrate foods, arts, or some aspect of the town's heritage. Even in winter, many towns deck themselves for the holidays. The little town of McAdenville has become famous for its holiday lights, and people travel from miles around to see it.

If you're planning a trip and have some time to travel the backroads, take an advance look at the map and see towns you might pass through. A call ahead to the Chamber of Commerce might give you some ideas about what you'll find. But some things will just turn up on their own.

Scene in Old Salem, a restored Moravian Village.

State Parks

Following is a list of parks and recreation areas owned and maintained by the State of North Carolina. Included are brief instructions on how to get there and details on what you will find. Parks are open year-round unless otherwise indicated. Some facilities, however, may be open only during season.

There are no entry fees, but fees are sometimes charged for camping.

Mountains

Mount Mitchell State Park: Northeast of Asheville; access via Blue Ridge Parkway to Milepost 355.4, five miles on N.C. 128 to parking area.

At 6,684 feet, Mount Mitchell is the highest peak east of the Mississippi. Great views, hiking trails. Campground open mid-May to mid-October; toilets and cold showers; first-come, first-served.

Stone Mountain State Park: Between Elkin and Sparta; access via U.S. 21, west for four miles on SR1002 (marked by park signs), south 2.5 miles on SR1784.

The principal feature is a 600-foot high granite dome. Hiking, fishing, rock climbing, waterfalls. Camping at family grounds, with RV facilities, toilets and hot-water showers. Primitive camping for backcampers, permit required. All sites first-come, first-served.

New River State Park and Scenic River: From Jefferson, eight miles southeast on N.C. 88 to SR1590 at Wagoner Baptist Church, then one mile to park entrance at Wagoner Road Access Area. Also from Jefferson, 7.5 miles on U.S. 221 to New River General Store and follow park signs to U.S. 21 Access Area. A third access area, the Alleghany County Access Area, is accessible only by canoe.

From the Wagoner Road Access Area 26.5 miles to the N.C.-Va. State Line, the New is classified as a State Scenic River and is protected as a federal Wild and Scenic River. Canoe and raft launching points are available at each access area, as are primitive camping grounds.

Mt. Jefferson State Park: Between Jefferson and West Jefferson; access via U.S. 221 to SR1152, three miles to summit parking lot.

Known for its panoramic views of neighboring mountain ranges and farm landscapes. Hiking and picnic grounds available.

Lake James State Park: Between Marion and Morganton; via I-40 then U.S. 70 to Nebo, east on N.C. 126, three miles to park entrance.

Lake James' area is 6,500 acres. It was created in the '20s by dams on the Catawba and Linville rivers as part of the Duke Power network. Swimming areas available, as are picnic and camping grounds, hiking trails and boat access ramps.

South Mountains State Park: Between Morganton and Shelby, via N.C. 18 until 10 miles south of Morganton, right onto SR1913 for 3.5 miles, left onto SR1924 for two miles, right onto SR1901 for 1.5 miles, right onto 1904 for 3.6 miles to park entrance.

Rugged terrain, with waterfalls and picturesque streams. Hiking and primitive camping, fishing. Open all year except for March.

Piedmont

Hanging Rock State Park: Near Danbury, park entrance is on Moore's Spring Road, (SR1001,) which connects N.C. 89 to the east and N.C. 66 to the west.

The park is in the Sauratown range and is named after a scenic overhang. Cliffs offer climbing, and hiking trails offer scenic views of waterfalls and distant ranges. Also available are fishing, swimming and boating. Camping facilities are first-come, first-served with toilets and hot showers available. A fee is charged. Cabins can also be rented April through November.

Pilot Mountain State Park: Park is 24 miles north of Winston-Salem via U.S. 52 and is in two sections. Pilot Mountain section access is from U.S. 52 to SR2053 to park gates. Yadkin River section is from U.S. 52 onto SR2065 at the Pinnacle Exit, then 8.2 miles to entry gate.

Pilot Mountain is a solitary peak rising 1,400 feet above the Piedmont and

Pilot Mountain, one of the state's most recognizable natural landmarks.

is visible for great distances. Hiking and horseback trails wind through the park, with climbing and camping available as well as canoeing and fishing in the Yadkin. Family campgrounds are first-come, first-served with a fee charged, but may be closed from mid March to mid-December.

Boone's Cave State Park: West of Lexington via I-40 to N.C. 150, northwest five miles to Churchland west on Boone's Cave Road (SR1165, 1162, 1167) for 4.5 miles to gate.

Daniel Boone is said to have lived with his folks in a house on property now within the park. Picnicking, hiking and fishing are available. Closed weekdays from Christmas to mid-March.

Duke Power State Park: Between Statesville and Charlotte, exit U.S. 21 at Troutman, then west on Wagner Road (SR1321) and State Park Road (SR1330) to park entrance.

Lake Norman is the main reason for a visit here, with boating, fishing, swimming, water skiing available, as well as hiking and camping. Campgrounds are first-come, first-served with a fee charged. Available are toilets and showers and an RV dump but no water or power hookups.

Crowders Mountain State Park: Park is six miles southwest of Gastonia via I-85, exit at US 29, 74 junction, turn south onto Freedom Mill Road (SR1125) to entrance.

Remnant of an ancient range that rises 800 feet above the Piedmont. Cliffs provide opportunity for rock climbing; hiking and fishing available. Group sites may be reserved; family sites are first-come, first-served. A fee is charged. Beautiful picnic grounds.

Eno River State Park: Park is four separate areas along the river in Durham and Orange counties. All are reachable by either Cole Mill Road (SR1569) or Pleasant Green Road (SR1567) exits off of I-85 near Durham. Focal point is Cate's Ford access area. Follow Pleasant Green Road three miles north and turn onto Cole Mill Road extension, a gravel road, for .9 mile to entry gate.

With Class II rapids, canoeing and rafting are popular on the Eno. Lots of hiking trails, picnicking and primitive camping available. Bring your own wood for fires, minimal facilities, with spaces first-come, first-served.

Kerr Lake State Recreation Area: Situated on 50,000-acre reservoir north of Henderson. Nine access areas can be reached via I-85, U.S. 1 or N.C. 39.

Boating access ramps are plentiful for all water-based sports. Campgrounds are located at each access area, most of them on the lake. Campsites may be reserved. A fee is charged. Most are open all year, but not all. For camping information, write the Recreation Area office at Rt. 3, Box 800, Henderson, NC 27536.

Jordan Lake State Recreation Area: In Chatham County on 14,000-acre lake on New Hope and Haw rivers; five access areas reachable off U.S. 64 between Apex and Cary.

Boating ramp access for all water sports; camping sites may be reserved with the main office, Rt. 2, Box 159, Apex, NC 27502. A fee is charged. Campgrounds are closed from mid-December to the end of March. Bald eagles may be seen from an observation platform in the park

Morrow Mountain State Park: East of Albemarle, via Badin Road (N.C. 740) for 3.6 miles, then right onto Morrow Mountain Road (SR1798) for four miles to park.

Focus is the ancient Uwharrie Mountain Range and Lake Tillery, with lots of hiking and horseback trails to take, and opportunities for fishing and boating. Several campgrounds with facilities ranging from primitive to modern; first-come, first-served with a fee charged except for a youth area where reservations can be made a month in advance by contacting the main park office at Rt. 5, Box 430, Albemarle, NC 28001.

Weymouth Woods/Sandhills State Nature Preserve: Located a mile southeast of Southern Pines on Fort Bragg Road (SR2074).

The only stand of virgin long-leaf pines left in the state was donated by the widow of author James Boyd, whose grandfather bought the property just to save the trees. Hiking trails and a museum tell the story here. No other facilities are available.

Raven Rock State Park: On the Cape Fear River nine miles west of Lillington via U.S. 421 to SR1314, then three miles to park entrance.

Cliffs of quartzite carved by the river are the main feature. Hiking and horseback trails wind through the park, and wildflowers are abundant in spring. You can canoe on the river. Campgrounds are primitive and can be reserved by contacting the park office at Rt. 3, Box 1005, Lillington, NC, 27546.

William B. Umstead State Park: Located between Durham and Raleigh, with access at two points: from U.S. 70 six miles northwest of Raleigh, and from I-40 via exit 287 and Harrison Avenue.

A 5,000-acre preserve in the middle of an urban growth area, the park provides an opportunity for hiking and horseback riding, fishing and boating. A picnic grounds and campgrounds are available. Campsites are first-come, first-served with a fee charged. But groups can reserve a camping area or a stay at Maple Hill Lodge by contacting the park office at Rt. 8, Box 130, Raleigh, N.C. 27612.

Falls Lake State Recreation Area: In Wake and Durham counties on the shore of 11,000-acre Falls Lake on the Neuse River. Four access areas can be reached, two each by N.C. 50 and N.C. 98.

Boat ramps allow access to all water-related activities. Amenities are relatively new, including a campground at the Rollingview Access Area. That is reached via N.C. 98 and either SR1803 or SR1807 to the park gates. For further information on facilities, write the park office at 12700 Bay Leaf Church Rd., Raleigh NC 27614.

Medoc Mountain State Park: In Halifax County between Roanoke Rapids and Rocky Mount. From N.C. 48 take SR1002 west for 1.5 miles to park entrance.

Medoc Mountain is actually a ridge, covered by forest, and the park features Little Fishing Creek which flows under 60-foot bluffs. Visitors can hike, canoe, fish or picnic in the park. Camping is available with toilets and solar heated water for showers. A fee is charged.

Coast

Jones Lake State Park: In Bladen County, four miles north of Elizabethtown on N.C. 242.

A 224-acre bay lake, Jones Lake is large enough for boating and water skiing. Fishing is allowed, and there are picnic grounds and hiking trails. Camping facilities with modern bathhouses and hot showers are open from mid-March to mid-November. Sites are first-come, first-served and a fee is charged.

Singletary Lake State Park: In Bladen, 14 miles southeast of Elizabethtown on N.C. 53.

A 572-acre bay lake with group camping available to organizations. For reservations and fee schedule write the park superintendent at Rt. 1, Box 63, Kelly, NC, 28448. Others can fish the lake only when group camping sites are

Canoeing in Merchant's Millpond State Park.

not in use.

Lake Waccamaw State Park: 12 miles east of Whiteville via U.S. 74/76, south on SR1740 for .3 mile, east on NC 214 for 1.1 miles, south on SR1757 for 1.2 miles, east on SR1947 for 2.6 miles, left onto Martin Road for 1.1 miles to gate.

Another of the eastern bay lakes. Facilities limited to hiking trail, picnic grounds and beach, boardwalk and pier for fishing. Primitive camping facilities are available. No boating access from within the park, but a Wildlife Commission ramp is on the above route.

Waynesborough State Park: West of Goldsboro off U.S. 117 Bypass.

Day park on the Neuse River, open Wednesday to Sunday except for fall and winter holidays. Picnic grounds, with canoeing, fishing and hiking available.

Cliffs of the Neuse State Park: Park is 14 miles southeast of Goldsboro on NC 111.

Featured are tall cliffs carved by the Neuse River. Fishing, swimming, boating and hiking are activities. Picnic grounds and an interpretive museum are on the grounds of the 750-acre park. A family campground is available with hot water showers. A primitive tent-camping area for youth groups is also available. For details, write the superintendent at Rt. 2, Box 50, Seven Springs, NC 28578.

Merchant's Millpond State Park: Gate is at U.S. 158 midway between Sunbury and Gatesville.

Park is 2,600 acres and features a lake and a swamp forest of massive cypress and gum trees. The water provides opportunities for fishing and canoeing, while picnic grounds and hiking trails are there for the land lovers. Family camping is available for a fee, with sites first-come, first-served. Primitive camping is available for hikers and canoe groups.

Pettigrew State Park: In Washington and Tyrrell counties, south off U.S. 64 seven miles via SR1142, SR1160 and SR1168 to park.

Park is 850 acres on 16,600-acre Lake Phelps another of the eastern bay lakes. Fishing, boating, picnicking and hiking are available. The unusual attraction at this park is Somerset Place, a restored plantation mansion and grounds, which can be toured daily at no charge. Camping is first-come, first-served with a centrally located bath house. A fee is charged. There is also a youth group campground, reservations for which can be made with the park superintendent at Rt. 1, Box 336, Creswell, NC, 27928.

Goose Creek State Park: From little Washington, take U.S. 264 east for 10 miles to SR1334, then south for 2.5 miles to park entrance.

Park is at junction of Goose Creek and the Pamlico River. Nine miles of river shore offer opportunities for boating, fishing picnicking and hiking. Primitive campsites offered with a fee charged for use.

Jockey's Ridge State Park: The entrance is off the U.S. 158 Bypass at Nags Head. Park features Jockey's Ridge, the highest system of unstabilized dunes in the east. A day-use park with no camping. Chief activities are climbing and hiking the dunes, hang-gliding, flying model planes and kites.

Ft. Macon State Park: From Morehead City, cross the bridge to Bogue Banks and turn east on SR1190 to its end.

The primary feature is the fort itself, built in the 1830s then lost at the beginning of the Civil War to Union forces. The fort is open for tours. Beaches are good for swimming and surf fishing, with a bath house and refreshment stand open from June to Labor Day.

Hammocks Beach State Park: On Bear Island off the coast near Swansboro via N.C. 24 to SR1511 then two miles to parking lot at ferry landing.

This an undeveloped barrier island where visitors can observe the effects of land, ocean and wind on the coastal environment. Bath house available for swimmers; surf fishing allowed. Picnic and primitive campgrounds are available. Park is open year-round, but the ferry runs daily only between June 1 and Labor Day and on weekends in May and September. Several boats come and go each day. At other times, you'll have to take a private boat to the island.

Carolina Beach State Park: Park is 10 miles south of Wilmington via U.S. 421 to Carolina Beach then right onto Dow Road (SR1573) for a short distance, following signs to the entrance.

On the Cape Fear River at Snow's Cut for the Intracoastal Waterway, the park provides hiking trails, picnic grounds and fishing and boating areas. Family campground sites are first-come first-served with a fee charged. Youth camping can be reserved in advance by writing the superintendent at P.O. Box 475, Carolina Beach, NC, 28428. The plant life along the hiking trails is interesting here. From spring to November, you're likely to stumble onto the Venus fly-trap, our most famous carnivorous plant. But be protective of them as their numbers are declining.

Ft. Fisher State Recreation Area: South of Carolina Beach five miles on U.S. 421.

For day use only, this is a four-mile stretch of beach on the Atlantic where visitors can swim, fish and hike. It is near the remains of Ft. Fisher, which protected the Cape Fear and Wilmington until the latter stages of the Civil War before falling to union troops.

Hunting and Fishing Licenses

If you're 16 or over and are fishing anywhere except a private pond, you'll generally need a fishing license.

The same holds true for hunting, but even a hunter under 16 must be with a licensed adult or carry a parent's license unless on family property. A hunter must always carry either a license or, if under 16, a valid safety certificate, issued on completion of a safety course required for every hunter in North Carolina.

Licenses can be bought in many places across the state, particularly sporting equipment outlets. They fall into five general categories. Within each category are a variety of special licenses, but the main points are listed here.

Prices and categories were applicable in 2001 and are subject to change along with regulations and season dates. The state Wildlife and Resources Commission publishes a brochure of hunting and fishing regulations, which can be obtained at licensing outlets or ordered through www.ncwildlife.org or by writing NCWRC, 1707 Mail Service Center, Raleigh, NC, 27699-1707.

Annual licenses: Licenses are good for 12 months from date of purchase.

Basic fishing and hunting licenses are $15 each, or $20 combined, for North Carolina residents. For non-residents, the fee is $30 for fishing and $60 for hunting.

Short-term licenses: For residents, only a one-day short-term license is available and costs $5. Non-residents can buy the one-day fishing license for $10 or a three-day license for $15. The non-resident six-day hunting license is $40, as is an additional six-day license that is required to hunt big game.

Additional privilege licenses: These licenses cover special hunting and fishing categories and must be carried in addition to the basic licenses.

Except for a big game hunting license – which is $10 for residents and $60 for non-residents – the special licenses cost the same: $10 for trout fishing, $10 for waterfowl hunting, $15 for controlled hunt preserves.

To hunt bear or wild boar, non-residents must also pay $125 for a license.

Lifetime licenses: Comprehensive fishing and hunting licenses are available to residents only for $250 each.

A sportsman's license for those 12 and over, which covers most categories of hunting and fishing available, costs $500 for residents and $1000 for non-residents.

A special sportsman's license is available for those aged 70 and over for $10.

For the disabled, a basic hunting and fishing license combined is $10. The legally blind can fish with a license issued at no charge.

Festivals

At the end of the next chapter on what we eat, we list a number of food-related festivals that take place during the year. Here are some of our other popular events. These have been going on at least 25 years;

Azalea Festival, Wilmington, early April.
International Whistlers Convention, Louisburg, mid-April.
Spring Festival, Pleasure Island, early May.
Spring Thing, Rutherfordton, early May.
Ole Time Fiddlers & Bluegrass Festival, Union Grove, late May.
National Hollerin' Contest, Spivey's Corner, mid-June.
Southeast Old Threshers' Reunion, Denton, early July.
Farmers Day, Robbins, late July.
Macon County Gemboree, Franklin, late July.
Mt. Mitchell Crafts Fair, Burnsville, early August.
Sidewalk Art Show, Hendersonville, early August.
National Balloon Rally, Hickory, late September.
Mule Days, Benson, late September
Autumn Leaves Festival, Mt. Airy, mid-October.

Many other communities have festivals as well. Contact a local Chamber of Commerce for information.

Books

Barefoot, Daniel W. *Touring the Backroads of North Carolina's Upper Coast.* 1995. Winston-Salem, John F. Blair.

Barefoot, Daniel W. *Touring the Backroads of North Carolina's Lower Coast.* 1995. Winston-Salem, John F. Blair.

Biggs, Walter C. Jr. and Parnell, James F. *State Parks of North Carolina.* 1993. Winston-Salem, John F. Blair.

Bledsoe, Jerry. *North Carolina Curiosities.* 1990. Old Saybrook, CT., Globe Pequot Press.

Paysour, Buck. *Tar Heel Angler.* 1991. Asheboro, Down Home Press.

Paysour, Buck. *Fly Fishing in North Carolina.* 1995. Asheboro, Down Home Press.

Sakowski, Carolyn. *Touring the Western North Carolina Backroads.* 1995. Winston-Salem, John F. Blair.

Taylor, Walter. *Wild Shores: Exploring the Wilderness Areas of Eastern North Carolina.* 1993. Asheboro, Down Home Press.

Turner, Ginny (Ed.). *North Carolina Traveler.* 1994. Winston-Salem, John F. Blair.

9

What We Eat — and Drink

Finally, here's a chapter you can sink your teeth into.

We're through with government and history and politics and all those weighty subjects.

Now, we can turn to food. Of course, that can be a weighty subject too if you're not careful.

In this chapter, we'll introduce you to barbecue and how two schools of barbecue cooking developed in North Carolina. We'll also take you to Calabash and tell you what's so special about the way the restaurants down there cook fish.

We'll discuss ramps — and how to select the best. Say you've never eaten a ramp? Well, we'll tell you about a festival where you can sample one.

We'll also cover other food-related festivals. That's a good way to sample what we consider the best of what we have to eat.

We'll also mention some of the foods available at the grocery which will give you a taste of the state — Lance Crackers, for instance, and Mount Olive Pickles.

To help you digest all this, we'll wash it down with a look at some of our soft drinks and wineries.

It's true that we share a lot of food habits with the rest of the South that may seem strange to northerners. They always seem to make a big issue out of grits, which we like to douse with butter and red-eye gravy.

We also share a lot in common with rural areas everywhere. Remember on *Hee-Haw,* when a chorus of voices would ask Grandpa Jones what was for supper, he would launch into a list of dishes involving fresh vegetables and meats and dairy products and biscuits that would just make your mouth water. They were more than likely simple dishes favored on the farm. And even though we're less and less a farm state those food preferences are a deep part of our heritage and linger on.

209

A plate of barbecue with all the fixins'.

Granted, we are changing. In North Carolina, we're becoming as prone as people in the next state to head for the nearest fast food joint or to open a can or frozen package of vegetables or meat.

But let's hope that those foods we consider special to North Carolina have a long and happy future.

Barbecue

There are two schools of barbecue cooking that stand out in North Carolina and each has its followers. One is known as Lexington style, the other as Eastern style.

With Lexington style, only the shoulder of the pig is used. With eastern, the entire pig goes in.

With Lexington, the meat is cooked slowly over smoking hickory charcoal. Down East, most restaurants have gone to electricity or gas. A handful cling to tradition, but they burn oak instead of hickory to produce their charcoal.

Lexington style barbecue is served with red slaw, which is made with ketchup, vinegar and sugar, no mayonnaise, while eastern North Carolina slaw is white or yellow, depending on whether it has a dab of mustard added with the mayonnaise, vinegar and sugar.

Now we all know that there are other styles of barbecue. We know they use beef in Texas and ribs in Memphis. We know that folks in Kansas City like their beef with a heavy dose of sauce and that the same goes for barbecued pork in states to the south of us. Just as long as the meat is cooked over wood coals we'll acknowledge that it's truly barbecue.

But we really are partial to our styles of barbecue. And one of the worst ways to introduce yourself to a North Carolinian is to claim that we really don't know what barbecue is, that when you were out in Kansas City, you etc., etc., and that we really should be using beef and blah-blah-blah. We've heard it all before.

The fact is that we like the faint taste of wood smoke in our barbecue. That's why we sauce it so lightly — with a vinegar based sauce that doesn't cover up the taste.

The other fact is that pork was the original meat for barbecue, cooked here long before they started pasturing beef cattle out west. Usually, the only beef on our settlers' farms was the milk cow, and they certainly weren't going to cook her up for barbecue. Besides, pigs were far more common.

As with most kinds of cooking, the origins of barbecue are lost.

But one of our eastern style restaurant families has been cooking it since about 1830. Pete Jones, proprietor of the Skylight Inn in Ayden, has been cooking barbecue since he was a child. He has remained faithful to the recipe and cooking methods developed by his great-great-grandfather, who cooked his meat at home and sold it out of the back of his wagon.

Jones was interviewed not long ago by the *New York Times* , which ran near-ly two full pages of stories and pictures on Eastern North Carolina barbecue. At the Skylight Inn, and at two other of our well-known barbecue restaurants, Wilber's and Scott's Famous Barbecue in Goldsboro, the writer was struck by the simplicity of the meal, how it was usually served on paper plates and so on. The photos showed newspapers neatly laid out to mark places for eaters at long tables, or simple four-place tables with metal and plastic cushion chairs, or counters lined with stools. These were not places that have to hang old farm tools or drink sign reproductions on the wall to make them look authentic. This is the real North Carolina, bud.

The *Times* article only briefly mentioned Lexington barbecue, saying "that it might be even better known." That wouldn't be even close to equal time for those fans of Lexington style who claim that barbecue cooked their way has no equal.

Perhaps because it has stuck with hickory, Lexington barbecue has a very good reputation that has been given lots of good press over the years. Its tra-dition is said to go back to the 1920s when two competitors, Sid Weaver and Varner Swicegood, set up tents and charcoal pits across from the courthouse and sold lunch on court days.

Warner Stamey eventually bought Swicegood out and established Stamey's in Greensboro that remained true to the Lexington style. Weaver sold out to Allen Beck, another Lexington purist. Many who worked for the two men would start new restaurants. Lexington has remained a bastion of pure barbe-cue and sustains more than a dozen barbecue restaurants. Around lunch, if you find yourself within a short drive of Lexington or Ayden or Goldsboro, you should treat yourself to this true taste of North Carolina.

Barbecue is generally sold chopped or in slices. You can buy a sandwich or get a plate, or tray, with the slaw and hushpuppies or cornbread. Sometimes a barbecue place will also serve Brunswick Stew. A good full meal is not going to cost you much, maybe five or six dollars at most. And that would include some-thing to drink.

Iced Tea

Here's something you need to know right off, in case reading about bar-becue and stew makes you want to run right out and get a bite before finishing this chapter.

It's this: If you order ice tea in a North Carolina restaurant, you'll proba-bly get it sweetened unless you say so otherwise.

That said, let's get on to ...

Seafood

Typically, North Carolinians like their fish lightly coated or battered and briefly fried. As with barbecue, we don't like to cover up the basic taste of the meat with too much bread or grease.

For coating, we use seasoned flour, cornmeal or cracker meal and sometimes dip the fish in egg beaten with a little water before frying. We like to use
a heavy skillet with a shallow bit of real hot fat, and turn the fish one time.

Whether the fish is salt-water or fresh-, this is how you'll find most of it
cooked at the fish camps that sit by the waterways from the coast to the
foothills. Generally, if you want your fish broiled you can get that too. But frying is the typical North Carolina way.

Our favorite fresh water fish are bass, bream, catfish and, of course, trout.
Some also favor carp. From the ocean, we have plentiful catches of bluefish,
drum (channel bass), croaker, flounder, grouper, mackerel, mullet, rock fish,
sea bass, sea trout, shad, red snapper and, in the last couple of years, tuna,
although that's rarely served fried.

In some coastal areas, they cook up what they call a muddle. Fish is boiled,
boned and then cooked in a pot with pork fat, onions, potatoes, tomatoes and
seasoning.

We have a good supply of shellfish, as well — shrimp, clams, scallops, blue
crabs and oysters. The Outer Banks claim its own distinctive style of clam chow-
der, made with clams, broth, onions, potatoes and pork fat drippings. Some
coastal restaurants also offer fritters, made by mixing chopped clams, oysters
and scallops with onions in a batter that is spooned into hot oil or butter and
lightly browned.

As for crabs, give us a potful steamed alive, a stack of old newspapers, a
bowl of melted butter and a device for cracking the claws, and watch us go at
them. We also favor crab cakes panned in butter.

Oysters can be fried, roasted, sauteed, cooked in a creamy-buttery stew, or,
best of all, steamed in the shells, then cut out and dipped into a melted butter
or cocktail sauce.

The North Carolina equivalent of the New England clambake is the oyster
roast. Line a pit in the ground or sand with rocks, then start a wood fire in the
pit. Put raw oysters in the shell on a rack above the fire, and in a few minutes
they're done.

Back in the '30s, two families in South Brunswick County used to hold oyster roasts on the beach for hungry travelers. They attracted more and more
people and finally moved their operations inside. Over the years, the menu
expanded, until they became full-fledged seafood restaurants — or fish camps,
as we call them. More and more came to eat in the restaurants in this little community, which was called Calabash, and other restaurants started popping up,
all serving roughly the same thing. Today, there are more than 30 restaurants,
and each night during the summer they attract huge throngs of people who
have to wait in line to get in. It sometimes seems as if everybody in Myrtle
Beach drives to eat in Calabash.

But that's because it's good, the North Carolina style of cooking seafood beating anything they can get in South Carolina.

Slaw

The only thing consistent about all the ways we make slaw is the cabbage.

Cabbage was a hardy vegetable, easy to grow, and it was always around. Cooks statewide — once they had chopped up the cabbage — did different things with it. As you read above, there is ketchup-based, mayonnaise-based, mustard-based slaw. It is the natural side dish in North Carolina. We even put it on hot dogs and hamburgers.

The only thing most of us don't do is call it coleslaw. There's nothing particularly wrong with that, but why use two syllables when you can get by with one?

Brunswick stew

We mentioned this in the barbecue section, but we need to chew it over a little more.

There is debate about the origin of Brunswick stew. Some say that it originated in Brunswick County in our state, others maintain that it comes from Brunswick, Georgia. Still others — and they may have the inside track — say it comes from Brunswick County, Virginia. Then again, that's right on the North Carolina line, so they may have snuck the recipe over to their side in the dark of night.

Regardless, we do like to eat it here. And the ingredients ought to be spelled out. A Brunswick stew consists of game — squirrel, rabbit, etc. — and chicken, with onions, potatoes, tomatoes, corn, lima beans and hot peppers. Stir it all in the biggest pot you can find, so as to feed the most that you can, and cook it slowly for hours on end.

Bread

Long before the arrival of Europeans, the native Americans ground their corn for a meal that was used in much of their cooking. Naturally, they made corn bread. They also mixed the meal with beans to make bean bread. And, when the chestnut trees were still around, they did the same thing with the boiled nuts to make chestnut bread. Generally, their corn bread was of a pone variety — corn meal mixed with water and baked in pottery over hot coals, or wrapped in leaves and dropped into boiling water as corn dumplings.

Corn was one of the crops adopted by the whites, as well as were native methods of planting. They grew a lot of it, because it was easy and sometimes they could work in a second crop in a single growing season. Early settlers in North Carolina exported a lot of corn to the northern colonies, but they kept much more for themselves. Even after wheat was grown in appreciable quantities, corn remained the preferred basic ingredient for bread.

(Of course, corn came in handy for other things too — beer and liquor, to mention two. And grits, perhaps the base of all Southern cooking.)

Like the natives, the colonists ground their corn into meal, but they developed their own forms of bread. Sometimes a thick-batter corn bread called ash cakes was baked on the hearthstones of their kitchen fires. One of the favorites of North Carolina settlers was cracklin' corn bread, into which crunchy bits of rendered fat were mixed. They also put cracklin's in corn dodgers, or hush puppies, as many Tar Heels prefer to call them. Hush puppies usually contain corn meal and wheat flour, plus onions, and perhaps even a little sugar. In whatever shape they take, the batter is deep fried to a golden brown.

Most people add a little flour, salt and baking soda when they make corn bread nowadays as well. You will still find that corn bread is frequently served in our homes. And no dinner on the church grounds is complete without several platters full.

To many North Carolinians, no meal is complete without biscuits. We like biscuits for breakfast, lunch and dinner. You will notice that all of the fast food restaurants serve biscuits for breakfast. You can't get that everywhere.

We like our biscuits big and fluffy, and we like them served hot, so that butter spread in them will run down the sides. We like to sop with them, too, so that we get every dab of juice or gravy on our plates.

Ramps

When mountain folks felt the need to clean out their systems they often turned to the ramp.

The ramp is a garlic-like vegetable that grows wild on the north slopes of the higher mountains, with the lowest ones found at about 4,700 feet. They also grow in Tennessee and other mountainous parts of the east, but it is in North Carolina that the ramp has a festival all its own.

Each year, on the first Sunday in May, the folks at the American Legion Post 47 in Waynesville cook up the ramps that they've dug from the hills. They open the gates at noon, and charge a modest fee for an afternoon of country music and square dances and speeches and, of course, all the ramps you can eat.

Before you eat a ramp, however, there are a few things you need to know. In the first place, a ramp is a heck of a lot stronger than any onion, stronger even than garlic. It will stay on your breath for several days. For that reason, ramp experts recommend that if you're going to eat one, your buddy ought to as well. And it *will* clean out your system, they say.

Cookie Wyatt, who is in charge of the Waynesville festival, says his cooks fix the ramps with eggs, fried potatoes and meat loaf. That makes ramp-eating more tolerable to the average person, he said. For the true enthusiasts, there is a ramp eating contest. The one who eats the most raw ramps in five minutes wins.

The knowledgeable ramp eater knows that those with a pink cast are the roughest. "White-arounds," says Cookie Wyatt, are the easiest to take.

For the timid, concession stands sell hot dogs and hamburgers without ramps, and they can still enjoy the music and speeches. For many years, the main address was given by Secretary of State Thad Eure, who was considered the "Ramp King." Thad Eure is gone now, and so far, no one has achieved a comparable prominence in the ramp world. The title is open.

But don't look to Cookie Wyatt to claim it. He won't eat a ramp. He tried some a few years back and they made him sick.

Country ham

We didn't quite dispose of the whole hog issue with the section on barbecue. We also need to speak of country hams.

As we said, the hog was the meat staple of farms going way back in our history. In the days before refrigeration, most farmers found it convenient to kill their pigs at the first frost. Just about every part of the pig was used in some way.

The fat was rendered into lard. The resulting cracklin's were used in corn bread.

The liver was ground and cooked with corn meal and spices for liver pudding, or liver mush, as it is called in some areas of the state.

Meat scraps went into sausage, which was spiced with sage, and red and black peppers.

Head cheese, scrapple, and souse meat were made from the head and various other less appealing parts. Even the brains were kept, usually cooked and preserved in Mason jars to be served with scrambled eggs. Canned pork brains can be found in almost every supermarket in the state, and brains and eggs remains a stable on the breakfast menus of many country cooking restaurants.

The feet were pickled.

That left the prime cuts to be salted down and cured, the side meat for bacon and fatback, the shoulders and hams to be smoked and cured with pepper and brown sugar. Country ham, as these hams were called, were prized above all other cuts. And country ham was the finest dish that could be served when company came. Few North Carolinians cure their own hams anymore, but commercial producers abound all across the state. Four can be found within a few miles of one another in Randolph County alone.

Moravian cookies

Old Salem, in Winston-Salem, is a restored Moravian village, where at Christmas you will find the characteristic Moravian cookies. The Moravians were from Germany and settled in Pennsylvania, then moved down to North Carolina early in our history.

The heritage of the Moravians has been preserved in many ways, and certainly in a wide range of cooking methods. The love feast, a meal at church in which participants are served a yeast bun and a mug of coffee, is one of the food traditions still observed. But the best known Moravian treat is the traditional Christmas cake we know as a Moravian cookie.

Beth Tartan's *North Carolina and Old Salem Cookery* gives a recipe for these cookies. The dough includes brown sugar, molasses, cloves, cinnamon and ginger which, when ripened overnight, is rolled out extra thin. After baking, the cookies should be stored in a tin to keep them crisp.

The combination of spices is very good and is what gives the cookies their uniqueness. The purists look for black Puerto Rican molasses for the mix, and those who like extra bite add more cloves.

Soft drinks

Over the years, North Carolinians have slaked their thirst with numerous home grown concoctions that have involved peaches, strawberries and you name it with effervescent sugared water. Only a couple have hung on to go into our Hall of Fame.

Pepsi Cola is the granddaddy of the Tar Heel soft drinks, having been developed by a druggist named Caleb Bradham in New Bern in 1903. He obtained a patent and developed a network of bottling plants in other states. Sugar supply problems in World War I brought him down. He went bankrupt and Pepsi passed into other hands.

Cheerwine is a Salisbury product with a syrupy cherry taste that has a cult of devotees. Those who move away from North Carolina coddle their Cheerwine connection. Friends are most welcome who come bearing a case or two of the cherry liquid and are always invited back.

Wineries

Efforts to make wine commercially in North Carolina have faced more than the usual difficulties of weather, pests and other factors generally afflicting the farmer. Another obstacle has been the temperance movement, which resulted in North Carolina going "dry" a decade before national prohibition went into effect.

Wine-making goes back into the 1700s, chiefly among Swiss, Italian and German immigrants. Successful enterprises in the late 1800s dotted the map from Valdese to Duplin County.

Today, the Biltmore House produces wines, as does Germanton Winery near Winston-Salem, which even makes a Bob Timberlake wine. But the largest winery is the Duplin Wine Cellars in Rose Hill, which offers tours and tastings year-round. Duplin Wine Cellars has won awards for its magnolia and scuppernong wines, made from native North Carolina grapes.

Home Grown Food Companies

With all of the products grown in our fields, all the experimenting that went on in the kitchen over the years and all the business opportunists out there, we were bound to have a strong food processing industry in the state.

Over the years, many food companies have started operations in the state. Some are listed below. Among them are companies that have achieved note outside of our borders. Others may not have, but are included here just because you should know about them.

House of Lance: The peanut butter cracker is a Tar Heel invention. A Mrs. S.A. Van Every of Charlotte should be given the credit. She liked the taste of peanut butter on crackers and suggested that her husband and his friend, Philip Lance, market the idea. Lance, a coffee salesman, and Van Every, who was in pickles, knew about selling and set up the House of Lance. The rest is snack food history.

Hardee's: The first Hardee's was opened in 1960 in Greenville, N.C. by a man named Wilber Hardee. It was a bald-faced imitation of McDonald's, but the 15-cent hamburger had struck a chord with the nation, and Hardee cashed in on it. The trouble, though, was that he cashed out too fast, selling out to partners he took in to expand the business, one of whom, Jim Gardner, later became a Congressman and unsuccessful candidate for governor. Gardner eventually sold out too. Today, Hardee's is a multi-national company based in Rocky Mount, and is consistently in the top handful of fast-burger chains.

Mt. Olive Pickle Co.: 1926 was a great year for cucumbers, especially in the Mt. Olive area in Wayne County. In the face of the cuke glut, some folks in town started a pickle company that is still a familiar brand in stores today.

Charles F. Cates Pickle Co. was started in 1898 in Alamance County, then moved to Faison in Duplin County in 1929 to be near the cucumber growers.

Luck's: Based in Seagrove, Luck's has been canning beans, meats and fruits for decades. It made its name by canning dried pinto beans with salt pork, and by its catchy jingle that ends "... why shucks, you eat country style when you bring home the Luck's."

Krispy Kreme Doughnuts: Many a Southerner has started a day with a cup of coffee and a couple of glazed doughnuts at the Krispy Kreme doughnut shop. The product was developed in Old Salem in Winston-Salem, but has become a real fad nationwide. The company went public in 2001.

Carnation: We may not have contented cows with that other brand of evaporated milk, but we do have Carnation. The company was started by one Elbridge Amos Stuart of Guilford County.

Waldensian Bakeries: In operation since 1919, this bakery makes Sunbeam, Roman Meal and Waldensian Heritage bread and rolls. The aroma of baked goods in this town is as distinctive as the smell of tobacco is to some of our cigarette manufacturing towns.

T.W. Garner Food Co. This Winston-Salem company makes the Texas Pete Hot Sauce. Actually, Garner started out with a barbecue joint, but his sauce was more popular than his cooking. The hot pepper sauce was a later creation, but its name caught on, and now all the company's sauces are marketed under Texas Pete.

Royal Cake Co. Another Winston-Salem company, Royal has been baking and packaging soft cakes for years. They were particularly noted for their cream-filled oatmeal cookies.

The Penrose Co. Staples of near-fine beer establishments everywhere are the pickled pigs feet, pickled eggs and pickled hot sausages produced by this Garner Company. Were Shakespeare alive today, he might write that a Penrose by any other name would taste as sour.

Food Festivals

Nearly every burg in the state now has a festival to draw people to town. Often these revolve around the foods that are unique to the locale. We believe that any excuse is fine to have a party, and food is probably the best excuse of all.

Here are few of the established festivals that will give you a reason to jump in your car, visit, party and, of course, eat. Call the local Chamber of Commerce for exact dates.

Shad Festival, Grifton, early April.
Robert Ruark Chili Cookoff, Southport, early April.
Herring Festival, Jamesville, mid-April.
Pig Cookin' Contest, Newport, mid-April.
Ham and Yam Festival, Smithfield, mid- to late April.
North Carolina Pickle Festival, Mt. Olive, late April.
Strawberry Festival, Chadbourn, late April-early May.
Ramp Festival, Waynesville, 1st Sunday in May.
Poultry and Pork Festival, Warsaw, early May.
Chicken Festival, Siler City, mid-May.
Croaker Festival, Oriental, early July.
Piedmont Berry Festival, Dobson, mid- to late July.
Watermelon Festival, Fair Bluff, late July.
Watermelon Festival, Murfreesboro, early August.
Seafood Festival, Corolla, early August.
Watermelon Day, Raleigh, early August.
Shrimp Festival, Snead's Ferry, mid-August.
Strange Seafood Exhibition, Beaufort, mid-August.
Barbecue Championship, Winston-Salem, mid-August.

Watermelon Festival, Winterville, late August.
Blue Crab Festival, Bayboro, early September.
Apple Festival, Hendersonville, early September.
Livermush Country, Shelby, mid- to late October.
Yam Festival, Tabor City, late October.
Apple Festival, Eden, late October.
Barbecue Festival, Lexington, late October.
Brushy Mountain Applefest, Wilkesboro, early December.

Books

Bledsoe, Jerry. *From Whalebone to Hot House/ A Journey Along North Carolina's Longest Highway*. 1986. Charlotte, Eastwoods Press.

Parris, John. *Mountain Cooking*. 1978. Asheville, Citizens-Times Publishing.

Sparks, Elizabeth Hedgecock (Beth Tartan). *North Carolina and Old Salem Cookery*. 1960. Kernersville.

Ulmer, Mary and Beck, Samuel E. Cherokee Cooklore. 1951. Cherokee, Museum of the Cherokee Indian.

10

Arts and Entertainment

North Carolina's rural heritage has had a profound impact on the forms of art and entertainment that we call our own.

Once we get past Bob Timberlake, most North Carolinians are hard-pressed to name one of our other painters. But there are many others, and exhibitions of their work show the powerful influence of North Carolina's landscapes and people. The more the artist's work reflects our personality the more we take to it.

Much more familiar to us are the craft arts — pottery, weaving, even black-smithing — than the classical arts of painting, sculpture or architecture. We can't always name our best potters either, but most of us are more comfortable picking out a piece of pottery or a quilt than a painting.

As for music, we do have our high-brow events such as the Eastern Music Festival at Guilford College, and the larger cities have their symphonies. These are important to us and are well attended. But North Carolinians are much more familiar with our country musicians, such as Arthur Smith or Doc Watson. Being a religious people, gospel music is also important, and in most of our households, our radios are more likely to pick up tunes by Shirley Caesar or George Beverly Shea than Luciano Pavarotti.

Each year, Durham hosts the American Dance Festival, and the finest dance companies in the country appear there. But our native dance is clog-ging, the natural response of leg and foot to the spirited playing of a fiddle or banjo. (Of course, some of us grew up dancing the Shag. But that and beach music are associated more with Myrtle Beach, which is in another state.)

Of all the fields of art, literature probably comes closest to combining pop-ular and critical tastes. The South in general has a strong literary tradition, and North Carolina is a part of that. Throughout our history we have depended a great deal on our storytellers for entertainment. The jokes and folk tales told on the back porch have had a much greater effect on our major literary works than, say, a three-fingered banjo tune has of influencing a symphony. It's probably safe to say that our state's writers are more likely to be reviewed in the *New York Times* than one of our musicians or artists. It's also more likely that the average North Carolinian has been exposed to their works.

We've responded particularly well to the outdoor drama, pioneered by Paul Green, who helps make our point. He was a North Carolinian who developed the stories and themes of our region, yet gained the outside recognition necessary to win the Pulitzer Prize. There are theatrical groups all over the state, but once we get beyond school plays, we're more likely to be in front of the outdoor stage, if any.

This chapter is to give you a working knowledge of our arts world — the visual arts, music and literature. We will present the highlights of the classical art world, but our emphasis will be on the folk arts.

The visual arts

Claude Howell, in a 1976 article on the history of painting in North Carolina, wrote about the scarcity of information on the subject but plowed ahead anyway. Much of what you'll read here has been taken from that article which was published in a book *200 Years of the Visual Arts in North Carolina* by the N.C. Museum of Art.

Howell wrote that our earliest painters were itinerants, who would set themselves up in the established towns of the east and paint the portraits of those wealthy enough to hire them. Most had no North Carolina connections. But there were several who took up residence here for extended periods — William Joseph Williams of New York, who painted in New Bern and died there in 1823, John Mare of New York and Edenton, William Ranney of New York and Fayetteville and William Garl Brown of Raleigh.

In Raleigh, an art school and museum were run by Jacob and Louisa Marling. He painted portraits of many folks around Raleigh and did a well-known oil painting of the first State House, which burned in 1831. William C. Frerichs, a European, taught art at Greensboro Female College and included wilderness scenes of the North Carolina mountains in his romantic paintings.

Two of the more prominent painters of the early 20th century were Elisabeth Augusta Chant, of Wilmington, and Elliott Daingerfield of Blowing Rock. Daingerfield studied in New York, and had a national reputation. He ran a summer art school in the mountains. Chant also taught art and influenced painters in Wilmington for many years. Among these were Howell, whose paintings were often of coastal subjects and who has been called the "Dean of North Carolina Painters."

Some of the groups that fostered art through exhibitions were the N.C.

Federation of Women's Clubs, the Professional Artists League in Chapel Hill and the North Carolina Art Society. During the Depression, the Works Progress Administration sponsored art centers throughout North Carolina and commissioned artists to paints murals in public buildings.

College level schools of art came into being in the '30s, nurturing North Carolina's budding artists. Prominent among the programs were Gregory Ivy's at Woman's College in Greensboro and Russell T. Smith's at Chapel Hill. An important school developed at Black Mountain under Joseph Albers, with most of the students from out of state, including Elaine de Kooning and Walter Gropius. Faculty members of the college art schools were among our most productive and influential painters.

Abstract painters who made a name for themselves in the '50s and '60s included Walter Thrift of High Point, Edith London and Robert Broderson of Durham, James Bumgardner and Willie Mangum of Winston-Salem, and Marvin Saltzman of Chapel Hill.

Landscape painters include Paul Bartlett of Charlotte, George Arnold of Greensboro, Philip Moose of Blowing Rock, and Henry Jay MacMillan of Wilmington. Maud Gatewood of Charlotte emphasized abstract landscapes, while W. Herbert Jackson of Davidson experimented with sky patterns.

Among the realist painters of the Piedmont who concentrated on the textures and objects of rural North Carolina were Ward Nichols, Robert Dance, Robert Doakes and Bob Timberlake.

Joe King (who signed his paintings "Vinciata") of Winston-Salem, painted portraits in a classical manner.

Natives who split their time between North Carolina and the art centers of the world and became known in art circles were Mabel Pugh of Morrisville, Francis Speight of Bertie County and William C. Fields III of Fayetteville

Over the years, a number of other artists have left the state to make names for themselves. These have included Frank London of Pittsboro, Charles Baskerville of Raleigh, Hobson Pittman of Epworth, Warren Brandt of Greensboro, Edward A. Bryant of Lenoir, Henry C. Pearson of Kinston, Kenneth Noland of Asheville, Romare Bearden of Charlotte, Lloyd Oxendine of Wilmington and Thomas Sills of Castalia.

Artists throughout the state continue to experiment with a variety of art forms. One way to keep up with what's going on is to attend the North Carolina Artists Exhibition held each year at the N.C. Museum of Art in connection with Culture Week.

Another way is to visit the museums — the N.C. Museum in Raleigh, the Mint Museum in Charlotte, the Witherspoon in Greensboro, Reynolda House in Winston-Salem and other smaller galleries across the state.

Bob Timberlake

Anyone contemplating a career change can take heart from the experience of Bob Timberlake. A more successful change in direction would be hard to imagine.

Timberlake was involved with several of his family's businesses, when a Life magazine spread on Andrew Wyeth kindled a flame to paint professionally. Timberlake had dabbled with art as a child and had won a prize for a decorative chest he built at age 15. But as a businessman, he had confined his painting to hobby status.

He began to take his art more seriously and worked to bring discipline to it. But before making a career change, he needed to have an objective opinion on his work. Was he good enough to forsake the business world for this new venture?

In 1969, he obtained an audience with Wyeth himself, got the encouragement he needed, and a year later launched his painting career. He bought a 200-year-old farm near Lexington — its buildings and natural features are seen in many of his paintings — and began to charm North Carolinians, if not the art critics, with his realistic, unglorifying interpretations of everyday scenes in rural North Carolina.

His paintings for the most part do not involve people. Rather, he paints weathered buildings with grainy, bare wood; flowers arranged in colorful enamelware with rust spots, old oaks with misshapen limbs, tools and implements past their prime but still functional. We're comfortable with his images because he have seen them all our lives and appreciate the honesty with which he paints them.

Timberlake has achieved national and international fame through his paintings which have been widely disseminated through books and gallery exhibits. He has extended his feel for our heritage into furniture designs and has even developed a wine. If you're looking for an artist who truly represents North Carolina, he is it.

John White

It's impossible to leave the section on painting without mentioning John White. He was the first to paint native North Carolinians in their daily activities.

Of course, our region wasn't known as North Carolina at the time. It was called Virginia, and White was a member of several English expeditions to the New World, including both attempts to colonize Roanoke Island. He was the governor of the second attempt, the Lost Colony, whose fate he escaped because he went back to England for supplies. He was detained there because of England's war with Spain and when he returned, he was unable to find the colonists, which included his daughter, her husband and their child, Virginia Dare.

White himself has been lost to history. We don't know his fate. But his paintings of the native life that he witnessed during his time on our soil are important to our heritage.

White sketched the village layouts, showed how the natives fished, cooked, ate, and otherwise went about their daily lives. He drew them in their different social roles, with their dress, ornamentation, weapons and the articles they used in their everyday lives. He also sketched the animals, fish and plants of the New World.

His work was published by the Flemish engraver De Bry along with Thomas Hariot's narrative on Virginia, and it gave the British and Europeans their first comprehensive look at what was across the sea. The work was reprinted in many languages, and White's drawings are as familiar to us today as the story of the Lost Colony. One of his drawings appears on page 8.

Craft arts

North Carolina's craft tradition developed mostly in the Piedmont during the early days of settlement.

The planters of the east had better access to the north via water routes and were more apt to import the articles they needed for their households. There were some furniture makers of note and silversmiths who thrived, but the need for potters, weavers, quilters, tinsmiths and so on was nil.

The Piedmont, on the other hand, was land-locked, and overland trade routes were more difficult. In addition, the small farmers who settled inland were generally not as well off as their eastern neighbors. So they made many of their own goods, or bartered what they could make for the work of other artisans in the area.

As settlers moved west into the mountains, they took along their crafts methods. The craft work of the Cherokees was also influential, and because handicrafts were encouraged as a commercial endeavor the mountains developed a strong crafts tradition of its own.

Pottery

English and German immigrant potters who settled the Piedmont in the mid-18th century immediately set up their wheels to turn out clay products for their fellow colonists. Chief among the pottery producing areas were the Moravian settlements in what is now Forsyth County, and in Rockingham, Alamance and Lincoln counties and, most prominently, in the Randolph-Montgomery-Moore county area.

Colonial potters brought with them the designs and production methods of the Old World. But the isolation of the Piedmont helped them develop their own styles. Since they were not continually affected by changing styles and tastes of our more "with it" coastal areas and urban centers of the North, the Piedmont potter traditions were based more on available materials and the

Unloading the kiln at a Seagrove pottery.

Melvin Owens shapes a bowl at his pottery in Moore County.

specific needs of their neighbors for vessels in which to cook or store food.

The Moravian potters Gottfried Aust and Rudolf Christ, who worked in Old Salem in the last half of the 18th century, did retain the old world look in their ceramics to a greater degree than others in the Piedmont. In the Catawba Valley, below Hickory, the pottery came to be identified by an alkaline-based glaze. In the lower Piedmont, a tradition of salt-glazed pottery evolved.

By the end of the 19th century, when glass and metal had replaced clay as the material of choice for vessels and as more modern methods of cooking and food preservation were being developed, pottery-making became a part-time enterprise conducted by "farmer-potters." As they died, the craft was in danger of dying out.

But individuals here and there have kept the tradition alive. In the Catawba Valley, for example Burlon Craig learned the farmer-potter ways of his Lincoln County area as a child-apprentice and went out on his own at age 15. For more than 50 years, he has dug his own clay, manufactured his glazes, used a treadle wheel and hardened his work in a wood-fired kiln. He has built such a following that kiln openings draw a crowd and his firing is usually sold out that day.

In the Seagrove area, the Jugtown enterprise begun by Jacques and Juliana Busbee during World War I revived a pottery tradition that had all but disappeared. The Busbees, of Raleigh, had connections in New York, and would sell there the work turned out by their "factory" of potters in North Carolina. Building on the primitive tradition, some of the potters added their own artistic touches which enhanced the pottery's reputation. Among these were Charles Teague and Ben Owen. Owen's work, in particular, became world famous, and he stayed at Jugtown until 1959 before starting a pottery of his own. Today, Jugtown continues to operate under Vernon Owens, who comes from a long line of potters, and his wife Pamela. In 1980, the late potters Walter and Dorothy Auman opened a museum in the old railroad station at Seagrove and with displays of pottery and photographs told the story of the area's history. Seagrove has the highest profile among North Carolina's pottery making areas.

But many visitors to North Carolina are also exposed to the native American tradition of pottery. Pottery making was practiced here long before the arrival of Europeans. John White's drawings made during his 16th century visits show supper cooking in stoneware pots. Shards help archaeologists date native sites. At Cherokee, a visitor can get a true understanding of Cherokee life and arts by visiting the Cherokee Museum, the Oconaluftee Indian Village and the Qualla Arts and Crafts Mutual. At the village, Amanda Swimmer has been demonstrating pottery-making for more than 35 years, and her work has won national recognition. She does not use a wheel, but molds her vessels — often beginning with coils of clay. She fires her pieces in an open pit, choosing different woods for fuels to achieve different effects.

Weaving and Quilting

As with pottery, weaving was a vital skill for communities of the early settlers. It also was in danger of dying out as a craft when it became more convenient to buy clothes than to make them from scratch. Weaving held its own for a longer time in the mountains, where the goods weren't as readily available and where there wasn't as much money to buy them.

As with many of the folk artists mentioned in this chapter, the late Wilma McNabb was honored with a Folk Heritage Award from the N.C. Arts Council, and is a good example of how the weaving craft was revived. She was born and raised on a farm in Cherokee County, where her ancestors had settled in the mid-1800s. They were weavers who passed the craft from generation to generation. Mrs. McNabb was introduced to the craft by her mother, but she dropped it for many years and didn't take it up again until she was around 40, when outsiders began to encourage mountaineers to ply their crafts for sorely needed income, thus spawning a crafts revival. But for more than half a century, she was known for her coverlets and other weavings and for her interest in teaching young weavers the intricacies of the loom.

The founder of America's oldest and largest crafts school was also a weaver, and it was weaving that Lucy Morgan taught to other mountain women when she began in a single log building at Penland in 1923. Over the years, the school grew. It now attracts students from around the world for classes in a variety of craft arts, including weaving, pottery, wood working, metal working, glass blowing, book arts and others. The school attracts top craftsmen to conduct classes. Many, charmed by the surroundings have decided to stay, such as Harvey K. Littleton, world renowned artist in studio glass.

Weaving was also an important component of the John C. Campbell Folk School, which was begun in 1925 by Mrs. Olive Dame Campbell to teach crafts and help the mountain people market them. That school, still in existence, is at Brasstown near Murphy.

Quilting is yet another craft that has a long and colorful history in the state. The practitioners of this craft number in the hundreds and can be found in any section of the state.

A North Carolina Quilt Project in the '80s conducted by Ruth Roberson and Erma Kirkpatrick documented more than 10,000 quilts in the state and resulted in a major exhibition and book, entitled *North Carolina Quilts* by UNC Press.

Wood and metal

Behind pottery and textiles, the craft arts that are apt to catch your eye are in wood or metal.

Woodcarvers practice throughout the state, with a lot of different styles emerging from the flying chips. In Cherokee, Virgil Ledford learned to carve animals under the tutelage of Amanda Crowe. His work is known for the character of the carvings and for the varied wood patterns that he works into his art. His sculptures are in a number of museums and private collections. One of his most prominent can be readily seen in Cherokee. It is the sculpture of the Cherokee hunter and eagle that is the emblem of the Museum of the Cherokee Indian.

Primitive toys are favorites of many of the mountain whittlers. If you're traveling in the mountains and come across a crafts co-op, stop in and tell them you want to see a gee-haw-whimmydiddle. They'll know what you're talking about and they'll probably be able to produce one for you.

Another mountain craft that is overshadowed somewhat is the making of musical instruments. The players, not the builders, bring the instrument to life and earn the mention on the playbills. But the workmanship that goes into the instrument is as traditional a craft as the playing. Leonard Glenn of Watauga County builds banjos and dulcimers that are known for their superior sound. It is a craft passed down through several generations of his family.

George Servance works out of his basement in Thomasville, carving everything from decorative walking canes to a full-sized cat to a slave in bonds. Demand is greatest for his dancing dolls, which he has been carving for thirty years and more. His own favorites are the carvings of biblical figures.

In Stacy, in Carteret County, Julian Hamilton Jr. and the late Homer Fulcher kept alive the decoy carving tradition of the coastal area. Their craft goes back to the mid-19th century when the birds that wintered in Core Sound were a major food source for local residents. With a decline in hunting and the availability of manufactured decoys, the craft went into decline. But Hamilton and Fulcher continued to carve, their work only a bit more decorative than the old working decoys and meant more for the mantel than the water.

Speaking of the coast, mention must also be made of the Harker's Island boat builders, who built shallow-draft boats from scratch. Among them was Julian Guthrie, who would scour the maritime woods for just the right building materials and build his skiff without plans. He went on to own and operate the Hi-Tide boat company and adapted his designs to 85-foot yachts and trawlers. But the "Guthrie Boat" of old is still recognizable in the types of craft of the southeastern coast.

The most enduring metal worker of our age is Bea Hensley, a blacksmith from Spruce Pine. He was born in 1919 at a time when most blacksmiths had gone on to other careers, many with garages or body shops to fix the cars that replaced the horses and buggies that were the mainstays of the blacksmithing trade. But a few smiths turned to ornamental work, and Hensley apprenticed under Daniel Boone VI, who restored the ironwork at Williamsburg. It was a project that Bea Hensley helped with, then finished. Hensley has passed the trade on to his son Mike and together they create decorative pieces that grace the homes of the famous and have been featured at the Smithsonian.

Music

If you're a fan of classical music, you will find plenty of opportunities to hear it in the cities of our state. A number of symphonies and opera companies are supported by citizen groups. Within each of the universities, talented musicians perform on a regular basis. You just have to seek them out.

The state supports the North Carolina Symphony, which travels across the state, presenting programs in schools. It also presents a season of concerts in Raleigh.

The Eastern Music Festival was begun in the 1960s by music patrons in the Piedmont Triad. Each summer, from mid-June to mid-August, talented students come to learn from visiting artists, who perform regularly in recitals on the Guilford College campus. Full orchestras and music ensembles are also invited to perform during the festival. Events are open to all who want to buy a ticket.

Notable music schools have been developed at the N.C. School of the Arts and at Brevard Music Center. Each sponsors concerts and programs to show off their students and faculty.

These classical events are important to us, and they are well attended. Without putting them down, it has to be said, however, that they don't get to the heart and soul of North Carolinians.

The music that speaks to our experience and traditions is found at the Merle Watson Festival in Wilkesboro in late April, or the Ole Time Fiddler and Bluegrass Convention at Union Grove in early April or the Mountain Dance and Folk Festival in Asheville in August. It can also be found in many small churches, at gospel sings, blues joints and country music clubs.

Country music

Country music is an umbrella term that can cover a lot of topics. In North Carolina, it generally includes old-time string music, bluegrass, *the Grand Ol' Opry* type of music, and even the slick country style that has developed from it. The music springs from themes of hard work and true or lost love, tall tales and crimes, religion, drinking, wandering and just living. The best of it — how it's written, how it's played — really hits us down deep.

Wherever settlers came from, they brought their music with them. In North Carolina, major influences on our country music came with the British, the Scots, the Irish, the German settlers and African slaves. Throughout our history, music was a solitary pastime for many isolated by geography. Music and dancing were also the main attractions when people gathered for recreation.

Radio broke the music out of its personal and regional isolation. Musicians met each other in the studios and experimented with each other's styles. The music, styles old and new, now reached more people than ever, and its popularity grew.

The radio age began in the '20s, and those who had radios, or could find a neighbor who did, started tuning in to the *Grand Ol' Opry* out of Nashville, the *National Barn Dance* out of Chicago or the *Saturday Night Shindig* out of Asheville. One of the most influential stations in our region was WBT out of Charlotte. It featured country music programs early on and eventually became a CBS Radio affiliate, thus able to give its listeners local talent as well as music originated on other CBS station programs.

Charlotte radio drew from a large pool of part-time musicians who made their livings on the farms and in the textile mills of the Piedmont. Textile work was especially advantageous in that a musician could fit in a radio appearance, maybe even an evening appearance in a high school auditorium nearby and make it to the mill in time for a late shift.

The most popular got paid for appearances, and some got their chance to cut records in one of several recording studios that cropped up in the Charlotte area. If a musician could piece together an income from radio, records and shows, he might be able to get out of the mill, and a few did.

Some of the names associated with early radio were fiddlers Homer Sherrill of Sherrill's Ford and J.E. Mainer of Concord. Also Dorsey Dixon, a guitarist from East Rockingham, who wrote "Wreck on the Highway," made famous by Roy Acuff, and Earl Scruggs of Flint Hill. But a lot of outside entertainers passed through Charlotte as well, to play on the *Crazy Barn Dance* show, sponsored by the Crazy Water Crystals laxative company, or to record on RCA Victor or Decca. Among these were Bill Monroe, the father of bluegrass, legendary banjo picker and singer Uncle Dave Macon, and the Carter Family.

For 20 years, from the mid '30s and the hey-day of country radio to the '50s, when rock and roll and television put a dent in the music and its medium, the Briarhoppers were a mainstay of WBT via the *Carolina Hayride* and other shows. The Briarhoppers spawned a number of entertainers, such as Fred Kirby, who made the transition to television, and Arthur Smith, who formed The Crackerjacks and carried the Piedmont country music tradition well into the television age. Among Smith's credits is the song "Duelin' Banjos," which became famous through the film *Deliverance* in 1972. But he had to sue before he got credit for it.

For a time, in the late '50s and '60s, the old-time country music took a back seat to rock and roll, as a new generation came along. But folk singers continued to work with the music, and Nashville's artists kept it going in one form or another. North Carolina couldn't match Tennessee in the number of performers on the *Grand Ol' Opry*, but we did supply Jim Shumate of Wilkes County, who played with Bill Monroe and Flatt and Scruggs, Stonewall Jackson of Tabor City, Ronnie Milsap of Robbinsville, Don Gibson of Shelby, composer of "Oh, Lonesome Me," and "I Can't Stop Loving You," and Don Schlitz of Durham, composer of "The Gambler." Other North Carolina country stars of note Are Billy "Crash" Craddock of Greensboro, Charlie Daniels of

Wilmington, George Hamilton IV of Winston-Salem, and Donna Fargo of Mt. Airy.

To the true fans, old-time music, bluegrass, fiddler's conventions and the like never disappeared. But they were rediscovered by the Baby Boom generation in the late '60s and '70s, and have been in the forefront of our consciousness ever since, thanks to the old-timers who seemed to appreciate this new audience and to revival bands such as the Red Clay Ramblers out of Chapel Hill.

Doc Watson is probably the most important figure in that revival. He was always around, but a younger generation took to him. Wherever he appears, he is received with enthusiasm.

One of the great joys of being a North Carolinian is going to one of Doc Watson's concerts and knowing that you share the same state with him and that the music is his and ours. No matter how large the crowd, the atmosphere at his concerts is one of intimacy because of the way he'll pause from singing and playing to talk about the music and about our musical heritage.

Watson, born in 1923, is from Deep Gap in Watauga County. Before his first birthday, he lost his sight to an illness. But growing up in a musical home, he learned to play the harmonica as a child, then a banjo. He became known first for his flat-picking and finger-picking method of playing acoustic guitar. After playing with his brother Linny, and for this band and that, Watson went on the road in the early '60s.

Watson has a varied repertoire, including sacred and secular songs, folk and classical music, family and rock and roll, blues and ballads.

His son Merle played with him until he was killed in a tractor accident in 1985. An annual festival at Wilkesboro Community College is a memorial to Merle and draws huge crowds. Doc Watson, in his seventies, still tours and records now and then.

Another stronghold of old-time music has been the area between Mt. Airy and Galax, Va. The quality and originality of the string bands there have made the area famous among followers of the music. Illustrious players who have sprung up in the area include fiddler Tommy Jarrell, and banjo players Fred Cockerham and Charlie Lowe. The band names are a little geography lesson of the area — the Camp Creek Boys, the Pine Ridge Boys or the Smokey Valley Boys. A couple of the Surry County standouts, who have consistently won top prizes at area fiddler's conventions, including those at Galax and Union Grove, are Earnest East and Benton Flippen. Both play a number of instruments but favor the fiddle. Both lead groups that are in hot demand at dances.

A number of those musicians and others who have preserved the music of the past have been honored by the Folklife section of the N.C. Arts Council. Among them were string musicians Ennice Dickens of Alleghany County, Ora Watson of Watauga, Carroll Best and Luke and Harold Smathers of Haywood, Mary Jane Queen of Jackson County, Lauchlin Shaw and A.C. Overton of

Harnett, and singers Quay Smathers of Haywood and Dellie Norton of Madison County. Also honored were Joe and Odell Thompson of Mebane, string-band musicians who melded traditional country-style music with their own African-American traditions.

Gospel, blues and jazz

Each weekend across the state bands of every kind pack into vans and buses and travel to their gigs. On Friday and Saturday nights, the dance bands hold sway, whether they're bluegrass, old-time country, pop country, rock and roll, or what have you.

Sunday is reserved for the gospel groups. When all the other groups have laid down their instruments and are sleeping late, the gospel groups are ready to come on stage. Just as with other bands, there is a circuit and the groups range from old-fashioned to rock-and-roll.

Making a joyful noise is important in our religions, and the best groups and individuals can develop big followings. A few from North Carolina have risen above the crowd.

Shirley Caesar of Durham is our most recognizable name in gospel music. In fact, she has been called the leading female gospel singer of her generation. Her "rock-gospel" sound is familiar to gospel fans worldwide.

She was born in 1938 into a singing family. Her father, "Big Jim" Caesar, was a professional gospel singer, and she began singing in church choirs at an early age. At 14, she began touring as "Baby Shirley" with various gospel groups. In 1958, she moved to Chicago to tour and record with a group called the Caravans.

Then in 1966, she moved back to Durham and formed the Shirley Caesar Singers, continuing to tour and record and reap numerous awards from the music industry. Unlike many who trace their beginnings to gospel, Caesar has not ventured into the pop music field and her repertoire remains strictly spiritual.

Two other gospel groups honored by the state in recent years are the Branchettes of Johnston County and the Badgett Sisters of Yanceyville. Both groups sing spiritual music without musical accompaniment.

The Badgett Sisters have been a part of the N.C. Arts Council's "Black Folk Heritage Tour," as has George Higgs, an Edgecomb County native who sings and plays the blues on guitar and harmonica.

A Piedmont blues tradition is traced back to Fulton Allen, known as Blind Boy Fuller, who was one of the most influential and best-selling blues artists of the 1930s. He was born in Wadesboro, moved to Durham and turned to music after his sight began failing. He recorded on the ARC label along with George Washington, known as Bull City Red, and harmonica great Sonny Terry, both of whom played around Durham.

Etta Baker, a Caldwell County native, was born into a musical family and played guitar, banjo, fiddle and piano. When she married, she put aside her music career. But after her husband died, she resumed playing in public and was recorded, becoming something of a cult figure among blues and folk revivalists.

Richard "Big Boy" Henry was a native of Beaufort on the coast, but grew up in New Bern listening to the blues played on street corners and in the juke joints. He tried his hand at music in the early '50s without success, and turned to crewing on the menhaden boats. He took up music again in the '70s, playing and teaching the blues. When folklorists became interested in the songs of the menhaden crews, Henry helped organize the Menhaden Chanteymen, a group of retired fishermen, who brought their old style of work music to a wider audience.

In the field of jazz, North Carolina has several greats: pianist Thelonious Monk was a native of Rocky Mount, and tenor saxophonist John Coltrane was born in Hamlet. Both left the state at early ages, however. The same was true with Dizzy Gillespie. He was born over the line in Cheraw, S.C., but came to Laurinburg Institute at an early age and was graduated from there in 1935. The school now maintains a museum in his honor. Jazz and blues singer Nina Simone, a native of Tryon, also found fame elsewhere. Alienated by racism, she left the U.S. to live in France. We did keep Loonis McGlohon, of Charlotte, however, as our current, most visible jazz representative.

In the '30s, in the era of the big bands, Kay Kyser of Rocky Mount hit it big in Chicago with his *Kyser's College of Musical Knowledge*. The show was picked up by the American Tobacco Company and broadcast nationwide.

In the popular music field, singer Roberta Flack, born in 1937 in Asheville, fled our coop at an early age. So did Clyde McPhatter, born in Durham in 1933, who founded the Drifters and sang "A Lover's Question" in 1958.

And so did James Taylor, singer and guitar player who rose to fame in the '70s and who divided his time between Massachusetts and Chapel Hill. He is more associated with Massachusetts now, but he did leave us with a song, "Carolina On My Mind," for which we are grateful.

A group known as the Royal Sons left Winston-Salem around 1950 to record their gospel songs in New York. But they became known in Rhythm and Blues circles as The Five Royales. Two of their songs "You Know I Know," and "Baby Don't Do It" made it to the top of the R&B charts in the early '50s. Songs by their composer-guitarist Lowman Pauling were recorded by others that the group influenced, including "Think" by James Brown, "To Tell the Truth" by Ray Charles and Ike and Tina Turner, and "This is Dedicated to the One I Love," by the Shirelles.

The group was not able to cross over to the popular music charts. They stopped touring in the early '60s and returned to Winston-Salem. More recently, the Five Royales have received some attention from the old beach music crowd, who shagged to their style of music in the '50s and '60s.

234

Chapel Hill has become a center for popular rock music, spawning the Squirrel Nut Zippers, whose album "Hot" propelled the band to fame with its blend of jazz and swing reminiscent of the big bands era. The band records on the Mammoth label, a Carrboro company that was bought in 1997 by Disney and which has other stars in its fold, such as Jason and the Scorchers and Juliana Hatfield.

Sugar Hill Records is a Durham label that records favorite blue grass and folk artists, as well as Americana and alternative country. It calls itself "The Sweet Alternative" and has in its fold the Austin Lounge Lizards and Tim O'Brien.

Dance

In many ways, North Carolina dance parallels the music world.

Groups interested in ballet, for example, have existed in the major cities of the state for many years. Youngsters study dance of all kinds from ballet to tap dancing. In 1978, the American Dance Festival moved from Connecticut to Durham, spurring an interest in modern dance in the state.

More to the point are the dances that spring from our heritage — the African-American, the rural Appalachian and Cherokee dances that either originated here or have been notably practiced by North Carolinians.

John Dee Holeman and Quentin "Fris" Holloway are from Durham, long an important stop for blues singers and musicians. Holeman, on guitar, and Holloway, on piano, have played with each other for years, taking the blues anywhere in the Piedmont they can get a gig. When they're not playing, they're dancing. And in their travels with the "Black Folk Heritage Tour," they have demonstrated the kind of buck dancing that fits in with their music. It actually is better performed without music, because the dance — usually done solo — emphasizes the sound created by the feet, accompanied by "patting," or creating percussion sounds with the hands on the body.

Walker Calhoun, a Cherokee arts preservationist, is credited with keeping alive the ceremonial songs and dances of his tribe. He formed the Raven Rock Dancers to perform at pow-wows and special events. For his work, he has received special awards from the Cherokees and from the N.C. Arts Council.

Robert and Myrtle Dotson have also been honored for their efforts to preserve traditional flatfoot and buck dancing styles of western North Carolina. Flatfoot is a smooth and light dance with feet kept close to the floor. Buckdancing involves higher and heavier stepping. The Dotsons have traveled widely to demonstrate and teach their dancing styles and have won just about every prize available in the mountain dance contests.

Clog dancing is a variation on the traditional styles, usually performed by teams, and Maggie Valley can make as good a claim as any place to being the clogging headquarters. Sam Queen, who came to be know as the grandfather of clogging, formed a dance team there in the '20s.

Kyle Edwards, of Maggie Valley, whose mother Elizabeth danced with Queen's group, once told an interviewer:

"The word clogging, as far as we can trace it back, just started being used in 1935 in Chattanooga, Tennessee. We always just called it mountain dancing up to that time. You see, here in these mountains, you've got a mixture. You've got the Dutch, you've got the German, you've got the Irish, the Indian, the black. What it was was just a cluster of dances and they mingled together. It's the oldest dancing I know that's been created in the United States."

Edwards opened a dance hall for clogging called the Stomping Ground in Maggie Valley. It's open during tourist season, has a huge dance floor and seats about 2,000 paying customers. You can join in the dancing or just sit and watch. However the spirit — or the band — moves you.

Another clogging team from North Carolina made a name as a mainstay with the *Grand Ol' Opry*. This was Ben Smathers and the Stoney Mountain Cloggers. Smathers and his wife Margaret were originally from Hendersonville, N.C., which has called itself "The Dancingest Little Town in the World."

Storytelling

Before moving into the section on North Carolina literature, we need to mention a few of the storytellers in the state who have helped preserve our traditional tales and probably even made up a few of their own.

Our best known is Ray Hicks, of Beech Mountain, a near-seven-footer who speaks in an accent reminiscent of the British Isles which landed him a spot on the PBS series *The Story of English.* He is the star when he appears at the National Storytellers Festival in Tennessee, and he has received a number of state and national awards for preserving and promoting the art of storytelling.

The late Louise Anderson of Jacksonville was celebrated for sharing the African-American experience of stories, poems and toasts that she learned over her lifetime in Georgia and North Carolina.

Donald Davis grew up in the mountains, although he has now relocated to the coast. He, like Hicks, appears at the National Storytellers Festival and travels widely, making up to 400 appearances a year.

Gary Carden, of Sylva, is popular at Elderhostel programs in the mountains for his story-telling abilities. He also created a program for public television, *Blow the Tannery Whistle.*

Drama

The father of theater in North Carolina was a Kentuckian — Frederick H. Koch (1877-1944), better known as "Proff," who came to UNC in 1918 to teach drama.

Among his students were Thomas Wolfe, Jonathan Daniels, Bernice Kelly Harris, Frances Gray Patton, Betty Smith and Joseph Mitchell, all of whom made their marks in the literary world. He encouraged their writing and produced their plays on the Carolina Playmakers stage. These he also compiled into three volumes of *Carolina Folk Plays.*

His star in the field of drama was Paul Green, whose *In Abraham's Bosom,* a 1927 play about a black schoolmaster, won the Pulitzer Prize for drama. Green also is known as the Father of Outdoor Drama. Beginning with *The Lost Colony,* first produced in 1937 in Manteo, Green combined music, dancing and history and a fictitious plot in his "symphonic dramas." His outdoor plays are also performed in three other states, and served as formulas for other dramatists.

Other symphonic dramas performed outdoors in the state are:

Unto These Hills at Cherokee, written by Kermit Hunter. The play is about the Cherokee removal of the 1830s.

Horn in the West at Boone, also by Hunter. It is about Daniel Boone and the activities of frontiersmen during the Revolutionary War.

Sword of Peace at Snow Camp, by William Hardy. The drama is about the Cane Creek Quakers during the Revolutionary War.

Worthy is the Lamb at Swansboro, a drama about the last days of Christ.

But North Carolina has indoor theater as well. Flat Rock Playhouse, the State Theater of North Carolina, has a season that runs from late May to late October. Flat Rock is near Hendersonville. The theater produces about nine plays during its season.

The Parkway Playhouse, in Burnsville, Yancey County, has a shorter season — July 4 to mid-August, during which about five plays are performed.

Most larger cities and universities have theater groups that produce plays on a regular schedule.

The North Carolina School of the Arts in Winston-Salem stages about 300 performances of 10 different plays a year on campus and around the state. The Stevens Theater, which seats nearly 1,400, also has hosted a Broadway Preview Series. Among the plays previewed for Broadway have been Neil Simon's *Lost in Yonkers* and *Jake's Women,* and, more recently, *State Fair.*

High Point hosts the North Carolina Shakespeare festival each summer, presenting three or four of Shakespeare's plays over a six-week season.

In addition to Andy Griffith, North Carolina has produced a few other notable actors, among them Ava Gardner of Smithfield and William Holden of Tarboro. Also include in that list character actors Nick Searcy of Sylva and the late W.C. "Mutt" Burton of Reidsville.

Literature

When you tell someone "You can't go home again," you're quoting a North Carolinian — the most famous of our writers, Thomas Wolfe.

When you sit in the amphitheater at Manteo and watch raptly as the drama of *The Lost Colony* unfolds, you're listening to the words of Paul Green, who "invented" the outdoor drama.

When you laugh over *The Ransom of Red Chief* or weep at *The Gift of the Magi* your emotions are being manipulated by O. Henry, also a North Carolinian.

For more than four centuries, North Carolina has provided the characters, setting and stories that our writers have passed on to others in works great and small.

Some, like Thomas Wolfe, found it confining and fled. Others, such as Paul Green of Lillington, lived here all their lives and found an unending source of literary material. Still others — Carl Sandburg, Inglis Fletcher, Harry Golden and Betty Smith — moved to North Carolina and found its atmosphere just the tonic for their work.

Here then are our state's major writers. In their works that are set in the state, you can learn much more about the basic character of the people here than from any other source.

Thomas Hariot (1560-1621) Even though the title was *A briefe and true report of the new found land of Virginia,* Hariot's book, published in England in 1588, was the first about the land that was to become North Carolina. He wrote this 48-page pamphlet from notes compiled during a year's stay with Sir Walter Raleigh's first attempted colony at Roanoke Island in 1585-86. It was a beguiling account of the plant and animal resources and the natives of the New World.

Charles W. Chesnutt (1858-1932) A black born in Cleveland to a family who had moved from Fayetteville before the Civil War, then returned there afterward. Chesnutt spent his formative years in Fayetteville, becoming an educator and writing on the side. He moved to New York at 25, and began getting published. His themes were Southern, and his first work, *The Conjure Woman,* published in 1899, was a rendition of folk tales. He wrote several other books, including more story collections and a biography of Frederick Douglass. Chesnutt moved to Cleveland and became an influential leader of the NAACP.

O. Henry (1862-1910) William Sidney Porter was born in Greensboro, worked in his uncle's drug store and became a pharmacist. But he was restless, went out West and got into trouble. While serving time for embezzlement in an Ohio prison, he began writing. He went to New York, where his short stories were published and became the most-read author in the nation at the turn of the century.

Horace Kephart (1862-1931) A librarian in St. Louis, Kephart dropped out in 1904 and lived in a cabin in a remote section of the Smokies. He came to know the mountaineers and wrote about them in *Our Southern Highlanders*. He also excelled as an outdoors writer and was instrumental in establishing the Great Smoky Mountains National Park.

Thomas Dixon Jr. (1864-1946) Born near Shelby, Dixon was a lawyer, preacher and writer. He was a white supremacist, chiefly known for his 1905 novel, *The Clansman: An Historical Romance of the Ku Klux Klan.* It became a broadway play and was the basis for the classic silent film, *The Birth of a Nation.*

Olive Tilford Dargan (1869-1968) A Kentucky native, she lived from age 27 in Swain County and in Asheville. She was a playwright and poet, but also wrote short stories and sketches, including *From My Highest Hill* about her life in the mountains. Under the pseudonym Fielding Burke, she wrote three novels about the 1929 textile workers strike in Gastonia.

Carl Sandburg. (1878-1967) As a poet of the Midwest and biographer of Lincoln, Sandburg's reputation was made well before he moved to Flat Rock in the mountains in 1946 to raise goats. But he lived his last 21 years here and considered himself a North Carolina writer. His *Complete Poems* won the Pulitzer prize in 1950. While a resident, he compiled another book of poems, *Honey and Salt,* completed his biography of Abraham Lincoln, and wrote two novels, *Remembrance Rock* and *Always the Young Strangers.* His home, Connemara, is a National Historic Site open to the public, and goats still roam the property.

Inglis Fletcher (1879-1969) Although she was not a North Carolina native, Fletcher was caught up in our history as she was researching her genealogy in Tyrrell County. She moved to a plantation near Edenton and, over 25 years, turned out twelve historical novels of colonial North Carolina that are avidly read still.

James Larkin Pearson (1879-1981) Named the state's poet-laureate in 1953, Pearson was a true son of the North Carolina soil. His earliest poetry he composed while plowing, when he would write down his verse at the end of each furrow. *My Fingers and My Toes* compiles his work.

James Boyd (1888-1944) Another transplant, Boyd wrote about Revolutionary North Carolina in his historical novel, *Drums.* He had become interested in the state during visits to Southern Pines as a child. He moved here in his 30s, wrote *Drums* and other historical novels and, for a time until his death, owned and wrote for the Southern Pines *Pilot.*

Paul Green (1894-1981) In addition to *The Lost Colony,* Green wrote 15 other "symphonic dramas" that combine music and dancing with fictional drama to relate an historic event. Many are still staged. But he was also known for his serious theatrical work that included *In Abraham's Bosom,* which won a Pulitzer Prize in 1926. The heroes of his workers were common southerners, black and white, who all had potential for greatness.

LeGette Blythe (1900-1992) A prolific writer from Huntersville, Blythe has published novels on the New Testament, including *Bold Galilean;* historic

Carl Sandburg

drama, *The Hornet's Nest;* and biography: *William Henry Belk: Merchant of the South.* He has also helped others tell their stories, among them *Gift from the Hills* which he co-authored with Lucy Morgan, founder of the Penland School.

W.J. Cash (1900-1941) Born in South Carolina, but raised in Boiling Springs, Cash went to Wake Forest, then wrote for the *Charlotte News.* But his reputation rides on *The Mind of the South,* published in 1941, which tries to explain what makes Southerners tick. It was a sensation and is still being argued, alternately embraced and rejected by historians. Cash committed suicide the year his book was published.

Thomas Wolfe (1900-1938) To have lived such a short life, Wolfe wrote an astounding number of words, which continued to be edited and published as novel, play, poetry and travelogue long after his death. *Look Homeward Angel,* his first and most famous novel, recounted his days as a sensitive youth in Altamont (Asheville) and as a student at Pulpit Hill (Chapel Hill). It won him international acclaim, but some Asheville citizens were bitter at how he'd portrayed them.

Harry Golden (1901-1981) Golden was 38 when he moved to Charlotte from New York, but he stayed and made his mark. His monthly newspaper, the *Carolina Israelite,* covered controversial topics of race and religion. He made the bestseller lists with *Only in America,* a collection of columns which was also made into a Broadway play.

Hugh Lefler (1901-1981) Born on a farm near Cooleemee, Lefler became at mid-century our state's pre-eminent historian. He co-wrote with Dr. A.R. Newsome *North Carolina: The History of a Southern State,* a complete text, in 1954. He wrote a number of other histories for children and adults.

Manly Wade Wellman (1903-1986) Born in Africa, where his father was an army doctor, Wellman settled in Chapel Hill in 1951 where he wrote and wrote and wrote. He published more than 80 books and countless articles in pulp magazines, comic books and magazines. He wrote science fiction, true crime and mysteries and turned to history in later years. *Dead and Gone* and *The Kingdom of Madison* are among his most notable books about the state.

Betty Smith (1904-1972) Another transplanted New Yorker, Smith wrote and taught in Chapel Hill. *A Tree Grows in Brooklyn,* based on her childhood, was a bestseller.

Joseph Mitchell (1908-1996) A native of Fairmont, Mitchell left UNC to become a reporter in New York City. In *McSorley's Wonderful Saloon,* he included a number of stories that were based on his youth in Robeson County.

Burke Davis (1913—) A recent resurgence of interest in the Civil War created a new demand for the histories written by this Greensboro historian, including *They Called Him Stonewall, Gray Fox* (on R.E. Lee's Civil War Years) and *To Appomattox: Nine April Days, 1865.* Davis has written fact and fiction about other periods of American history and several books for students.

Randall Jarrell (1914-1965) A native of Nashville, Tenn., Jarrell was a recognized poet when, after serving in World War II, he began teaching writing at Woman's College (now UNC-G) in 1947. He won the National Book Award for *The Woman at the Washington Zoo,* one of several of his books of poetry. He has also written books for children, including *The Bat Poet.*

John Parris (1914—) A native of Jackson County, Parris was a war correspondent, then returned home to write a column for the Asheville Citizen-Times. Collections of his columns have been published under a number of titles, the first of them *Roamin' the Mountains* in 1957.

Lilian Jackson Braun (1914—) Author of the *Cat Who ...* mysteries, Braun was a newspaperwoman in Detroit when she began writing her series that features a detective named Qwilleran and his cats named Koko and Yum Yum. She is now a resident of Tryon.

Sam Ragan (1915-1996) For years North Carolina's poet laureate, Ragan was a native of Berea in Granville County. He was a newspaperman, having worked for the *Raleigh News & Observer* and the *Pilot* in Southern Pines, which he bought in 1969. He began publishing poetry anonymously in the newspapers, then compiled his works into books, *The Tree in the Far Pasture* in 1964, *To the Water's Edge* in 1972 and *Journey into Morning* in 1981.

Robert Ruark (1915-1965) Still popular 35 years after his death, Ruark was born in Wilmington and became a star columnist for Washington, D.C. newspapers. His books spoofed the historical novel, collected his best columns or told stories of big game hunting. But his most enduring are *The Old Man and the Boy* and *The Old Man's Boy Grows Older,* which are reminiscences of time he spent as a boy with his grandfather in Southport.

John Foster West (1918—) Born in Champion in the North Carolina mountains, co-founder of the *Carolina Quarterly,* West retired from teaching at Appalachian State University. His biographical novel *Time Was* was published in 1951. West also published *The Ballad of Tom Dula* in 1970, and *Lift Up Your Head Tom Dooley/ The True Story of the Appalachian Murder That Inspired One of America's Most Popular Ballads* in 1993.

William S. Powell (1919—) Powell, of Statesville, has succeeded Hugh Lefler as the state's foremost historian. He has been curator of the North Carolina collection at the UNC library and has written and edited a number of important books Among his works are *The North Carolina Gazetteer, Colonial North Carolina* (with Lefler), *North Carolina: A Bicentennial History* and *North Carolina: Through Four Centuries.*

David Stick (1919—) If you want to know more about the history of the N.C. coast, there is no better way to learn it than to read Stick's works. Born in New Jersey, he moved to Dare County at age nine. His major works include *Graveyard of the Atlantic,* in which he documents more than 600 shipwrecks along the coast, and *The Outer Banks of North Carolina.*

Wilma Dykeman (1920—) An Asheville native whose ancestors pioneered the settlement of western North Carolina, she has turned her mountain knowledge into several well-known works, including *The French Broad,* of the popular Rivers of America series, and the novels, *The Tall Woman* and *The Far Family.*

John Ehle (1925—) Born in Asheville, Ehle has set his fiction in North Carolina locales, primarily in the mountains. His works include *The Land Breakers,* about the mountains' first settlers, *The Road,* about the building of the railroad up the mountain from Old Fort to Ridgecrest, and *The Trail of Tears* about the Cherokee removal. In the early '60s, Ehle worked with Gov. Terry Sanford to launch or promote the Governor's School, the North Carolina Film Board, the Advancement School, the Learning Institute of North Carolina, the North Carolina Fund, and the North Carolina School of the Arts. Two of his works, *The Winter People* and *The Journey of August King* have been made into movies.

Guy Owen (1925-1981) Owen, from Bladen County, was a poet, novelist and professor of English at N.C. State. He created a rascally character in *The Ballad of the Flim-Flam Man* that George C. Scott brought to life on film. *Journey for Joedel,* about a Croatan boy, also brought Owen note.

A.R. Ammons (1926—) Poet Ammons was born in Columbus County and served in the Navy during World War II. His tour at sea and his later professional experience as a school administrator, business executive and professor gave him a wide field of knowledge from which to draw for his poetry. His *Collected Poems 1951-1971* won the 1973 National Book Award for poetry.

Maya Angelou (1928—) From St. Louis, Angelou now lives in Winston-Salem, where she is a professor at Wake Forest. She is well-known for her poetry and autobiographies, including *I Know Why the Caged Bird Sings.* She read her poem, *A Rock, A River, A Tree,* at President Clinton's inauguration.

Doris Betts (1932—) Betts, a native of Statesville, launched her career with a book of short stories, *The Gentle Insurrection,* in 1954, and has published consistently since then. Often her works explore the predicament of Southern women who are trapped by their upbringings. In *Heading West,* which brought her national notice, her Southern heroine escapes her situation through a kidnapping, then finds her own direction as a result of the experience.

Reynolds Price (1933—): A native of Macon, Price has drawn on his state for the characters and settings of his novels. His first, *A Long and Happy Life,* won critical acclaim for its characterization of a young Southern girl. After a bout with cancer in 1984, he learned self-hypnosis to counter pain and discovered that it unlocked lost memories that he has used in his later novels and autobiography. He has influenced others, including Anne Tyler, through his teaching, primarily at Duke University.

Fred Chappell (1936—): A native of Canton, now of Greensboro, where he teaches writing at UNCG, Chappell has excelled as a poet, novelist and short-story writer. His works often explore his Southern and mountain roots and their relationship to modern life. Chappell has won numerous awards, including the Bollingen Award in 1985 and is poet laureate for the state.

Gail Godwin (1937—): Grew up in Asheville, now lives in New York. Her first novel was *The Perfectionists* published in 1970. She has had a steady output since, many of her works based in the South, but generally featuring female characters who work to resolve various dilemmas.

Sylvia Wilkinson (1940—): This Durham native won national acclaim with her first work, *Moss on the North Side,* in 1966 and has continued a prize-winning literary career since. Her stories explore the development of intelligent Southern women who seek different paths through life from the ones taken by their elders which have prevented their fulfillment.

Jerry Bledsoe (1941—) A former columnist for the *Greensboro Daily News* and *Charlotte Observer,* Bledsoe is best known for his true-crime thriller, *Bitter Blood, A True Story of Southern Family Pride, Madness and Multiple Murder.* He operates Down Home Press in Asheboro.

Sue Ellen Bridgers (1941—) A native of Winterville, Bridgers now lives in Sylva and continues writing books for young people. She has won several national awards for her books, including *Home Before Dark* and *Permanent Connections.*

Anne Tyler (1941—) This best-selling novelist was born in Minnesota, but grew up in Raleigh and was graduated from Duke, where she studied under Reynolds Price. Her characters are often quirky, affected by odd families. A strain of humor runs through her works that tempers the poignancy and sadness of some of her stories.

Rick Boyer (1943—) An Illinois native who lives in Asheville, Boyer won the Edgar Award for Best Mystery of the Year (1990) for *Billingsgate Shoal,* the first of a series of mystery novels featuring his hero, Doc Adams. He also co-writes the bestselling *Places Rated Almanac* which first appeared in 1981.

Kathryn Stripling Byer (1944—) Poet from Cullowhee who draws inspiration from the women's voices of her adopted mountains and from her own heritage of growing up in a Georgia farm family.

Lee Smith (1944—) A Virginia native, but North Carolina resident since the mid-'70s and faculty member of the English Department at N.C. State University, Smith has written a number of novels, including *Oral History* and *Fair and Tender Ladies,* and collections of short stories. Her characters tend to be ordinary folks who are always looking for some sort of excitement or romance in their lives.

Clyde Edgerton (1944—) After a stint in the Air Force, Edgerton, a Durham native, took to writing short stories and developed a novel *Raney* out of a couple of his characters. It sold 200,000 copies after it was published in 1985 and created a ready market for several novels that followed.

Alan Gurganus (1947—) A native of Rocky Mount, he achieved recognition with *Oldest Living Confederate Widow Tells All.* He also has published a collection of short stories under the title *White People.*

Charles Frazier (1950—) This Asheville native, who now lives in Raleigh, won the National Book Award in 1997 for *Cold Mountain.* His character deserts from the Confederate Army and makes his way home on an eventful 300-mile journey. Chapters on his sweetheart and her difficult life at home in the North Carolina mountains are interspersed. The best-seller was praised for its authentic portrayal of mid-19th century life in the Appalachians.

Orson Scott Card (1951—) A science-fiction writer from Greensboro, Card won the Nebula and Hugo awards (1985-86) for his novel, *Speaker for the Dead,* and several other national writing awards. He is a senior editor of Compute! Books.

Tim McLaurin (1953—) The author of *Woodrow's Trumpet, Cured by Fire,* and *Lola* is a native of Fayetteville and served in the Marines and as a Peace Corps volunteer. He writes about the changing South, and the loss of Southern things that are truly valued.

T.R. Pearson (1956—) A native of Winston-Salem, Pearson invented Neely, N.C. in his first novel *A Short History of a Small Place* and revisited it in subsequent works. He finds comedy and serious meanings in the day-to-day existence of life in the rural south.

Jill McCorkle (1958—) McCorkle has produced steadily since 1984, when her novels *The Cheer Leader* and *July 7* were both published. She is a native of Lumberton who now lives in Chapel Hill.

Kaye Gibbons (1960—) Born in Nash County, her first novel was *Ellen*

Foster, published in 1987. In it, her character makes a life for herself after running away from an abusive father. Self-reliant women and their challenges are a consistent theme of her novels.

Jan Karon (? —) A Hickory native, Karon gave up an advertising career and moved to Blowing Rock to write. Her books take place in the fictional town of Mitford, and her portrayal of small town life has made her a best seller.

Margaret Maron (?—) A native of Greensboro, now a resident of Willow Spring, she won an Edgar Award for her mystery *Bootlegger's Daughter,* based in North Carolina.

The Media

There are 20 or so television stations located in the major cities of the state, representing all three of the major networks as well as the Fox network.

The public television station, WUNC-TV, originates in Chapel Hill. Translators throughout the state get the signal out to most North Carolina homes.

Several programs originate with WUNC-TV that are a great help in learning about North Carolina, among them the legislative reports when the General Assembly is in session, a news-feature program called "North Carolina Now" and a program featuring former UNC President William Friday on which he interviews North Carolinians of every stripe.

The largest newspaper in the state is the *Charlotte Observer,* which because it is so close to the line covers South Carolina as well as North.

The *Raleigh News & Observer* has the largest circulation within the state and is the paper most looked to for coverage of North Carolina state government.

Other larger papers are located in Greensboro, Winston-Salem, Wilmington, Durham and Asheville. Of these, only Durham is locally owned.

A couple of magazines have statewide audiences — *Our State* and *Business North Carolina* — and many local and regional magazines and special interest newspapers can be found in the cities and tourist areas.

Books

Bain, Robert, Flora, Joseph M. and Rubin Jr., Louis D. *Southern Writers/ A Biographical Dictionary.* 1979. Baton Rouge, LSU Press.

Foushee, Ola Maie. *Art in North Carolina/ Episodes and Developments, 1585-1970.* 1970. Chapel Hill, UNC Press.

Walser, Richard and Peacock, Mary Reynolds. *Young Readers' Picturebook of Tar Heel Authors.* 1981. Raleigh, Division of Archives and History.

Walser, Richard, and (Assisted by) Malone, E.T. Jr. *Literary North Carolina.* 1986. Raleigh, Division of Archives and History.

11

Haunts, Mysteries, Legends and Wonders

North Carolina is full of good folk tales, so many that books upon books have been written about them. Here are a handful of our favorite stories. Most North Carolinians are familiar with them and you should be too.

The Brown Mountain Lights: No one has ever been able to explain the mysterious reddish lights that sometimes glow over Brown Mountain on the Burke and Caldwell county line. At times, they just add a tinge to the sky. At other times, they seem to move, dance and divide. The lights have been written about since the early 1800s, with some saying they're caused by swamp gas, others by atmospheric reflections. To see them, two spots in McDowell County are ideal — one at a marked lookout on Jonas Ridge on NC 181; the other at Wiseman's View, just off NC 105.

The Devil's Tramping Ground: In Chatham County, near Siler City, there's a circle on the ground about 40 feet in diameter in which nothing grows and never has, at least for the 250 years or so that people have noticed it. Legend has it that the devil comes here to pace and brood at night. The site is 10 miles south of Siler City on SR1100, about a mile north of its intersection with NC 902, and is marked by a gravel pulloff.

The Maco Light: Shortly after the Civil War, train conductor Joe Baldwin was at his post at the rear of a passenger train when his car became uncoupled. As it slowed to a crawl, he was overtaken by a high-balling express. He waved his lantern back and forth, but the engineer of the express either didn't see it or couldn't react in time. Joe's car was smashed to pieces, his lantern sent arcing through the air. Joe himself was decapitated. His body, but not his head, was found and buried. Now sometimes at night, a light can be seen bobbing up

246

Tom Dula's grave near Ferguson in Wilkes County.

and down along the tracks and occasionally it will go arcing through the air. The light, they say, is Joe Baldwin's lantern carried by Joe's ghost as he looks and looks for his head.

Old Buck: A Spanish grandee, banished from his native country after being involved in a plot to overthrow the throne, packed all of his worldly goods into a galleon and set off in the mid-16th century to start a new life in America. He brought with him a magnificent bull, named Bucca, who was taken over in mid-voyage by the boisterous wandering spirit of the dragon slain by St. George several centuries before. Bucca became violent and nearly destroyed the ship, but a hurricane in the Atlantic took care of that. Passengers and crewmen were lost as the ship sank, but Bucca worked free and swam for shore with two boys, who had watered and fed him, clinging to his horns. Exhausted, he eventually made shore on Hatteras Island and went off into the woods to recover. The two boys settled with a native tribe on the island and their descendants became known as the "mustees" with blue eyes and fair hair.

247

Today, a much more placid Buck shows up each year as the residents of Rodanthe celebrate Old Christmas on January 6, which they say was the real Christmas before they started moving the calendar around back in the 1600s. To the children of these families, the appearance of Old Buck is as welcome as Santa. He does his bit, then goes back into the woods to rest.

Legend of the Dogwood: According to the Cherokees, the dogwood came to be because of the greed and meanness of a chief. The chief had four daughters and for a time was approached by interested suitors. The chief demanded they bring him gold and he would allow them to court a daughter. But when they delivered the gold, the chief disposed of them. As suspicions grew, the young men of the tribe stopped coming, and the chief's daughters grew to be old maids. The chief was mean to them and finally, the Great One punished the chief by turning him into a twisted, barren tree. But the tree was too ugly, even for the Great One, and he adorned it with a cross of delicate white flowers, one petal for each of the daughters, with a bit of the chief's ill-gotten gold at the center.

Tom Dula: Remember the old Kingston Trio tune, "Hang Down Your Head Tom Dooley"? Well, the murder that was the basis for that song took place in Wilkes County. The victim was named Laura Foster, one of two women that Tom Dula (that's the correct name) was seeing after he returned from the Civil War. The other woman was Ann Melton, Laura's cousin, whom Tom had known before the war but who had married while he was away. Anyway, Laura disappeared, and so did Tom who was pursued to Tennessee, arrested on suspicion of murder and returned to jail in Wilkesboro. When Laura's body was found, it was evident that she had been stabbed through the heart. Tom was tried and convicted and hanged on May 1, 1868. Many observers of the day believed Tom innocent, that he took the rap for Ann who killed Laura when she learned of her plans to run off with Tom.

She Done Him Wrong: Charlie Silver, said his wife, ran off with another woman and that's why neighbors didn't see him around anymore. Charlie's father didn't believe it, however, and he consulted a seer who said Charlie had been murdered. The Burke County cabin in which they had lived was searched and pieces of Charlie were found here and there — bones in the fireplace, bones near the spring, a pool of blood under the floor boards and his heart under the front steps. Poor Charlie had been done in with an axe and his wife, Frankie Silver, was charged with the murder. She never did confess. But in the Morganton jail, while awaiting her hanging date, she wrote a ballad about the murder that seemed to be an admission of guilt. After she was hanged, on June 12, 1833, Frankie's ballad worked its way into our repertoire. A later version, with Charlie's name changed to Johnnie, and the weapon now a .44 pistol, became famous as "Frankie and Johnnie." You've heard that one.

Siamese Twins: Chang and Eng were the original Siamese twins because they were born in Siam, now Thailand. They made their way to the United

States in 1829, toured with P.T. Barnum then went out on their own. But they grew tired of the grind. In their late 20s, when they were doing a show in Wilkesboro, they decided to settle in the Blue Ridge foothills and became farmers and woodcutters. At several points in their lives, they tried to get doctors to separate them, but were always told it was too risky. Chang and Eng married and had children. They built separate houses and would divide their time at each home. They were very different. Chang drank, Eng didn't. Chang was grumpy, Eng even tempered. But they both had a good sense of humor which helped them get along. Rough times came with the Civil War, and Chang and Eng went back on tour. After a trip to Europe, Chang had a stroke, and he began to drink more heavily as his health deteriorated. Finally, one morning, he died. Eng died a couple of hours later. They were 63. Chang and Eng were buried in a common grave which can be seen at the Old White Plains Baptist Church on old U.S. 601 two miles west of Mt. Airy.

Books

Carden, Gary and Anderson, Nina. *Belled Buzzards, Hucksters, and Grieving Specters/ Appalachian Tales: Strange, True & Legendary.* 1994. Asheboro, Down Home Press.

Chase, Richard. *The Jack Tales, told by R.M. Ward and his kindred in the Beech Mountain section of Western North Carolina..* 1943. Boston, Houghton-Mifflin.

Davis, Donald. *Jack Always Seeks His Fortune/ Authentic Appalachian Jack Tales.* 1992. Little Rock, August House.

Galloway, Mary Regina Ulmer (Ed.). *Aunt Mary, Tell Me a Story/ A Collection of Cherokee Legends and Tales* as told by Mary Ulmer Chiltoskey. 1992. Cherokee, NC. Cherokee Communications.

Harden, John. *The Devil's Tramping Ground and Other North Carolina Mystery Stories.* 1949. Chapel Hill, UNC Press.

Harden, John. *Tar Heel Ghosts.* 1954. Chapel Hill, UNC Press.

Roberts, Nancy. *Ghosts of the Carolinas.* 1967. Charlotte, McNally and Loftin.

West, John Foster. *Lift Up Your Head, Tom Dooley/ The True Story of the Appalachian Murder that Inspired One of America's Most Popular Ballads.* 1993. Asheboro, Down Home Press.

Whedbee, Charles Harry. *Outer Banks Mysteries and Seaside Stories.* 1978. Winston-Salem, John F. Blair.

12

Notable Crimes and Disasters

Jeffrey MacDonald: On the night of February 17, 1970, claimed Dr. Jeffrey MacDonald, a group of hippies chanting, "Acid is Groovy; kill the pigs," invaded his Fort Bragg apartment and murdered his pregnant wife and two young children.

But the jury didn't buy that. At his trial in 1979, jurors agreed with prosecutors who said MacDonald killed his wife and one of the girls in a rage, then killed the other child because she saw it. MacDonald was convicted on one count of murder in the first degree and two in the second and is still serving time.

Bitter Blood: A custody dispute ended in unbelievable horror when a North Carolina woman, her two sons, and the cousin who was her lover died as a car-bomb detonated while they were being pursued by police near Greensboro in June, 1985.

The police were after the cousin, Fritz Klenner, a gun-loving, CIA-posing son of a Reidsville doctor who had fooled his family into thinking he was going to med school. Klenner, police knew, had killed the mother and sister of the husband involved in the dispute, then had killed the parents and grandmother of his cousin, Susie Newsom Lynch, the mother of the two boys, Jim and John.

The cousins fed off each other's paranoia, and the murders were Klenner's way of removing obstacles to Susie's total control of the children. When it became apparent the game was up, Klenner apparently wired his vehicle and blew it up as police watched in horror. The case became a best-selling book, *Bitter Blood,* and a TV mini-series.

Velma Barfield: Velma Barfield was 52, a grandmother, when she was executed by lethal injection in 1984, the first woman to be put to death by the state since 1944.

She had been convicted of poisoning her fiance. She admitted also poisoning her mother and two elderly patients she had cared for as a private nurse.

After her appeals were denied, Gov. Hunt — involved in a U.S. Senate race with Jesse Helms — was pressed to grant clemency but did not.

James Jordan: The 56-year-old father of basketball star Michael Jordan was killed as he rested along a highway near Lumberton during a trip home to Charlotte from a funeral in Wilmington. His body was found floating in a creek in McColl, S.C., and his $40,000 Lexus found in woods near Fayetteville shortly after he disappeared on July 22, 1993. Two teenagers were charged. One, Larry Demery, pleaded guilty to first-degree murder and testified against his friend, Daniel Green, who was convicted and sentenced to life in prison in February, 1996.

Mine Explosion: 53 men were killed in an explosion at the Carolina Coal Mine in Coalglen, in southern Chatham County, on May 27, 1925.

Hamlet Fire: The second worst workplace disaster in North Carolina history took place in a fire at the Imperial Food Products plant in Hamlet on Sept. 3, 1991.

Exits to the plant had been locked because of the theft of chicken nuggets, and 25 people died because they were unable to get out as fire swept the plant. The fire was caused when hydraulic fluid leaking from a conveyor belt ignited in a gas-fired chicken fryer, sending a fireball through the plant.

The owner of the plant, Emmett Roe, pleaded guilty to two counts of involuntary manslaughter in 1992 and was sentenced to nearly 20 years in prison.

Air Disasters: Three major airplane crashes have been recorded in North Carolina.

July 19, 1967 — A Cessna 310 carrying three people and a Piedmont Airlines 727 with 79 on board collided in mid-air over Hendersonville shortly after takeoff from Asheville-Hendersonville airport. All 82 on board the two planes were killed, among them John T. McNaughton who had been nominated as U.S. Secretary of the Navy.

Sept. 11, 1974 — An Eastern Airlines jet crashed in woods three miles short of the airport at Charlotte, killing 72 of the 82 passengers on board. Among the dead was John Merriman, news editor for the CBS Evening News.

July 2, 1994 — A USAir jet crashed during a thunderstorm after pilots attempted to abort a landing at the Charlotte Airport. Of the 57 on board the DC9, 37 were killed.

Sea disasters: In 1951, David Stick wrote a book called *Graveyard of the Atlantic/Shipwrecks of the North Carolina Coast.* In it, he accounted for more than 600 vessels of more than 50 tons lost in the treacherous waters off the Outer Banks.

Here are a few of the most calamitous.

Home. Oct. 9, 1837. This steamboat had been drawing attention for its initial speedy runs between New York and Charleston, and an estimated 130 people had jammed aboard for its third voyage. The *Home* ran into a hurricane known as the Racer's Storm that had churned into the Gulf of Mexico, then reversed direction, crossed the Southern states and returned to the Atlantic off the North Carolina coast. The boat was taking water as it rounded Cape Hatteras. The captain attempted to beach the steamer on Ocracoke Island, but ran aground on a bar offshore. As the boat broke up, passenger and crew were tossed into the turbulent sea. Only two life preservers were on board, and 90 of those on board were lost. The toll resulted in a law that required a preserver for each person on board a vessel.

Pulaski. June 14, 1838. Another speedy packet, the *Pulaski* was steaming north out of Charleston bound for Baltimore with nearly 200 passengers and crew. The ship was about 30 miles off the coast of the New River inlet when a boiler exploded. The explosion killed a number of people and blew a hole in the vessel, which eventually broke in two. Only 59 survived, making their way to shore in lifeboats or clinging to pieces of wreckage and makeshift rafts to be picked up at sea.

Huron. Nov. 24, 1877. A U.S. Navy survey ship, the *Huron* sailed out of Hampton Roads into a gale that had most other ships staying sheltered in port. But the steamer was new, with reinforced hull, and the captain elected to follow the coastline as it moved south along the banks. As most of the 132 men on board slept, the *Huron* ran aground about 1:30 a.m. some distance offshore near Kitty Hawk. Helpless against the storm, the ship listed and took on water as wave after wave washed over her. Men trying to make their way to safe areas of the ship or to lower boats were washed away and drowned. Only 34 made it to shore. The toll of 103 dead included five in a small boat that had been launched from a rescue vessel and was attempting a landing on shore.

Train Wrecks: The 19th century's train wrecks were disasters on par with the jetliner crashes of today, and were given huge play in the nation's newspapers. But North Carolina was spared the headliner wrecks. Instead it waited until the 20th century to get on the rail accident map.

Dec. 16, 1943: An Atlantic Coast Line train derailed on tracks between Rennert and Buie near Lumberton, and a second train plowed into the wreckage after the engineer failed to see a fireman's warning signal. The death toll was 72.

Hurricanes: North Carolina's position on the Atlantic Coast makes it vulnerable during the hurricane season. In most cases, we are ready. Coastal residents know to board up their windows and evacuate the islands to safety. But occasionally, we get surprised —especially when a hurricane is so strong that its destructive forces are felt far inland — and these are the storms we remember. Here are a few:

Hazel — Oct. 15, 1954. For many years, this was the storm that we measured all others by. It came ashore at the North-South Carolina border with such force that it ranged northward as far as Canada, spreading destruction from winds and floods along its route. All told it killed 98 in the Caribbean and 249 on the continent, including 19 in North Carolina.

Camille — Aug. 17, 1969. One of the strongest hurricanes ever to hit the mainland, Camille came ashore near Biloxi, Miss., and took the back door route up the Appalachian chain into Virginia. It caused extensive flooding in the mountains.

Hugo — Sept. 22, 1989. Hugo came ashore at Charleston with 135 mph winds and was strong enough to cause major damage in the Charlotte area before spending itself in North Carolina.

Fran – Sept. 5-6, 1996. Fran came ashore at Bald Head Island and, on a nighttime jaunt over Wilmington and up I-40 to the Raleigh area, did an estimated $6.5 billion in damage and caused 22 deaths. Piers, beach houses and commercial buildings were destroyed by high winds and hurricane-driven water that flooded coastal islands. Thousands of trees, including many century oaks, were toppled by winds in Raleigh, Durham and Chapel Hill.

Floyd – Sept. 16, 1999. The worst natural disaster in state history killed 51 people, most by drowning, and caused $6 billion in damage. Floyd dumped 15-20 inches of rain across a wide area of eastern North Carolina that had been saturated 10 days earlier by rains from Hurricane Dennis. After winds subsided and the sun peeked through, things seemed to be returning to normal. Then that night, the Tar, Neuse, Roanoke, and Pamlico Rivers (and their tributaries) overran their banks and spilled over into urban areas, trapping people on the roofs of their homes and washing away roads. The waters flowed into agricultural and livestock farms, drowning millions of chickens and hundreds of thousands of pigs. Floods swept through sewage plants, contaminating the water supply in many communities. The waters finally crested as high as 24 feet above flood stage along the Tar River, where they all but erased the town of Princeville. In all 8,000 homes were destroyed and 67,000 damaged.

Floods: In July 1916, tropical storms hit western North Carolina from both directions, creating the greatest flooding in the region's history.

The rain began in Asheville on Friday night, July 7, and fell for the next four days, as a hurricane came ashore along the Gulf Coast and moved north into Illinois. By Tuesday, 3.8 inches had fallen at Asheville — more on the headwaters of the French Broad — and the river in the city was reported at nine feet above normal.

The skies were clearing and the waters abating when another storm came ashore the next weekend in South Carolina, moved over Charlotte and across the state, dumping more water on the sodden land. Again, the rain began on Friday night in Asheville and by early Sunday was flooding riverside structures. In some spots, 19 inches of rainfall were measured.

Three dams failed upstream from Asheville, and the raging water knocked bridges out along its course. In Asheville, the river crested at 22 feet above normal on Monday, as residents watched homes, warehouses and debris float by. Forty to 50 lives were lost and hundreds were left homeless.

13

Education

North Carolina's system of higher education is as old as the state's Constitution, which said that "all useful learning shall be duly encouraged and promoted in one or more universities."

In 1789, a Board of Trustees was appointed and a crossroads site at Chapel Hill was chosen for the first university, which we know today as the University of North Carolina at Chapel Hill.

The "at Chapel Hill" was added a quarter century ago during a consolidation of state-supported schools, and some of the older alumni still chafe at the "new" name.

The cornerstone of Old East on the Chapel Hill campus was laid in 1793 and Hinton James, the first student, arrived in 1795. It was the first state-supported college to open its doors in the United States and the only one to graduate students in the 18th century.

Because it had an earlier charter, folks in Georgia say that theirs is the oldest state-supported university. But the facts in the above paragraph are irrefutable, and that's what we base our case on.

Prior to the opening of UNC, students who wanted college-level studies had to find private schools or go out of state.

An attempt was made to gain a royal charter for Queen's College in Charlotte before the Revolution. The charter was never granted, but the school operated anyway under various names — the last, Liberty Hall — until Cornwallis' arrival in 1780.

The Rev. David Caldwell, a Presbyterian missionary, operated a "Log College" near Greensboro. He gave his students the equivalent of two years of college, and some went on to Princeton or, after 1795, to UNC.

The first religious institution of education for men was Davidson, established by the Presbyterians in 1837. Other denominations soon followed. The

Baptists opened Wake Forest in 1838. The same year, Methodists and Quakers opened Union School in Randolph County, which was the predecessor of Trinity College and, later, Duke University.

The first college-level training for women was offered by the Moravians at Salem College in 1802. Greensboro Female College (Methodist), St. Mary's in Raleigh (Episcopal) and Charlotte Female Institute (Presbyterian), which is today's Queen's College, were all founded in the two decades prior to the Civil War.

Enrollment during that period grew rapidly. In 1840, there were four colleges with an enrollment of about 280. In 1860, nineteen colleges were teaching a total student population of 2,400. The Civil War interrupted this growth, of course, as teachers and student-aged men went off to fight. And in the divisive Reconstruction period, UNC had to close for five years for lack of money.

The 15 years after the end of Reconstruction saw five new state-supported universities established: State Colored Normal School at Fayetteville (now Fayetteville State), the State Agricultural and Mechanical College in Raleigh (now N.C. State), the State Normal and Industrial School in Greensboro (now UNC-G), North Carolina Agricultural and Mechanical College for the Colored Race (now A&T), and the Elizabeth City Colored Normal school (now Elizabeth City State).

Denominational schools for blacks were also begun after the Civil War, among them Bennett Seminary (now Bennett College) for women in Greensboro in 1873 by the Methodist Episcopal Church and Livingstone College in Salisbury in the 1880s by the A.M.E. Zion Church.

In 1931, the state began the process of combining schools that led to the UNC consolidated system of today. Then, UNC was redefined to include the universities at Chapel Hill, Raleigh and Greensboro. It operated with one board of trustees and one president. By 1969, three more campuses had been brought under the UNC umbrella. By 1971, the 10 remaining state-supported senior institutions were included.

The 16-campus system is operated by a Board of Governors, appointed by the General Assembly, which elects a president. Each school is headed by a chancellor appointed by the Board of Governors and responsible to the UNC president. Each school also has a board of trustees, with duties delegated by the Board of Governors.

Molly Broad, the first woman president of the UNC system, was inaugurated in April, 1998. She formerly was an administrator with the California State University

Today, students who want to go to college can choose from 53 institutions, including junior colleges and a seminary. In addition, there are 58 community colleges and technical schools across the state that offer advanced training for a variety of careers and preliminary courses that can be transferred to degree-granting schools. There are also five Bible colleges to choose from.

Colleges and universities

Here is a list of the 53 colleges and universities, a brief history, and recent information on their tuition and enrollments.

Tuition figures (preceded with a "T") are for undergraduates for a full academic year and include required fees. For state-supported universities, out-of-state tuition ("OT") plus required fees is also given. Enrollment figures (Preceded by an "E") represent a total residential student headcount. All figures are for Fall, 2000, and are taken from the Stistical Abstract of Higher Education in North Carolina, 2000-01.

Appalachian State University: Boone, 28608. (828) 262-2040. Formed in 1903 as a state-supported institution in Boone on the site of Watauga Academy. For the first six years, state support of the school, known as Appalachian Training School, was given as a matching grant with a local fund drive raising half. In 1929, the name was changed to Appalachian State Teachers College. B.B. Daugherty was at the helm of the school from its founding until 1955. It joined the consolidated university system in 1967. T $1,988   OT $9,258   E 13,227.

Barber-Scotia College: Concord, 28025. (704) 786-5171. Founded in Concord as Scotia Seminary by the Presbyterian Church in 1867 to train women in education and social services. The name was changed to Scotia Women's College in 1960, then Barber-Scotia after merging with Barber Memorial of Anniston, Alabama in 1930. The next year, Barber-Scotia became a standard junior college, and in 1942 became a four-year school. It opened the doors to both sexes in 1954. T $8,700 E 543

Barton College: Wilson, 27893. (252) 399-6300. Formerly Atlantic Christian College. Established in 1902 in Wilson by the North Carolina Christian Missionary Convention, which had purchased the Kinsey Seminary the previous year. T $11,462 E 1,202

Belmont Abbey College: Belmont, 28012. (704) 825-6700. Opened in 1978 as St. Mary's College by the Roman Catholic Church, who sent monks of the Order of St. Benedict down to Belmont from Latrobe, Pa. The name was changed to Belmont Abbey in 1913, became a junior college in 1928 and a senior college in 1952. T $12,713 E 917

Bennett College: Greensboro, 27401-3239. (336) 273-4431. Founded in 1873 as Bennett Seminary on Greensboro property purchased by freed slaves and named for one of its early benefactors, Lyman Bennett, who died during a fund-raising drive. The school was operated by the Freedmen's Aid and Southern Education Society of the Methodist Episcopal Church. In 1926, Bennett was reorganized as a college for black women under the joint operation of the Methodist Episcopal church and the Women's Home Missionary Society. T $9,222 E 619

Brevard College: Brevard, 28712. (828) 883-8292. Junior college. An outgrowth of Brevard Institute, founded by Methodist Rev. and Mrs. Fitch Taylor to educate mountain young people, and bolstered by the merger of two other Methodist schools, Rutherford College and Weaver College. T $12,175 E 710

Campbell University: Buies Creek, 27506. (910) 893-1200. Established in 1927 as a junior college and named after J.A. Campbell, who nurtured Buies Creek Academy for 40 prosperous years before the property was sold to the Baptist State Convention. In 1962, Baptists made the school a four-year, coeducational college. T $11,548 E 3,490

Catawba College: Salisbury, 28144-2488. (704) 637-4111. Founded in Newton in 1851 by the Reformed Church as a school for men. The college became co-ed in 1880. It was moved to its present campus in Salisbury in 1922. T $13,330 E 1,342

Chowan College: Murfreesboro, 27855. (252) 398-4101. Opened in 1848 as Chowan Baptist Female Institute. Its name was changed in 1911 and operated as a junior college except from 1943 to 1949, when World War II caused a shortage of students. It changed to a four-year school in 1992. T $11,870 E 774

Davidson College: Davidson, 28036. (704) 892-2000. Organized in 1837 by a group of Presbyterian laymen and named for Gen. William Lee Davidson, a patriot killed during the Revolutionary War. It was one of two Southern schools to remain open during the Civil War. Its growth was spurred when in 1925 it became a yearly recipient of money from the Duke Endowment. T $23,095 E 1,679

Duke University: Durham, 27706. (919) 684-8111. Formed as Trinity College in 1850 as an outgrowth of Union Institute, a Methodist-Quaker school established at what is now Trinity, near High Point. It was moved to Durham in 1892 and renamed after James B. Duke, the tobacco magnate, who endowed the institution. A Women's College was formed in 1925. T $25,630 E 12,176

East Carolina University: 103 Spilman Building, Greenville, 27853-4353. (252) 328-6212. Begun in Greenville in 1907 as a co-ed school to educate teachers. It became a four-year school in 1920 and was made one of the regional universities in 1967. T $2,257 OT $10,120 E 18,750

Elizabeth City State University: Parkview Dr., P.O. Box 10, Elizabeth City, 27909 (252) 335-3230. Established by the legislature in 1892 as a training school for blacks and named Elizabeth City Colored Normal and Industrial Institute. It became a four-year teachers college in 1937 and one of the state's regional universities in 1969. T $1,686 OT $8,104 E 2,035

Elon College: Elon College, 27244-2010. (800) 334-8448. Established in 1890 as a four-year co-ed Christian college near Burlington by the Southern Christian Convention. Denominational mergers have put the college under the domain of the United Church of Christ. T $13,781 E 4,138

Fayetteville State University: Fayetteville, 28302. (910) 486-1141. Begun in 1877 when the General Assembly voted to support Howard School in Fayetteville and changed its name to State Colored Normal School. Floated for 30 years until present campus was purchased. Became a four-year school in 1939. T $1,620 OT $8,890 E 4,487

Gardner-Webb University: Boiling Springs, 28017. (704) 434-2361. Begun by Baptists as a Christian high school, then became a two-year college in 1928. Became a four-year school in 1969. T $11,780 E 3,194

Greensboro College: Greensboro, 27401-1875. (336) 272-7102. Chartered in 1838 as Greensboro Female College and built upon a school for girls established in 1833 by a Methodist Minister. Its main building burned during the Civil War, and its classes were held in other towns. It was merged with Davenport College of Lenoir in 1938 and became coeducational in 1956. T $12,780 E 973

Guilford College: Greensboro, 27410. (336) 316-2000. Founded in 1837 as New Garden Boarding School and became a four-year college affiliated with the Quakers under its present name in 1888. It is the oldest co-ed college in the South and was one of the few to remain open through the Civil War. T $16,815 E 1,255

High Point University: High Point, 27261. (336) 841-9000. Dates itself to 1856 with the founding of Yadkin College by the Methodist church. Yadkin was closed in 1924 in favor of a new campus at High Point. T $12,440 E 2,788

Johnson C. Smith University: Charlotte, 28216-5398. (704) 378-1000. Organized in Charlotte in 1867 by the Presbyterian Church and named Biddle Memorial Institute after an early benefactor. Renamed in 1922 for a Pittsburgh man whose widow provided an endowment and funded the construction of several buildings. T $11,605 E 1,576

Lees-McRae College: Banner Elk, 28604. (828) 898-5241. Founded in 1900 on site of a Presbyterian day school, with its first teacher a Mrs. Elizabeth McRae. Its motto is "In the Mountains, of the Mountains, and for the Mountains." T $11,340 E 713

Lenoir Rhyne College: Hickory, 28603. (828) 328-1741. Opened as Lenoir College in 1891 on a campus in Hickory that was a gift of a Capt. Walter Lenoir. The Evangelical Lutheran Synod sponsored the school in 1895. In 1923, the school added to its name in honor of D.E. Rhyne who provided a large endowment. T $13,356 E 1,439

Livingstone College: Salisbury, 28144. (704) 638-5500. Opened in 1880 in a parsonage in Concord, the school, established to teach black men self-reliance, moved to Salisbury in 1882. It was named after David Livingstone, the missionary and explorer, and became a college in 1885 under the sponsorship of the A.M.E. Zion church. T $8,820 E 1,018

Louisburg College: Louisburg, 27549. (919) 496-2521. Traces its beginning to Franklin Academy, chartered in 1787, which became coed in 1813. Through several closures and fires, the Louisburg institution has survived and is today a standard junior college sponsored by the Methodist church. T $9,300 E 543

Mars Hill College: Mars Hill, 28754. (828) 689-1111. Opened in Mars Hill by mountain settlers in 1856 as the French Broad Baptist Institute and chartered by the state under its present name three years later. Became a four-year school in 1962 under the auspices of the N.C. Baptist State Convention. Its Community Development Institute, which combines academics and community betterment, has been nationally recognized. T $12,800 E 1,219

Meredith College: Raleigh, 27607-5298. (919) 829-8600. Opened in 1899 as Baptist Female University, renamed in 1909 after Thomas Meredith, 19th century advocate of a female seminary. Moved from downtown to a campus west of Raleigh in 1926. T $9,840 E 2,595

Methodist College: Fayetteville, 28301. (910) 630-7000. Opened in 1960 after the Methodist church accepted a 600-acre tract and $2 million offer from Fayetteville citizens to start a four-year college. The campus has been recognized for its architecture. T $13,340 E 2,134

Montreat-Anderson College: Montreat, 28757. (828) 669-8011. Opened in 1916 as Montreat Normal School on the grounds of the General Assembly of the Presbyterian Church at Montreat. It became Montreat-Anderson in 1959 in honor of Mr. and Mrs. R.C. Anderson, school official and principal benefactor. T $11,730 E 1,203

Mt. Olive College: Mt. Olive, 28365. (919) 658-2502. Opened as Mount Allen College in 1952 by the Free Will Baptist State Convention at the denomination's assembly grounds at Cragmont, near Asheville. Moved to Mount Olive and renamed in 1956. Its present campus was begun in 1964. T $9,100 E 1,026

N.C. Agricultural and Technical State University: 312 N. Dudley St., Greensboro, 27411. (336) 334-7940. Established by the legislature as the agricultural and mechanical school for blacks in 1891. Classes were held at Shaw University until 1893 when the first buildings were ready on its Greensboro campus, the site for which was donated by several citizens. The school was given its "A&T" name in 1915. It awarded its first master's degree in 1941 and graduated its first School of Nursing graduates in 1957. It was made a part of the regional university system in 1967. T $1,939 OT $9,209 E 7,748

N.C. Central University: P.O. Box 19617, Shepard Station, Durham, 27707. (919) 560-6104. Founded in 1909 by Dr. James E. Shepard as a private school, the National Religious Training School and Chautauqua. It received state support in 1923 and was renamed North Carolina College for Negroes with a mission to educate teachers and principals for black schools. Graduate degrees were authorized in 1939 and a Law School opened in 1940. It joined the regional university system in 1969 under its current name. T$1,975 OT $9,245 E 5,476

N.C. School of the Arts: 200 Waughton St., P.O. Box 12189, Winston-Salem, 27117-2189. (336) 770-3200. Opened in 1965 on a renovated, former high school campus in Winston-Salem. Its first president was Vittorio Giannini, a prime mover behind the idea who picked up the support of Gov. Terry Sanford, the arts community and, finally, the legislature. The school for the performing arts accepts students from junior high through college in five areas: academics, dance, drama, music and design and production. The school is supported by the state in combination with private funds. T $2,592 OT $11,220 768

N.C. State University: P.O. 7001, Raleigh, 27695-7001. (919) 515-2191. Opened in 1889 as the state's school for agriculture and technology. As one of the nation's "land grant" colleges, it received federal support to operate as part of the national agricultural experiment station and extension service systems. It is the state's primary institution for teaching agriculture, engineering, design and forest resources. T $2,814 OT $11,980 E 28,619

N.C. Wesleyan College: Rocky Mount, 27804. (252) 985-5100. Opened in 1960 as a liberal arts college on a new campus in Rocky Mount. Support for the school was shared by citizens of Nash and Edgecombe counties and the North Carolina Conference of the Methodist Church. T $9,236 E 894

Peace College: Raleigh, 27604. (919) 832-2881. School for women established by the Presbyterian Synod and named for William Peace, who donated the Raleigh campus and money to start construction. Civil War and Reconstruction delayed the opening until 1872. The junior college came under the auspices of the First Presbyterian Church of Raleigh in 1969. T $9,924 E 603

Pfeiffer College: Misenheimer, 28109. (704) 463-1360. Established in Misenheimer in 1910 after moving from Lenoir, and had various names in honor of early benefactors. It was named Pfeiffer Junior College in 1935 after Mrs. Henry Pfeiffer of New York City, who gave the school money for five new buildings. It became a four-year college in 1954. T $11,380 E 1,496

Queens College: Charlotte, 28274-0001. (704) 337-2200. With breaks in service and through several name changes, a link can be made to Queens College established during Gov. Tryon's administration in 1771. Offically, the school traces its origin to 1857 as Charlotte Female Institute, a Presbyterian liberal arts school for women. It became Queen's College in 1912 and was moved to its present campus in 1914. T $10,680 E 1,596

St. Andrews College: Laurinburg, 28352. (910) 276-3652. Opened on a new campus in 1961, it consolidated Flora MacDonald College in Red Springs and Presbyterian Junior College in Maxton. T $14,235 E 515

St. Augustine's College: Raleigh, 27610. (919) 516-4000. Founded in 1867 in Raleigh as a normal school and college for blacks by the Freedmen's Commission of the Protestant Episcopal Church and a group from the North Carolina Diocese. The school evolved into a junior college and, by the early '30s, a degree-granting institution. T $7,900 E 1,465

Salem College: Winston-Salem, 27108. (336) 721-2600. Begun in 1722 by the Moravians as Salem Female Academy, a day school. It survived the Revolutionary War and the Civil War, and today is a four-year college in Winston-Salem, with Salem Academy, a college prep school as an offshoot. T $14,205 E 1,027

Shaw University: Raleigh, 27611. (919) 546-8200. Begun in 1865 as Raleigh Institute for theological study, and became Shaw College in 1872 in honor of benefactor Elijah Shaw. Today, Shaw University operates with income from endowment and trust funds and from various Baptist sources. T $7,430 E 2,527

Southeastern Seminary: Box 1889, Wake Forest, 27588-1889. (919) 556-3101. Opened in 1951 by the Southern Baptist Convention to train theologians, it occupies the campus vacated by Wake Forest when it moved to Winston-Salem. T $1,360 E 1,858

UNC-Asheville: Asheville, 28804-3299. (828) 251-6500. Developed from Asheville-Biltmore College, a junior college supported by the City of Asheville and Buncombe County. It was given state support in 1955, and two years later became the first community college. A new campus opened in 1961. The school received four-year accreditation in 1967, and became part of the regional university system in 1969. T $1,993 OT $8,839 E 3,292

UNC-Chapel Hill: 103 South Building, Campus Box 9100, Chapel Hill, 27599. (919) 962-1365. Chartered in 1789 and opened six years later, the university has operated since, with the exception of five years during Reconstruction. Classes in law were begun in 1845, with medical and pharmaceutical studies starting in 1879. Women were first admitted in 1897. T $2,710 OT $11,876 E 24,892

UNC Charlotte: UNCC Station, Charlotte, 28223. (704) 547-2201. Started in 1946 by UNC to give returning veterans of World War II the first two years of college. It was then taken over by the city as a community college, and received state support again in 1957. In the early '60s, it occupied a new, 1,000-acre campus and began offering four-year degrees. It was made part of the consolidated university in 1965. T $2,134 OT $9,404 E 17,241

UNC-Greensboro: 1000 Spring Garden St., Greensboro, 27412. (336) 334-5266. Established in 1891 as the first state-supported university for women largely after acrusade by Charles D. McIver. It was opened on a 10-acre site in Greensboro as the State Normal and Industrial College. It became the Woman's College of UNC in 1931, and UNCG in 1963. Male students were first accepted in 1964. T $2,309 OT $10,763 E 13,125

The Old Well, South Building at the University of North Carolina at Chapel Hill, probably around 1880.

UNC-Pembroke: College St., Pembroke, 28372. (910) 521-6201. Established by the state in 1887 as a normal school for the Indians of Robeson County. Over the years, elementary, then high school classes were eliminated and in 1940, the first college degrees were awarded. That year, the school became known as Pembroke State College for Indians. It became one of the state's regional universities in 1967. T $1,860 OT $9,130 E 3,445

UNC-Wilmington: 601 South College Rd., Wilmington, 28403-3297. (910) 395-3630. Established as Wilmington College in 1947 with county support. It was accredited as a junior college in 1952, then began receiving state support as a community college in 1958. Its first four-year degrees were awarded in 1965, and it was made part of the UNC system in 1969.
T $2,360 OT $9,710 E 10,100

Wake Forest University: Winston-Salem, 27109. (336) 759-5000. Founded in 1834 by the Baptist State Convention in Wake Forest, near Raleigh. It opened a law school in 1894, a school of medicine in 1902 and a graduate school of business in 1969. To become eligible for an annual grant from the Z. Smith Reynolds Foundation, the school moved to its Winston-Salem campus in 1956. T $22,410 E 6,173

Warren Wilson College: Asheville, 28815-9000. (828) 298-3325. Established as a high school and junior college in 1942 in Swannanoa by combining Asheville Farm School for boys and Dorland-Bell School for girls, both started by the Presbyterian Church in the 1890s. It was named for a national church official. The school began offering degrees in 1968, and reserves a large portion of its enrollment for overseas students. T $14,375 E 799

Western Carolina University: Cullowhee, 28723. (828) 227-7100. Founded in Cullowhee in 1889 as a high school, and became Cullowhee Normal and Industrial School with some state funding in 1905. It became a junior college in 1912 and a four-year school in 1929 as Western Carolina Teachers College. It was made part of the regional university system in 1967. T $2,102 OT $9,372 E 6,699

Wingate University: Campus Box 3001, Wingate, 28174. (704) 298-3325. Established by the Union Baptist Association in 1897 and operated as a high school, then as a junior college and today is a four-year school, still associated with the Baptists. T $13,050 E 1,283

Winston-Salem State University: Winston-Salem, 27110. (336) 750-2041. Founded as Slater Industrial Academy in 1892, and charted by the state as Winston-Salem Teachers College in 1925. Adoted its current name in 1969 and joined the UNC system in 1972. T $1,805 OT $8,223 E 2,857

Community colleges and technical schools

In 1957, the Community College Act opened the way for a system of junior colleges and technical schools that offer vocational, technical and college parallel programs. Communities set up fund-raising drives and used their ingenuity to find local land and buidings for campuses. With local and state support, 58 of these schools now exist across North Carolina. Young people have more ways to enter college through this program and adults can continue their educations more easily.

Here is a list of the community colleges and how to reach them. Most operate on a quarterly system and will be glad to send you course schedules once they have been prepared.

Tuition for all of the schools in the community college system in 1994-95 was $557 for in-state students and $4,515 for out-of-state students.

Alamance Community College: P.O. Box 8000, Graham, 27523. (336) 578-2002.

Anson Community College: P.O. Box 126, Polkton, 28135. (704) 272-7635.

Asheville-Buncombe Technical Community College: 340 Victoria Rd., Asheville, 28801. (828) 254-1921.

Beaufort County Community College: P.O. Box 1069, Washington, 27889. (252) 946-6194.

Bladen Community College: P.O. Box 266, Dublin, 28332. (910) 862-2164.

Blue Ridge Community College: Flat Rock, 28731. (828) 692-3572.

Brunswick Community College: P.O. Box 30, Supply, 28462. (910) 754-6900.

Caldwell Community College and Technical Institute: 1000 Hickory Blvd., Hudson, 28638. (828) 726-2200.

Cape Fear Community College: 411 N. Front St., Wilmington, 28401. (910) 251-5100.

Carteret Community College: 3505 Arendell St., Morehead City, 28557. (252) 247-6000.

Catawba Valley Community College: Rt. 3, Box 283, Hickory, 28602. (828) 327-7000.

Central Carolina Community College: 1105 Kelly Dr., Sanford, 27330. (919) 775-5401.

Central Piedmont Community College: P.O. Box 35009, Charlotte, 28235. (704) 330-6719.

Cleveland Community College: 137 South Post Rd., Shelby, 28150. (704) 484-4000.

Coastal Carolina Community College: 444 Western Blvd. Jacksonville, 28546. (910) 455-1221.

College of the Albemarle: P.O. Box 2327, Elizabeth City, 27909. (252) 335-0821.

Craven Community College: 800 College Court, New Bern, 28562. (252) 638-4131.

Davidson County Community College: P.O. Box 1287, Lexington, 27292. (704) 249-8186.

Durham Technical Community College: P.O. Drawer 11307, Durham, 27703. (919) 686-3300.

Edgecomb Community College: 2009 W. Wilson St. Tarboro, 27886. (252) 823-5166.

Fayetteville Technical Community College: P.O. Box 35236, Fayetteville, 28303. (910) 678-8400.

Forsyth Technical Community College: 2100 Silas Creek Parkway, Winston-Salem, 27103-5197. (336) 723-0371.

Gaston College: 201 Highway 321 South, Dallas, 28034. (704) 922-6200.

Guilford Technical Community College: P.O. Box 309, Jamestown, 27282. (336) 334-4822.

Halifax Commmunity College: P.O. Drawer 809, Weldon, 27890. (252) 536-2551.

Haywood Community College: Freedlander Drive, Clyde, 28721. (828) 627-2821.

Isothermal Community College: P.O. Box 804, Spindale, 28160. (828) 286-3636.

James Sprunt Community College: P.O. Box 398, Kenansville, 28349-0398. (910) 296-1341.

Johnston Community College: P.O. Box 2350, Smithfield, 27577. (919) 934-3051.

Lenoir Community College: P.O. Box 188, Kinston, 28501. (252) 527-6223.

Martin Community College: Kehukee Park Road, Williamston, 27892. (252) 792-1521.

Mayland Community College: P.O. Box 547, Spruce Pine, 28777. (828) 765-7351.

McDowell Technical Community College: Route 1, Box 170, Marion, 28752. (828) 652-6021.

Mitchell Community College: West Broad Street, Statesville, 28677. (704) 878-3200.

Montgomery Community College: P.O. Box 787, Troy, 27371. (910) 576-6222.

Nash Community College: P.O. Box 7488, Old Carriage Road, Rocky Mount, 27804-7488. (252) 443-4011.

Pamlico Community College: Highway 306 South, Grantsboro, 28529. (252) 249-1851.

Piedmont Community College: P.O. Box 1197, Roxboro, 27572. (336) 599-1181.

Pitt Community College: P.O. Drawer 7007, Greenville, 27834. (252) 321-4200.

Randolph Community College: P.O. Box 1009, Asheboro, 27204-1009. (336) 633-0200.

Richmond Community College: P.O. Box 1189, Hamlet, 28345. (910) 582-7000.

Roanoke-Chowan Community College: Route 2, Box 46-A, Ahoskie, 27910. (252) 332-5921.

Robeson Community College: P.O. Box 1420, Lumberton, 28359. (910) 738-7101.

Rockingham Community College: Wentworth, 27375. (336) 342-4261.

Rowan-Cabarrus Community College: P.O. Box 1595, Salisbury, 28144. (704) 637-0760.

Sampson Community College: P.O. Drawer 318, Clinton, 28328. (910) 592-8081.

Sandhills Community College: 2200 Airport Doad, Pinehurst, 28374. (910) 692-6185.

Southeastern Community College: P.O. Box 151, Whiteville, 28472. (910) 642-7141.

Southwestern Community College: 275 Webster Rd., Sylva, 28779. (828)

586-4091.

Stanly Community College: Rt. 4, Box 55, Albemarle, 28001. (704) 982-0121.

Surry Community College: P.O. Box 304, Dobson, 27017. (336) 386-8121.

Tri-County Community College: P.O. Box 40, Murphy, 28906. (828) 837-6810.

Vance-Granville Community College: Box 917, Henderson, 27536. (919) 492-2061.

Wake Technical Community College: 9101 Fayetteville Rd., Raleigh, 27603. (919) 662-3400.

Wayne Community College: Caller Box 8002, Goldsboro, 27533-8002. (919) 735-5151.

Western Piedmont Community College: 1001 Burkemont Ave., Morganton, 28655. (828) 438-6000.

Wilkes Community College: P.O. Box 120, Wilkesboro, 28697. (336) 838-6100.

Wilson Technical Community College: P.O. Box 4035-Woodard Station, Wilson, 27893. (252) 291-1195.

Bible Colleges

Heritage Bible College: P.O. Box 1628, Dunn, 28335. (910) 892-4268.

John Wesley College: 2314 N. Centennial St., High Point, 27265. (336) 889-2262.

Piedmont Bible College: 716 Franklin St., Winston-Salem, 27101-5197. (336) 725-8344.

Roanoke Bible College: 714 First Street, Elizabeth City, 27909. (252) 338-5191.

Winston-Salem Bible College: Box 777, Winston-Salem, 27102. (336) 744-0900.

Public schools

As with most states, every school-age child who lives in North Carolina has the right to go to a public school.

This will tell you basically how to get your child enrolled and tell you a bit about the public school system.

The state requires students to go to school for 180 days, but it leaves the calendar to the discretion of local school boards across the state. So you have to check the local papers or call the school office to find out when school starts.

A child must reach five years old on or before Oct. 16 of the year in which he or she is enrolled. The first year is the kindergarten year. Proof of a child's birth date must be provided at enrollment. A child also needs proof of immunization against diphtheria, tetanus, whooping cough, polio, mumps, and red and German measles.

The state has a compulsory attendance law which requires a student to attend school until the 16th birthday. The state is phasing in end-of-grade test standards that must be met before a child can be promoted. The new standards take effect for 5th graders in 2000-01, for 3rd and 8th graders in 2001-02. To graduate, high school students must pass a computer skills test beginning in 2001 and and an essential skills test beginning in 2005.

Children may attend approved private schools or, if properly registered, can be taught at home. In addition, there about 100 charter schools across the state.

14

Motor Vehicle Registrations

Driver's Licenses

Within 60 days of becoming a permanent resident, you are supposed to get a North Carolina driver's license.

With nearly 150 licensing offices in the state, there is one within a short drive of just about anyplace you live. To find it, look up "North Carolina, State Of" in the phone book and run your finger down to Driver's License Office. Or just ask someone. Most everyone knows the location.

If you were licensed to drive in another state, getting your North Carolina license is a fairly simple matter. A road skills test is generally waived for already licensed drivers.

But you will have to take a multiple choice written test, a road sign recognition test and a vision test. To bone up for the written and road sign tests, each office has a Driver's Handbook that you can borrow. It contains everything you need to know, including practice questions.

Although it's not always necessary, you can make an appointment to take the test when you pick up the handbook.

Bring with you your old license, cash to pay for your new license (they won't take a check or credit card) and, if you own a car, Form DL-123 from your insurance company that proves you have auto insurance. You must also provide a document that includes your Social Security number.

North Carolina is establishing a five-year license renewal plan, so your new license will be good for the number of years (with a minumum of three) that gets you to an age divisible by five. For instance, if you are 28, your new license will be good for 7 years so that you can renew at age 35. The cost for the license is $2.50 a year, so for 7 years you would need to pay $17.50.

This is not official, but long-time North Carolinians know that you can miss four questions on the written exam and still pass. You should study, but don't worry too much about it.

After you've taken the written exam, you're shown to a machine where your vision is checked as well as your ability to recognize highway sign shapes and colors. If your vision is not at least 20/40 in each eye, you'll have to wear corrective lenses to drive.

If you do have to take a road test, you must take it in your own car.

Your reward for all this is a plastic-laminated license with one of those awful mug shots taken moments before just as your face twitched.

Exceptions: First-time license applicants must bring two forms of identification, with at least one showing a date of birth, and will have to take the driving test. Those 16 or 17 must have their applications signed by a parent or guardian and certify that they've passed a driver education course.

If you are 16 or 17 and have a license from a state that does not require a driver education course, that won't do here. You have to take the driving course. But you can get a temporary permit until you take it.

Fees and requirements vary for licenses: for taxis, buses and commercial trucks, for example.

North Carolina has adopted a Graduated Licensing plan for drivers under 18.

Fifteen-year-olds who have taken a driver education course and pass the written, signs and vision test, qualify for a Level One Limited Learner Permit. For the first six months, driving is limited to 5 a.m. to 9 p.m. while accompanied by a supervising driver.

At 16 and after holding the Level One permit for 12 months, a Level Two permit can be obtained if there have been no moving violations within the preceding six months. A supervising driver must be present except between 5 a.m. to 9 p.m., or unless the licensee is driving directly to and from work.

After six months at Level Two and if there are no moving violations, a driver is eligible for a Level Three Provisional License until turning 18. This differs from a conventional license primarily in that a provisional licensee cannot drive after or while consuming alcohol or drugs.

A new law is in effect to discourage high school dropouts. Driver license applicants under 18 must have a "driving eligibility certificate", high school diploma or its equivalent to be eligible for a North Carolina driving permit or license. The certificate must be signed by the applicant's school administrator who certifies that the applicant is enrolled in school or that substantial hardship would be placed on the applicant or family if he does not receive a driver license.

The license of anyone under 18 will be revoked if it is notified by school authorities that the person is no longer eligible for a certificate. This revocation remains in effect until the person's 18th birthday or until the required standards are met and a driving eligibility certificate is obtained.

Also, if a student is suspended for more than 10 consecutive days or is assigned to an alternative educational setting due to disciplinary action for more than 10 consecutive days, he must give up his driver's license.

Motorcycle riders must have an endorsement stamped on their driver's license. This requires an extra written test and on-cycle skills test. The endorsement costs an extra $1.25 a year.

Some rules of the road

North Carolina's laws may vary a bit from those in the state where you're used to driving.

It is a "right-on-red" state, which means you can turn right after stopping at a red light and determining that no traffic is coming. You can do this at any light unless there is a sign specifically prohibiting it.

If the level of alcohol in your blood exceeds 0.08 percent, you can be charged with Driving While Impaired. At minimum, you will lose your license for a year if convicted (and 92 percent are in this state), with no restricted driving privileges for at least 30 days. A second DWI will result in losing your license for four years. Also, if you refuse to take a breathalyzer test the results are the same as if you'd been convicted.

You do not have to call the police to the scene of an accident unless the total damage is $1,000 or more. Of course, at today's body repair rates, that's not a great deal of damage. But, if you decide to deal with it without police, you should swap this information with the other drivers involved: name, address, driver's license number, auto registration number and name of insurance company.

Drivers and all passengers in the front seat must be wearing seat belts and shoulder straps. All children under 12 must be buckled up, with those under four in special seats.

If you are using your windshield wipers, you must have on your headlights.

Motorcycle riders must wear helmets and shine their headlights whenever they are traveling on the road.

Like most states, North Carolina has a point system to keep track of a driver's traffic violations. Points range from one for littering to five for passing a stopped school bus. Most violations, such as speeding, running red lights or stops signs, etc. are assessed three points.

If you accumulate seven points during a three-year period, you're likely to be sent to a Driver Improvement Clinic, which costs $25. After you've completed the course, three points are subtracted. If you collect 12 points in the three-year period, your license can be suspended for 60 days.

Your license can also be suspended for periods ranging from 30 days to permanently. Speeding more than 15 miles per hour in a 55 mph or higher zone can get you the 30 day suspension, while permanent revocation can result for a third conviction for driving while impaired or a conviction for manslaughter while driving impaired.

Twice, since 1966, prosecutors in North Carolina have obtained first degree murder convictions against drunken drivers who caused accidents resulting in deaths. Both defendants are serving mandatory life sentences.

These are some of the highlights of North Carolina's rules of the road. All of this and much more is covered in the Driver's Handbook.

Vehicle registration

Within 30 days of moving to North Carolina, or of getting a job here, you also must register your vehicle and get a state license tag. For this, you have to prove two things: that you own the car and that you have insurance coverage.

You need only certify that you have insurance by signing a document naming your insurance company and giving the policy number.

The state will check this, and insurance companies are required to notify the state if your insurance lapses. If that happens, you are subject to a fine and to having your tag seized.

For new, unregistered vehicles, the tag office requires a Manufacturer's Certificate of Origin, properly assigned, and a bill of sale showing price and trade-in credit.

For new or used vehicles already registered, the owner must produce his certificate of title. If the title is owned by a lienholder, the owner must provide evidence of this and his registration to get a tag.

Some states are classified as non-title states because in certain circumstances —say, for older vehicles— no proof of purchase is required to get a plate. North Carolina isn't that easy. If your car was registered under those circumstances, you must have notarized paperwork establishing a chain of ownership to you before you can get a tag. Bills of sale or papers showing three consecutive years of registration will generally do.

On all vehicles 10 years old and newer an Odometer Disclosure Form is required ao that the new buyer will have documented evidence as to how far the car has been driven. Some federally approved forms have a box for odometer readings, and in this case the separate form is not required.

The state's title fee is $35. A 3-percent Highway Use Tax of not more than $1,500 is charged on all new and used vehicle sales, the taxable amount being the purchase price, or book value, less the trade-in.

New residents must pay a Highway Use Tax of up to $150 to register their cars in North Carolina.

In addition, there are fees for registering your car and for your license tag. Fees vary over a wide range, depending on the kind of title work needed and for the kind of vehicles registered.

Unlike the Driver's License Office, the state offices handling registration and license tags will take checks as well as cash. But you will need two forms of identification.

When you register your vehicle, you will get a state registration card, a metal license plate with letters and numbers, as usual, and two stickers — one for the month and one for the year. You will need to update your registration and get a new sticker for your tag each year. For passenger cars, the cost for this is $20.

Our license tags, by the way, picture the Wright Brothers plane that first flew at Kitty Hawk in 1903 as it soars over a waving line of sea oats. The motto "First in Flight" and the name of our state also appear on the tag.

You can also get tag with some college names on them for $25.

And, if you want, you can get a personalized tag for $20 extra. You can choose any 8 letters, numbers or punctuation marks for your tag.

It used to be that all license tags in North Carolina expired in February. There were long lines at the tag counters and long waits as the deadline approached. Today, the expirations occur monthly according to the date you first register your vehicle. Procrastinators don't have the problem they once did.

The license tag office is another one that almost all people know, so you can usually ask around for its location. Or, you can look under "North Carolina, State of" again and run your finger down to License Plate Agency for the location.

One more thing. When you register, the Department of Motor Vehicles forwards that registration to the county tax office where you live, so that the county can send you a property tax bill on your vehicle. If you don't pay this, the county can block you from registering your car next time around.

Insurance

North Carolina requires every vehicle to be registered and insured for liability insurance. Proof of insurance is necessary to register a vehicle.

Minimum liability limits are:

$25,000 for bodily injuries to each person,

$50,000 for bodily injuries in each accident,

$15,000 for property damage.

With medical costs and the price of vehicles as they are, car owners might consider getting more coverage.

If you lease a vehicle, most dealers will require that you raise the coverage to $100,000/$300,000/$50,000 for the above categories.

Automobile insurance is priced using base rates times factors based on points, which are assigned after conviction of road violations. Refer to the driver's license section for a rundown of the points system.

If drivers have a reasonable driving record, if there are no youthful drivers in the household, or if a high-powered car isn't involved, insurance companies will generally insure voluntarily — each company has different rules.

If, after shopping around, you can't find a company to insure you, there is a way out. Because it requires drivers to be insured, the state developed a North Carolina Reinsurance Facility to cover the uninsurable. Individual companies write the insurance, but cede the risk to the NCRF, which is funded by law through premium assessments based on the market share of the different companies. This is called the assigned risk plan. Rates are higher and the coverage is more limited. You can't get collision through the facility.

Auto insurance rates in North Carolina are low, according to a 1994 study by the National Association of Independent Insurors. At the time, North Carolina ranked 42nd among the states in the cost of auto insurance. Why? The study also showed that the state ranked 48th in the number of uninsured drivers, 44th in hospital room charges, 38th in auto thefts, 37th in average payment for injuries and 33rd in average household income. It also is low in relation of lawyers to citizens. Nationally, there was a lawyer for every 340 people. In North Carolina the average was one lawyer for every 800 citizens. Don't let this get out.

Inspections

Now that you have your driver's license, your registration card and license tag, you need to do one more thing: that is to have your vehicle inspected.

A lot of service stations, garages and auto dealerships can do this. The business just needs to be certified by the state and will display a sign that designates it an Official North Carolina Vehicle Inspection Station.

Inspections items include: brakes, lights, horn, steering mechanism, windshield wipers, turn signals, tires, rear view mirrors, exhaust system and window tint. The cost for this is $9.25.

In nine counties, an emissions inspection is required along with the vehicle inspection. This costs an extra $19.40, and applies to any non-diesel-powered vehicles, model 1975 or newer. The counties are Cabarrus, Durham, Forsyth, Gaston, Guilford, Mecklenberg, Orange, Union and Wake.

If your vehicle passes the required inspections, you will get a color-coded sticker for the lower left corner of your windshield that gives the month and year that your next inspection is due. That way, if you happen to forget your inspection deadline, a law enforcement officer can remind you.

15

Taxes

To all of you newcomers, allow us to extend our hand in friendship and to give you a warning.

Right behind us will come the State of North Carolina, and in many cases the counties, also extending their hands — for whatever tax money they can get.

Whether you have come to North Carolina to live permanently or just to pay a visit, you must sooner or later face the grim reality of taxation.

If you've just come for a visit and happen to go shopping, you'll have to pay sales tax. If you spend the night, there usually will be a room tax. If you're just passing through and happen to gas up, well that will be a pretty stiff gasoline tax, please.

Resident, part-time resident or non-resident, if you earn money in North Carolina or from property or a business in North Carolina, you'll have to pay an income tax. And if you are living here, there's property tax too.

Tax information contained in this chapter was based on rates in effect as of October, 2001.

The income tax

This chapter is to acquaint you with our tax structure in a very general way. The state publishes instructions for filing income taxes each year. Certainly, complicated tax questions should be directed to the state tax information line or to an accountant.

Tax lines are open 8 a.m.-5 p.m. Monday through Friday. To order tax forms, call (919) 715-0397. For other questions call (919) 733-4684.

In general, if you are a resident of the state you must file a state income tax form. If you are a part-time or non-resident and had North Carolina earnings, you must file. If you are married and filed a joint U.S. tax return, you must also file a joint state return.

Taxes are due on April 15, the same day federal returns are due.

Income levels required for filing range from $5,500 for a single person and $10,000 for married couples filing a joint return to $6,250 for a single person over 65 and $11,200 for married couples who are both over 65. In some cases, dependents who have their own sources of income also need to file a state tax return.

In North Carolina, taxable income is based on the taxable income that an individual or couple calculates for federal returns.

Some additional deductions are allowed. Among them are interest on debt instruments received from national, North Carolina and local government sources; Social Security benefits; state, local and foreign income tax refunds, and up to $4,000 in retirement benefits.

But the state also calls for some income additions, including interest from debt instruments issued by other states and their local governments; lump-sum distributions from a pension or profit-sharing plan; any state, local or foreign tax deducted on the federal return and federal cost-of-living adjustments for personal exemptions and standard deductions.

The state allows exemptions of $2,500 for each taxpayer and dependent unless federal taxable income is above levels that range from $60,000 for single filers to $100,000 for married couples filing joint returns.

The standard deduction is $3,000 for single taxpayers. For married taxpayers, the deduction increases from $5,500 in 2002 and $6,000 in 2003. An additional deduction is given taxpayers over 65 or who are blind.

A child tax credit increases from $60 per dependent child to $75 in 2002 and $100 in 2003. In addition, tax credits are available for dependent care expenses, for income taxes paid to other states on North Carolina taxable income, for installation of solar energy equipment, for the disabled and for a number of other expenses related to specific economic development activities.

Tax rates are as follows:

For couples filing jointly and for qualifying widows and widowers:
On income not above $21,250, tax is a straight 6 percent;
On income between $21,251 and $100,000, tax is $1,275 plus 7 percent of income over $21,250.
On income above $100,000, tax is $6,787.50 plus 7.75 percent of income over $100,000.

For qualifying Head of Household:
On income not above $17,000, tax is a straight 6 percent.
On income between $17,001 and $80,000, tax is $1,020 plus 7 percent of income over $17,000.
On income above $80,000, tax is $5,430 plus 7.75 percent of income over

$80,000.

For single taxpayers:
On income not above $12,750, tax is a straight 6 percent.
On income between $12,751 and $60,000, tax is $765 plus 7 percent of ncome over $12,750.
On income above $60,000, tax is $4,072.50 plus 7.75 percent of income over $60,000.

For married taxpayers filing separately:
On income not above $10,625, tax is a straight 6 percent.
On income between $10,626 and $50,000, tax is $637.50 plus 7 percent of income above $10,625.
On income above $50,000, tax is $3,393.75 plus 7.75 percent on income above $50,000.

For tax years 2001 through 2003 only, tax will be 8.25 percent for taxable income exceeding $100,000 for married people filing separately, $120,000 for singles, $160,000 for heads of households and $200,000 for married couples filing jointly.

Employers are required to withhold state income tax from wages, which is reported on a W-2 form along with other taxes withheld. If a taxpayer's estimated tax bill is $500 more than what is withheld, he must pay an estimated income tax in advance of filing a return. The first estimated tax payment is generally due on April 15.

Property taxes

County and municipal governments raise most of their operating revenues from taxes on real estate and tangible personal property. The state does not levy property taxes.

Tax rates vary among localities, but may be lower than you are accustomed to mainly because the state pays most of the cost of operating the public schools and for building and maintaining highways. The average tax rate for rural property in 1996-97 was 72.1 cents per $100 of appraised valuation. The average rate for municipal property was $1.20.

By law, appraised value is supposed to be full market value but, because property must be revalued only every eight years, the appraised value will often fall behind.

For those over 65 and for the disabled, a $20,000 homestead exemption is allowed if annual household income is not above $15,000.

Sales and use taxes

A 6.5-percent tax is levied on purchases of all tangible commodities, room and cottage rentals and laundry and dry-cleaning services. The state will take four 1/2 percent of this until July 2003, and four percent thereafter. The difference is returned to counties where the purchase takes place. The tax does not apply to prescription medicines, false teeth, eyeglasses, or coin operated laundries. Food is taxed at four percent, with state and local governments each getting two percent. A three-percent state tax is levied on electricity and piped natural gas. A five-percent tax is levied on satellite television services. Taxed at six percent is local phone service, as well as in-state and out-of-state long distance calls. Sales of boats and aircraft are taxed at three percent, with a maximum of $1,500. Mobile homes are taxed at two percent, with a maximum of $300 per section.

Vehicle and gasoline taxes

The state levies a three-percent tax on motor vehicles sales, with a maximum of $1,000 for certain commercial vehicles. The difference between the price of the car and your trade-in allowance is what is taxed.

The state also charges an annual $20 license and registration fee per vehicle. Municipalities may add a fee between $5 and $25.

The state gasoline tax was 22.6 cents per gallon through December, 1997. This is the total of a motor fuels tax of 17.5 cents per gallon plus a seven percent tax on the average wholesale price per gallon. This part of the tax was 5.1 cents per gallon in the last six months of 1997, and is readjusted every six months by the Secretary of Revenue.

Also, for scrap tire disposal, the state has a one- to two-percent sales tax on new automobile tires.

Other taxes on sales

White goods: The state taxes sales of new large appliances, such as refrigerators, freezers, washing machines, dishwashers, clothes dryers, ranges and air conditioners. The tax is $10 if the item contains chloroflourocarbon refrigerants, $5 if it does not.

Tobacco products: A five cents excise tax is levied on each pack of cigarettes. Other tobacco products are taxed at two percent.

Soft drinks: An excise tax of one-fourth cent per bottle is charged on soft drinks. Syrups, fountain drinks and soft drink mixes are also taxed. This phased out in 1999.

Alcoholic beverages: Beer is subject to a tax equivalent of five cents per 12-ounce bottle or can. Wine is taxed at 21 to 24 cents per liter depending on alcohol content. Effective Dec. 1, 2001 a six-percent tax was levied on liquor sales.

Real estate transfer tax

An excise stamp tax is levied on real estate transfers at the rate of $1 per $500 of the value of the property. Seven coastal counties — Dare, Camden,

Chowan, Currituck, Pasquotank, Perquimans and Washington — can levy a local real estate transfer tax of $1 per $100 of value.

Occupancy tax

Some counties and municipalities levy a tax on hotels, motels and inns that usually goes to promote travel and tourism in the area. The tax, which is authorized by the state but administered by the local governments, varies but is usually about three percent.

Occupational Licenses

State and local governments charge a variety of license fees for occupations and businesses. The state limits fees on certain businesses and prohibits them for others, but in most cases local governments use their discretion.

Inheritance Taxes

The state taxes property or interest that changes title through death to heirs or beneficiaries. The tax rates vary, with direct descendants paying the least and non-related heirs the most according to tax schedules that increase the higher the amount passed down.

Exemptions include property passing to a surviving spouse, bequests or insurance payable to charitable, religious or educational institutions, and proceeds of insurance policies paid by the U.S. government to beneficiaries of U.S. veterans.

In addition, tax credits are available to direct descendants.

Gift Tax

Gift taxes are similar to the same beneficiary and rate schedules that govern the inheritance tax. Gifts of up to $10,000 per year to an individual are not taxable.

Also, a lifetime exemption of $100,000 is allowed each donor for gifts to direct descendants.

Books

Young, Jane, J. *Settling Estates in North Carolina.* 1993. Asheboro, Down Home Press.

Index

B

D